PROVERBS 1–9
A STUDY OF INNER-BIBLICAL INTERPRETATION

SOCIETY
OF BIBLICAL
LITERATURE

DISSERTATION SERIES
Michael V. Fox, Old Testament Editor
Pheme Perkins, New Testament Editor

Number 150

PROVERBS 1–9
A STUDY OF INNER BIBLICAL INTERPRETATION

by
Scott L. Harris

Scott L. Harris

PROVERBS 1–9
A STUDY OF INNER-BIBLICAL
INTERPRETATION

Scholars Press
Atlanta, Georgia

PROVERBS 1–9
A STUDY OF INNER-BIBLICAL INTERPRETATION

Scott L. Harris

© 1995
The Society of Biblical Literature

Library of Congress Cataloging in Publication Data
Harris, Scott L.
    Proverbs 1-9 : a study of inner-biblical interpretation / Scott L.
Harris.
        p.   cm. — (Dissertation series ; no. 150)
    Revision of the author's thesis (Ph. D.)—Union Theological Seminary,
1988.
    Includes bibliographical references.
    ISBN 0-7885-0147-X (alk. paper). — ISBN 0-7885-0148-8 (pbk. :
alk. paper)
    1. Bible. O.T. Proverbs I-IX—Criticism, interpretation, etc.
I. Title. II. Series: Dissertation series (Society of Biblical
Literature) ; no. 150.
BS1465.2.H37   1995
223'.7066—dc20   95-34238
                                                        CIP

Printed in the United States of America
on acid-free paper

To Karen, Matthew, Andrew, and Elizabeth

Contents

Preface .... xi-xxi

Chapter I.   Prov 1:8–19; 1:20–33; and 6:1–19.
   Introduction 1–3
   Recent Interpretation of Proverbs 1–9:
      The Egyptian Connection. 3–6
   R. N. Whybray: Proverbs 1–9 and an "Egyptian
      Lesson-Book." 7–10
   Christa Kayatz and the Resemblance of Egyptian
      Speech Forms and Motifs in Proverbs 1–9. 10–15
   W. McKane: Proverbs 1–9 and the International
      Form of "Instruction." 15–21
   Summary. 21
   A Proposed Approach. 22–31

Chapter II.   Prov 1:8–19, Genesis 37, and Inner-Biblical Interpretation.
   Translation. 33–34
   Introduction. 34–37
   Proverbs, Torah, and Prophets: Examples of
      Editorial Redaction. 37–41
   Prov 1:8–19 and Evidence of Editorial Redaction. 42–45
   Prov 1:8–19 and the Role of Direct Discourse
      in Inner-Biblical Interpretation. 45–46
   M. Bakhtin and M. Sternberg: Double-Voiced
      Discourse and Inner-Biblical Interpretation. 46–52
   Prov 1:8–19 and Genesis 37: A Case of
      Inner-Biblical Interpretation. 52–61
   Prov 1:8–19, Genesis 37, and Rabbinic Commentary. 61–65

Chapter III. Prov 1:20–33, Jeremiah 7, 20, and Inner-Biblical
        Interpretation.
    Translation. 67–68
    Introduction. 68–70
    Prov 1:22–23: Problems in Translation and Interpretation. 71–79
    Prov 1:20–33 and the Identification of
        Quoted Speech. 79–83
    The Different Layers of Speech in Prov 1:20–33. 83–86
    P. Trible's Analysis of the Structure of Prov 1:20–33. 86–87
    Preliminary Observations Concerning the Similarities
        Between Proverbs 1:20–33 and Jeremiah 7 as seen
        by Contemporary Commentators. 87–93
    Prov 1:20–33 and the Reutilization of
        Traditions from Jeremiah 7 and 20. 93–100
    Prov 1:20–33, Jeremiah, and Rabbinic Commentary. 101–102
    Contemporary Research in the Reutilization of
        Jeremianic Traditions in Zechariah and the
        Parallels with Prov 1:20–33. 102–108
    Summary. 108–109

Chapter IV. Prov 6:1–19 and the Joseph Story.
    Translation. 111–112
    Introduction. 112–115
    The Compositional Unity of 6:1–19. 115–117
    Separate Units and Perceived Unity: The
        Composition of Prov 6:1–19. 117–126
    Prov 6:1–19: Mimetic Representation By Means
        of Actional and Descriptive Speech. ....
        Introduction. 126–128
        Action and Description: Quoting the Unspoken. 128–134
    Prov 6:1–19 and Judah's Role in the Joseph Story. 134–135
        The Parallel Expressions lĕrēʿekā, "for
            your neighbor," (RSV) and lazzār, "for
            a stranger," in Prov 6:1–15. 135–139
        A Proposed Translation and Interpretation
            of lĕrēʿekā and lazzār. 139–142
    Prov 6:1–19, the Joseph Story, and Mimetic. 142–143
        Representation via Actional Discourse.
            ʿăśēh zōʾt ʾēpôʾ Prov 6:3/ʾēpôʾ zōʾt ʿăśû Gen 43:11. 143
        The "Reversed" Framework of Prov 6:1–19
            and Judah's Role in the Joseph Story. 144–146
        The Pairing of Surety and Agricultural Readiness
            in Prov 6:1–11 and Events from the Joseph Story. 147–149
        Third Person Discourse, a "Worthless Man" (inter alia),
            and Judah's Role in the Joseph Story. 149–153
    Prov 6:1–19, the Joseph Story, and Rabbinic Commentary. 153–154
    Summary. 155–156

Chapter V. The Implications of Our Analysis for Proverbs 1–9.
    Introduction. 157
    The Opening and Closing of Proverbs 1–9. 157–162

Parental Warnings About "Sinful Men" and
     "Strange/Foreign Women:" The Role of Prov
     1:8–19 and 1:20–33 as Introduction...162–168
Prov 6:1–19 and Its Interrelationship with Proverbs 5. 169–172

Chapter VI. Conclusion..173–178

Bibliography 179–190

Appendix 191–193

PREFACE

This book is my Ph.D. dissertation as accepted by Union Theological Seminary in 1988, with minor revisions. I have been able to take into account a few valuable publications that have appeared since the dissertation was completed; in substance, however, the work remains unchanged. This work has benefited from the support and encouragement of many people. I wish to thank Union Theological Seminary for its generous graduate fellowship and the Division for World Mission and Ecumenism of the Lutheran Church in America for its financial assistance. Their combined support allowed me the freedom to pursue my graduate studies.

I am grateful to the following faculty members for their help. To the members of my dissertation committee, Professors George Landes and Phyllis Trible of Union Theological Seminary, Professor Gerald Sheppard of the University of Toronto, Professor Burton Visotzky of the Jewish Theological Seminary, New York, and Professor Ellen Davis of Yale University, I wish to express my deep gratitude for their guidance and assistance in the writing of this dissertation. A special word of thanks goes to Professor Edward Greenstein of the Jewish Theological Seminary for his initial help and encouragement in my research and to Mr. Seth Kasten of Burke Library at Union for his unstinting assistance.

More recently, Professor John Schmitt of the Theology Department at Marquette University deserves mention for urging me to submit my dissertation for publication. Without his persistent efforts and genuine interest my research would still be in an unpublished dissertation form. I continue to value his insights and friendship.

I thank the editor of the SBLDS, Professor Michael V. Fox, for suggestions about revisions and for allowing me to make mention of more recent literature.

While it is not so much impossible as it is impractical to thank by name each member of the congregation where I serve as Senior Pastor, some recognition is due them. I consider myself to be in an enviable situation wherein I serve a congregation of committed Christians whose support and affirmation of my ministry is rooted in a deep involvement in Scripture. In my time of serving the people of Dr. Martin Luther Church (ELCA), we continue to learn how our lives are shaped and formed by the beauty and wisdom of Scripture. My deepest thanks goes to them.

Most of all, my wife Karen has been a constant source of loving support throughout my graduate studies and ministry. Without her I doubt that my work could have been completed. To her and to our children, Matthew, Andrew, and Elizabeth, this work is dedicated.

EASTER, 1995

1

PROVERBS 1:8–19; 1:20–33; AND 6:1–19.

INTRODUCTION

The purpose of this study is to show how portions of the first nine chapters of the book of Proverbs draw upon earlier traditions from the Torah and the Prophets for their form and content. Although scholars have noted a degree of similarity between Proverbs and earlier canonical literature, no one has yet sought to provide a systematic analysis of the discourse in Proverbs 1–9 in light of other biblical traditions. Our analysis will concentrate on select units of discourse in Proverbs 1–9 in order to show how traditions from the Torah and the Prophets are refashioned so as to conform to a new sapiential context.

Specifically, the texts that we will analyze are Prov 1:8–19; 1:20–33; and 6:1–19. Our reasons for choosing these texts relate to the unique characteristics that they display in the first nine chapters of Proverbs. As the opening didactic lesson, Prov 1:8–19 occupies the potentially important role of introducing the reader to issues addressed elsewhere by the parent. We know from other examples in the Hebrew Bible that an opening discourse can initiate a point of view that is developed further in a text.[1] Given the fact that the parent in vv 8–19 introduces us to the words of the "sinners," and not wisdom, signals an importance to their discourse that has hitherto gone unrecognized by contemporary scholars.

As for Prov 1:20–33, it is the only example of prophetic forms of speech and content found in the book of Proverbs. While the prophetic cast of these verses has not gone unnoticed by scholars, the prophetic characteristics of the text, which conform to a wisdom context, merit closer analysis and interpretation. Of chief interest for us is how the text combines levels of sapiential and prophetic speech.

Our last example is Prov 6:1–19. Because these verses are perceived as an interpolation in the context of Proverbs 5–7, little effort is made by scholars to interpret them. In contrast to current treatments of 6:1–19, our analysis is presented as an attempt to describe the sophisticated nature of the parent's lesson and how it relates to a broader biblical context. Even though our initial interest is mainly in three discourse units in Proverbs 1–9, we will work with an eye toward the broader implications of our research not only for Proverbs 1–9 but also for the larger canonical context of the book of Proverbs.

Our concentration upon select units of tradition within Proverbs 1–9 is an attempt to contribute to the continuing analysis of these chapters and to account for the unique role that they play. Many scholars refer to Proverbs 1–9 as the "Introduction" to Proverbs 10–31.[2] The basis for such

---

[1] For example, the following scholars have offered their own analyses of how opening units of tradition play central roles in introducing topics, themes, and issues that are developed later in a text. R. Polzin, *Moses and the Deuteronomist: A Literary Study of the Deuteronomic History* (New York: The Seabury Press, 1980) esp. pp. 75–80; idem, "The Speaking Person and His Voice in 1 Samuel," *VT* 36 (1985) 218–229; esp. p. 219; J. L. Mays, "The Place of the Torah-Psalms in the Psalter," *JBL* 106 (1987) 3–12; and G. Sheppard, *Wisdom as a Hermeneutical Construct: A Study in the Sapientializing of the Old Testament* (Berlin/New York: Walter de Gruyter, 1980) 136–143.

[2] Cf. O. Plöger, *Sprüche Salomos* (Neukirchen Vluyn: Neukirchener Verlag, 1984) xxxvi; H. Ringgren, W. Zimmerli, *Sprüche/Prediger* (Göttingen: Vandenhoeck and Ruprecht, 1980) 8; S. R. Driver, *An Introduction to the Literature of the Old Testament* (New York: Meridian Books, 1960) 395; R. B. Y. Scott, *Proverbs, Ecclesiastes: A New Translation with Introduction and Commentary* (AB, 18; Garden City, New York: Doubleday and Company, 1965) 15; idem "Wise and Foolish, Righteous and Wicked," *VT* 23 (1972) 146–165. B. S. Childs, *Introduction to the Old Testament as Scripture* (Philadelphia: Fortress, 1979) 552–553, speaks of Proverbs 1–9 as forming the "framework" and "prism" through which the remaining chapters of Proverbs are read: "Although chs. 10ff. are usually regarded as the clearest example of Israel's 'old wisdom' and historically the earliest, in its present order this earliest level is now read through the prism of chs. 1–9. The effect is far-reaching." Also: "As we have suggested, chs. 1–9 serve as a hermeneutical guide for reading what follows"(p. 553). See: W. Zimmerli, "Zur Struktur der alttestamentlichen Weisheit," *ZAW* 10 (1933)

an assessment lies in the content, topics, and themes introduced in the parent's discourse in Proverbs 1–9 which are subsequently found scattered throughout the remaining chapters of Proverbs 10–31. While we recognize the introductory role played by Proverbs 1–9, we will argue further that chapters 1–9 do more than introduce the reader to topics found elsewhere in Proverbs. We shall also argue that, as the latest level of tradition, Proverbs 1–9 re-introduce us to persons and events from Israel's history by means of its carefully crafted discourse, thus forming a bridge between Israel's historical traditions and the book of Proverbs.

Before we present our own analysis it is necessary to see first how other scholars have analyzed and interpreted our texts. In the following sections, we will offer a brief summary of current interpretation for the book of Proverbs. Special attention will be given to the interpretation of Prov 1:8–19; 1:20–33; and 6:1–19. Afterwards we will turn our attention to these same texts in the hopes of presenting a new reading.

RECENT INTERPRETATION OF PROVERBS 1–9: THE EGYPTIAN CONNECTION.

Since the mid 1920's, research in the book of Proverbs has been dominated by models based on comparative studies from ancient Near Eastern literature. Traditions from Egypt have had an especially prominent role. Indeed, the one event which signaled a sea change in the study of Proverbs was the correspondences discovered by E. A. W. Budge in 1922 between the Egyptian text of Amenemope and Prov 22:17–24:22.[3] Up until the time that Budge first published the text of the *Wisdom*

189, "Concerning the Structure of Old Testament Wisdom," translated by B. Kovacs in J. Crenshaw *Studies in Ancient Israelite Wisdom*, (New York: KTAV, 1976) 185, where he speaks of Proverbs 1–9 as the "interpretative canon" for Proverbs 1off. Hereafter, *SAIW=Studies in Ancient Israelite Wisdom*.

[3] E. A. W. Budge, "The Precepts of Life by Amen-em-Apt, the Son of Ka-nekht," in *Recueil d'études égyptologiques dédièes á la mémoire de Jean-Francois Champollion* (Paris: E. Champion, 1922) 431–446. Cf. also A. Erman, "Eine ägyptische Quelle der 'Sprüche Salomos,'" in *Sitzungsberichte der preussischen Akademie der Wissenschaften*, Phil.-hist. Kl. 15 (1924) 86–93, who argues that Prov 22:17–23:24 is based directly upon Amenemope. Budge's discovery and Erman's further argument generated a debate concerning the question of which tradition borrowed from the other. D. C. Simpson, "The Hebrew Book of Proverbs and the Teaching of Amenophis," *JEA*, 12 (1926), 232, and W. O. E. Oesterley, *The Wisdom of Egypt and the Old Testament in the Light of the Newly Discovered 'Teaching of Amen-emope'* (London: Methuen and Co., Ltd. 1927) 105, posit a common semitic source for both Amenemope and Prov 22:17–24:22. R. O. Kevin, "The Wisdom of Amen-em-Apt and its Possible Dependence upon the

4 PROVERBS 1-9: A STUDY OF INNER-BIBLICAL INTERPRETATION

of Amenemope, scholars were mainly concerned with such things as the numerous text-critical details of the book of Proverbs, the dating of the various divisions of the book, and the number of corresponding features between Proverbs and Sirach.[4] Seen as a thoroughly ahistorical book in

---

Hebrew Book of Proverbs," *JSOR* 14 (1930) 115–157, mounts a detailed case for arguing that Amenemope actually borrowed from Proverbs. Kevin's argument was again taken up by E. Drioton, "Sur la Sagesse d'Aménémopé," in *Mélanges bibliques rédiqués en l'honneur de Andrè Robert*, ed. by H. Cazelles (Paris: Bloud and Gay, 1957) 254–280; and again by Drioton in "Le Livre des Proverbes et la Sagesse d'Aménémopé," in *Sacra Pagina. Miscellanea biblica congressus internationalis Catholici de re biblica*, ed. by J. Coppens, A. Descamps, É. Massaux (Paris/Gembloux: Éditions J. Duculot, 1959) 1. 229–241. See: R. J. Williams, "The Alleged Semitic Original of the *Wisdom of Amenemope*," *JEA* 47 (1961) 100–106, who finds Drioton's argument wanting because of the lack of clear lexical connections between the two. At this point in time, it appears that the evidence shows that portions of the book of Proverbs are clearly dependent on Egyptian traditions. Cf. also, H. Gressmann, *Israels Spruchweisheit in zusammenhang der Weltliteratur* (Berlin: Verlag Karl Curtius, 1925); A. Alt, "Zur literischen Analyse der Weisheit des Amenemope," *VTS*, 3 (1960) 16–25. Recently I. Grumach, *Untersuchungen zur Lebenslehre des Amenemope* (MÄS, 23; Münich: Münchener Universitätsschriften, 1972) attempts to reconstruct the "original" core tradition in Amenemope. In the process she describes the phenomenon of how Amenemope seems to be a composite piece made up of older traditions that have been expanded and reworked to fit in their new context. R. B. Y. Scott ("The Study of Wisdom Literature," *Int* 24 [1970] 23–24) says the following about the impact made by Egyptian studies on the study of Proverbs: "The groundwork for the present fuller appreciation of the wisdom movement was laid in an intense burst of scholarly activity in the twenties and thirties. . . . What occasioned this remarkable degree of attention to one corner of the Old Testament field which had previously been neglected or inadequately tilled, is quite clear. It was the publication in 1923 by Wallis Budge of *The Teaching of Amén-ém-opé* from the Hieratic papyri in the British Museum, and its republication in German by Adolf Erman in 1924 and by O. H. Lange in 1925. This document, with its obviously close yet problematical relationship to a distinct section in the Book of Proverbs, 22:17–24: 22, opened the eyes of scholars to the fact that the literary forms, ideas, motives, and emphases of the biblical Wisdom books were not particularly Hebrew." Scott continues (p. 25): "The main lines of present-day understanding of the Wisdom Literature were staked out, as already noted, in about a dozen years following the teaching of *Amén-ém-opé* in 1923. Scholarly work in this area since then has been pretty much an amplification of those earlier basic studies."

4 For example, see the following "pre-Amenemope" commentators: A. J. Baumgartner, *Étude critique sur l'état du texte du livre des Proverbes d'apres les principales traductions anciennes*, (Leipzig: Imprimerie Orientale W. Drugulin, 1890); F. Delitzsch, *Proverbs, Ecclesiastes, Song of Songs*, trans. by J. Martin (Grand Rapids: W. B. Eerdmans, 1986), originally published as *Das Salomonische Sprüchbuch*, in Keil and Delitzsch, *Biblische Commentar über das AT*, (Leipzig: Verlag von S. Hirzel, 1873); W. Frankenberg, *Die Sprüche übersetzt und erklärt* (Göttingen: Vandenhoeck & Ruprecht,

terms of its failure to mention any of the major events or persons from Israel's history, Proverbs received scant attention from scholars who concentrated on Israel's early history and on the history of the biblical text. But with the discovery of the parallels between Amenemope and Proverbs, scholars began to reassess the historical context of Proverbs. Even though scholars recognized the difficulty in dating Amenemope, the period of Solomon's reign soon became the focal point for the analysis of the earliest traditions in Proverbs.[5]

1898); J. K. Gasser, *Die Bedeutung der Sprüche Jesu Ben Sira für die Datierung des althebräischen Spruchbuches* (Gütersloh: Druk und Verlag C. Bertelsmann, 1904); D. Steurnagel, "Die Sprüche," in *Die heilige Schrift des alten Testaments*, ed. by E. Kautzsch (Tübingen: Verlag von J. C. B. Mohr, 1910) 249–293; P. Lagarde, *Anmerkungen zur griechischen übersetzung der Proverbien* (Leipzig: A. A. Brockhaus, 1863); A. Müller and E. Kautzsch, *The Book of Proverbs: Critical edition of the Hebrew Text with Notes* (Leipzig: J. C. Hinrichs' Svhe Buchhandlung, 1901); W. Nowack, *Die Sprüche Salomo's* in *Kurzgefasstes exegetisches Handbuch zum Alten Testament* (Leipzig: Verlag von S. Hirzel, 1883); C. H. Toy, *A Critical and Exegetical Commentary on the Book of Proverbs* (ICC, Edinburgh: T & T Clark, 1899); D. G. Wildeboer, *Die Sprüche* (Leipzig/Tübingen: J. C. B. Mohr, 1897).

[5] G. von Rad (*Wisdom in Israel* [London: SCM Press, 1972] 9) makes reference to the change that takes place in Proverbs research with the discovery of the correspondences between Amenemope and Proverbs: "The investigation [that placed Proverbs in the post-exilic era and treated it in a disparaging manner] did not emerge from the shadow of these unfortunate, religious judgments until scholars became aware of wisdom texts in the great cultures which were neighbour to Israel and of the relationship of these texts to Israelite material. Particularly in ancient Egypt, wisdom books existed dating from the third millenium BC right up to the later period. A somewhat revolutionary effect was produced by the discovery that a whole passage from the wisdom book of Amenemope had been taken over almost word for word into the biblical book of Proverbs (Prov. 22.17–23.11). The assumption that wisdom was a religious phenomenon of post-exilic Israel proved to be completely wrong. Wisdom, it was now clear, was a phenomenon common to the ancient East, a cultural commodity with respect to which Israel was to a great extent a recipient and not a donor. At the same time, the suspicion against its early dating in the period of the monarchy was seen to be unjustified. It followed logically that a great comparison of the wisdom materials should begin then and there." See U. Skladny (*Die ältesten Spruchsammlungen in Israel* [Göttingen: Vandenhoeck and Ruprecht, 1962) who concentrates solely on Proverbs 10–29. His work is another illustration of how influential comparative studies from Egypt have been in determining the focus of contemporary Proverbs research. He says: "Die alttestamentliche Wissenschaft hat sich seit Beginn dieses Jahrhunderts—vor allem unter dem Einfluss derin den letzten Jahrzehnten aufgefundenen Zeugnisse der ausserisraelitischen (besonders der ägyptischen und babylonisch-assyrischen) Weisheitsliteratur—in steigendem Masse mit der 'Weisheit' Israels beschäftigt, wobei sich das Interesse in erster Linie auf die *Anfange*, also auf die *ältere* Weisheit konzentrierte"(p. 5). See also: H.-J. Hermission, *Studien zur Israelitischen Spruchweisheit* (Neukirchen-Vluyn: Neukirchener Verlag,

Because a detailed summary of the scholars who have endeavored to find other parallels between biblical wisdom traditions and Egyptian literature is beyond the scope of our work, we shall first summarize how some biblical scholars have tried, since Budge's discovery, to offer a systematic analysis of Proverbs 1–9 in terms of its parallels with Egyptian traditions. In chronological order, the works of R. N. Whybray, C. Kayatz, and W. McKane exemplify the most concerted efforts to interpret Proverbs 1–9 in the context of Egyptian traditions.[6] Even though other scholars have offered their own interpretation of Proverbs by referring to common features from Egyptian and other ancient Near Eastern traditions,[7] the work of Whybray, Kayatz, and McKane in terms of scope and ingenuity cannot be matched.

1968); H. H. Schmid, *Wesen und Geschichte der Weisheit, Eine Untersuchung zur altorientalischen und israelitischen Weisheitsliteratur* (Berlin: Alfred Töpelmann, 1966); W. Richter, *Recht und Ethos, Versuch einer Ortung des weisheitslichen Mahnspruches* (Müchen: Kösel-Verlag, 1966); M. Fox. "Two Decades of Research in Egyptian Wisdom Literature," *ZÄS* 107 (1980) 120–135. See G. S. Sheppard, *Wisdom as a Hermeneutical Construct*, p.7, where he discusses briefly the impact that comparative studies of wisdom in its ancient Near Eastern context had on von Rad's dating of Proverbs 1–9.

[6] R. N. Whybray, *Wisdom in Proverbs*, (SBT, 45; London: SCM Press, 1965); C. Kayatz, *Studien zu Proverbien 1–9: eine form- und motivgeschichtliche Untersuchung unter Einbeziehung ägyptischen Vergleichsmaterial* (WMANT 22; Neukirchen-Vluyn: Neukirchener Verlag, 1966); W. Mckane, *Proverbs: A New Approach* (London: SCM Press, 1970).

[7] J. Crenshaw, *Old Testament Wisdom, An Introduction* (Atlanta: John Knox Press, 1981) offers a sweeping assessment of Israelite wisdom literature in which he lumps together both canonical and non-canonical wisdom traditions under the banner of a group of "sages"/"skeptics" (Crenshaw at times uses the terms interchangeably) who, in the case of Proverbs, search for knowledge(pp. 66–99). Crenshaw recognizes the importance of the international role of wisdom, but he minimizes Egyptian influence upon Israel's wisdom traditions. He places the discussion of Egyptian wisdom traditions in the last chapter in his book in contrast to many scholars who initiate a discussion of Israel's wisdom with reference to wisdom from Egypt. Crenshaw does not provide a detailed analysis of the book of Proverbs as we find in the works by Whybray, Kayatz, and Whybray. See also, B. Lang,*Wisdom and the Book of Proverbs: An Israelite Goddess Redefined* (New York: Pilgrim Press, 1986). There is some confusion in the title for Lang's book. On the inside title page the subtitle reads, *A Hebrew Goddess Redefined*. We have not included Lang in our discussion because Lang makes use of Egyptian traditions only to the extent that they provide him with a hypothetical school system which, as Lang argues, was adopted by Israel's sages in the post-exilic period. Lang also alludes to Canaanite religious traditions which are still in evidence within the book of Proverbs. Lang's selective analysis of the traditions within Proverbs 1–9 does not result in a comprehensive interpretation of the traditions. C. Camp's recent book, *Wisdom and the Feminine in the Book of Proverbs*

R. N. WHYBRAY: PROVERBS 1–9, AND AN "EGYPTIAN LESSON-BOOK."

In his book, *Wisdom in Proverbs*, R. N. Whybray provides the first concerted attempt to account for the traditio-historical background of Proverbs 1–9 in light of Egyptian influences. Whybray hypothesizes that the original form of Proverbs 1–9 was made up of "Ten Discourses" and divides Proverbs 1–9 into the following "Discourses:" I) Prov 1:8–19; II) 2:1, 9, 16–19; III) 3:1–2, 3bc, 4–10; IV) 3:21ba-24, 27–31; V) 4:1–3, 4abc-5bB; VI) 4:10–12, 14–18; VII) 4:20–26; VIII) 5:1–8, 21; IX) 6:20–22, 24–25, 32; X) 7:1–3, 5, 25–27.[8] The considerable amount of variation in length and content in the ten discourses is due to the fact "that they are derived from a common basic form, which in some cases has been expanded by additions which introduce new and originally extraneous ideas."[9] That basic form is found in Prov 1:8–9. Being essentially "similar in form and content" in the ten discourses, its closest parallel is *not* within Hebrew scripture, but within the "pedagogical instructions in Egyptian wisdom literature. . . The closest parallel is with *Amen-em-opet. . . .*"[10]

Whybray is careful to note that whatever resemblances there are between the ten discourses and the other portions of Hebrew scripture, they are purely accidental.[11] As such, Prov 1:8–19, the first discourse, was at one time a portion of a larger body of Egyptian discourse which is now lost.[12] At best Prov 1:8–19 is an abbreviated form of the larger

---

(Sheffield, England/Decatur, Georgia: Almond Press, 1985) is a study of "personified wisdom" and "female imagery" in portions of the book of Proverbs and the Hebrew Bible at large. Comments about Proverbs 1–9 are scattered about in the various discussions of the topics of "personified wisdom" and "female imagery." Her book offers a number of intriguing observations about the figure of wisdom within the book of Proverbs.

[8] *Wisdom in Proverbs*, 33. A year later Whybray in "Some Literary Problems in Proverbs I-IX," *VTS* 16 (1966) 482–496, supplemented his book by offering more detail to his analysis of the discourses which he isolates in Proverbs 1–9. His original argument and analysis in *Wisdom in Proverbs*, is not altered by his later article.

[9] *Wisdom in Proverbs*, 33.

[10] *Wisdom in Proverbs*, 35.

[11] *Wisdom in Proverbs*, 37: "But while there may be biblical reminiscences in a few cases, the parallels with *Amen-em-opet* are in general much closer than the biblical parallels. . . . There can be no doubt that the discourses in Proverbs 1–9 stand firmly in the tradition of international wisdom and are not derived from, though they may have been to some extent influenced by, the Yahwistic tradition." For a contrasting opinion see: G. H. Wilson, "'The Words of the Wise': The Intent and Significance of Qohelet 12:9–14," *JBL* 103 (1984) 175–192.

[12] See Whybray, *Wisdom in Proverbs*, 46, where he concludes that Prov 1:8–19 is one of the "original discourses."

discourse not able to stand on its own within the book of Proverbs because these verses are theologically unorthodox.[13] Only by a succession of two reinterpretations is Prov 1:8–19 able to correspond to the rest of Proverbs. The first reinterpretation, termed group 1 by Whybray, is achieved by the addition of Prov 1:20–28, 30–33. The second reinterpretation, group 2, has been achieved by the addition of a single verse, v 29.[14] In other words, Whybray argues, Prov 1:8–19 represents the "alien" tradition which had its literary roots in an Egyptian lesson-book. The lesson-book was then appropriated by Israel's "wise men" and subsequently reinterpreted in two different stages. The outcome of the process of reinterpretation is that Prov 1:8–19 is now accorded a theological role under the rubrics of Israelite religion found in 1:20–28, 30–33, and most especially v 29.

As we have noted, Prov 1:8–19 counts for Whybray as one of the original Ten Discourses in Proverbs. But because Whybray is primarily concerned with identifying the additions which subsequently reappear as the building blocks of the final form of Proverbs 1–9, he does not question the details of the traditio-historical additions. By narrowing the focus of his work, Whybray disregards any questions concerning the broader traditio-historical development of the passages themselves. Hence, Whybray suggests that 1:20ff and other additions "*may have originally been independent poems* which were inserted because they were considered appropriate to the context"[15] (emphasis added). And in conjunction with 1:8–19, the two groups of additions serve to align the "Discourse" with Israel's theological traditions.[16]

For the additional traditions, he shifts from *describing* the discourses, to *explaining* the hermeneutic process of raising the alien discourses to the level of acceptable theological orthodoxy by means of the additions. Acceptable theological orthodoxy is achieved by the adding of two layers of tradition. However, what appears abundantly clear is that the process of adding traditions was caused by the necessity to reconcile two traditions which were potentially competitive.[17] The group 1 passages,

---

[13] *Wisdom in Proverbs*, 71.

[14] *Wisdom in Proverbs*, 73.

[15] *Wisdom in Proverbs*, 79.

[16] *Wisdom in Proverbs*, 76. As Whybray says: "The motives for the twofold expansion of the Book of Discourses are thus reasonably clear. Each stage represents an attempt to re-interpret the teaching of the discourses"(p. 76).

[17] *Wisdom in Proverbs*, 97.

then, represent the so-called concept of wisdom additions which derive from one educational context.[18]

Whybray summarily discounts any role for a form of hypostatized wisdom and instead speaks of the figure of wisdom as providing a lively didactic example for an otherwise droll teacher.[19] The addition of the group 2 passages are all characterized by the "concept" of "the fear of the Lord." The passages in group 2 represent the latest step in the traditioning process.[20] The end result of the wedding together of the two concepts of "wisdom" and "the fear of the Lord" is that the heretofore alien discourses are embraced and reinterpreted by a traditio-historical and theological editing of the traditions which rests in an educational context.

Whybray's schematic analysis of the traditions has the effect of smoothing over the rough edges in the tradition. For example, his treatment of 1:20–33 too facilely dismisses the prophetic form and content of the material. If, in fact, 1:20–33 was at one time an independent poem which has been inserted here, as Whybray argues, is it possible that further investigation into its independent status could highlight the traditioning process within the verses? Moreover, Whybray fails to demonstrate that 1:29 is actually a later addition that can bear the weight of theologically reinterpreting the whole of 1:8–33. In contrast to Whybray's argument, 1:29 appears to fit smoothly into its present context. It does not have the markings of an addition nor does it stand out as the theological keystone for all of 1:20–33. In addition, there are no textual variants which would indicate the presence of an addition. Lastly, Whybray does not discuss the nature of speech and the problems

---

[18] R. N. Whybray, *Wisdom in Proverbs*, 74: "The passages in group 1 are entirely concerned with something called 'wisdom', and they have been added in such a way as to expand and interpret the teaching of the discourses by identifying wisdom—which is in some cases wholly or partly personified—with the purely human teaching of the discourses for which the teacher makes such absolute claims."

[19] *Wisdom in Proverbs*, 94–95.

[20] "The 'Fear' of Yahweh." Of the seven passages in this group, four (1.7; 1.29; 2.5; 8.13a) identify wisdom with the 'fear' or 'reverence' (*yirʾā*) of Yahweh. This phrase is mainly confined to the wisdom literature, of which it is a characteristic expression. It occurs five times in almost identical phrases defining the nature or essence of wisdom or knowledge. An examination of the use of the verb 'to fear' (*yārēʾ*) and the noun 'fear' (*yirʾā*) in connexion with Yahweh show that this concept, like that of wisdom, was clearly associated with *education*. The two phrases 'wisdom' and 'fear of Yahweh' signify two originally distinct types of education in Israel: the teaching of wisdom schools and the ordinary religious education of the Israelite given by parents or by the religious authorities"(*Wisdom in Proverbs*, 95–96).

in the change of person in 1:24-33 and how such a change reflects an educational context.

As for Prov 6:1-19, even though these verses meet his criterion of a formulaic introduction which uses the introductory expression "my son," Whybray discounts vv 1-19 as a discourse unit. Whybray says: "The word 'my son' in 6:1 stands at the head of a new section, but this section (6.1-19) is rightly held by many commentators to be an independent collection of proverbs which had no place in the original book."[21] Instead of analyzing 6:1-19 according to his own criteria, Whybray accepts uncritically what other scholars have said about vv 1-19. In addition, the point of his analysis for the ten discourses is that none of them formed a part of the "original book." As a result, each discourse has undergone a process of gathering further content over and above the basic form. If such is the case, Whybray's exclusion of 6:1-19 is not consistent with his proposed method.

Furthermore, where Whybray allows for expansion in the form of "additions which introduce new and originally extraneous ideas"[22] for the other ten discourses, similar characteristics in 6:1-19 are used to argue *against* incorporating the verses in the purportedly original lesson-book! More baffling, however, is the fact that while other scholars before Whybray noted the similarity between portions of Prov 6:1-19 and Amenemope—the same Egyptian tradition which Whybray argues represents the closest parallel to Proverbs 1-9—Whybray says nothing about the similarities between Proverbs 6 and Amenemope.[23] His silence leads us to question his treatment of 6:1-19.

CHRISTA KAYATZ AND THE RESEMBLANCE OF EGYPTIAN SPEECH FORMS AND MOTIFS IN PROVERBS 1-9.

Like Whybray, Kayatz is also heavily dependent on models drawn from Egyptian sources for her interpretation of Proverbs 1-9. As a result, Kayatz pays little attention to close text-critical details in Prov 1:10-19, 20-33; and 6:1-19. The title of her book indicates the direction of her work: *Studien zu Proverbien 1-9: eine form- und motivgeshichtliche Untersuchung unter Einbeziehung ägyptischen Vergleichsmaterials.* She

---

[21] *Wisdom in Proverbs*, 33, n. 1. Cf. pp. 30, 48.

[22] *Wisdom in Proverbs*, 33.

[23] See W. O. E. Oesterley's comments (*Proverbs*, 43) where he notes the similarities between Prov 6:16-19 and sections from Amenemope. See also, C. Pritchard, *Ancient Near Eastern Texts*, 3rd edition (Princeton: Princeton University Press, 1969) 423.

approaches the text from the point of view of the shared forms and motifs between Egyptian literature and Hebrew scripture.

Kayatz argues that Proverbs 1–9 and 10–29 co-existed in the period of the so-called Solomonic Enlightenment. Proverbs 1–9 is markedly theological in content and outlook, while Proverbs 10–29 is experientially oriented. The difference between the two divisions of Proverbs is explained by the change in the historical and theological climate around the time of Solomon. Because the demand for a theologically oriented wisdom during the time of the Solomonic Enlightenment could not be met by *die Erfahrungsweisheit*, (i.e., the proverbial traditions in Proverbs 10–29) Kayatz posits a process of assimilation from Egyptian didactic traditions to Israel's wisdom literature as found in its final form in Proverbs 1–9. The carrier of the assimilation process is what Kayatz calls an *einfache Form* (basic form) of speech. The *einfache Form* functions not only as the medium for detecting shared forms of speech between Egyptian and Israelite traditions but as the hermeneutic key which indicates a commonly shared theological understanding of the world.

As for Prov 1:10–19, these verses represent for Kayatz a prime example of the *einfache Form* which links up form-critically with the divinely created order of the world. Hence, in the world which is founded upon an order best summarized as *Tun-Ergehen-Zusammenhang*,[24] (deed-result relationship), Kayatz uses Prov 1:10–19 to demonstrate not only that Prov 1:10–19 and select portions of Egyptian literature share the same thought-world, but also that this theological thought-world is couched in shared forms of expression. By a circuitous route of predication of speech forms as exemplified in "Ptahotep 19"[25] (*sic*) where the content of Ptahotep is linked to speech forms of Maat, Kayatz posits a similar process of predication among the speech form of Prov 1:10–19, the "order" (*Tun-Ergehen-Zusammenhang*) of the world, and, finally, wisdom. Such a process is not an example of the dependency of Israelite traditions upon Egyptian traditions, but rather an example of a shared thought-world.[26]

Kayatz pays little attention to the content of Prov 1:10–19 other than to note that the sinners are characterized by their speech patterns and by their actions. Central to her argument is the relationship between the *Mahnreden* (speech patterns) and the purported god-given order of creation. Whenever we detect corresponding speech forms between

---

[24] *Studien zu Proverbien 1–9*, 6–7; 30.

[25] See *Studien zu Proverbien 1–9*, 30–31, where Kayatz has a section on "*Begründung durch Prädikation.*"

[26] *Studien zu Proverbien 1–9*, 138. Cf.: *Einführung in die alttestamentliche Weisheit*, pp. 93–95.

Egyptian traditions and Proverbs 1–9, Kayatz argues, we can conclude that we have evidence that Proverbs not only contains the same kind of "language" as Egyptian traditions do, and expresses the same kind of thoughts as expressed in Egyptian traditions, but that in all likelihood we have evidence of indirect Egyptian influence upon Proverbs 1–9. The corollary to Kayatz's argument is that the source for the *Mahnreden* form need not be founded upon the shorter proverbial forms in Proverbs 10–29.

Kayatz's analysis of Prov 1:20–33 is far more detailed than her analysis of Prov 1:10–19 because, as she admits, vv 20–33 are difficult to place under the general umbrella of Egyptian traditions.[27] Kayatz pays close attention to the form and content of Prov 1:20–33 especially since "Einen ganz andersartigen Charakter als in Prov. 8 hat die Rede der Weisheit in Prov. 1, 20–33."[28] In her analysis of this text, Kayatz alerts the reader that her analysis will begin with Old Testament resources and then turn to comparable Egyptian traditions.[29]

Kayatz first offers a detailed verse by verse classification of Prov 1:20–33 where she analyzes the *Schelt- und Mahnpredigt* forms (invective and admonitory speech forms), the address to the *Einfaltigen Spotter und Toren* (simple ones, scoffers and fools), and the *Verheissung* (promise).[30] After calling attention to the parallels with prophetic traditions and prophetic forms of speech, Kayatz concentrates on the striking similarities between Deutero-Isaiah, Trito-Isaiah, the deuteronomic portions of Jeremiah, and Prov 1:20–33.[31] Having shown the similarities in form and content between Prov 1:20–33 and prophetic traditions, she raises the question of the direction of influence in a surprising way: Is the influence from the prophets to wisdom or from wisdom to prophets?[32]

To answer the question of influence Kayatz calls attention to R. Bultmann's 1923 essay concerning "Der alten Mythos von der Weisheit."[33] For our purposes, it is only necessary to note that Bultmann does not attribute the content or form of Prov 1:20–33 to prophetic traditions but to an unknown myth of wisdom seeking a place on earth. Not finding one, wisdom returns to its origin. Of interest for Kayatz in

---

[27] *Studien zu Proverbien 1–9*, 119–134.

[28] *Studien zu Proverbien 1–9*, 119.

[29] *Studien zu Proverbien 1–9*, 122: "Wir beginnen mit dem alttestamentlichen Befund und ziehen anschliessend ägyptisches Vergleichsmaterial heran."

[30] *Studien zu Proverbien 1–9*, 120.

[31] *Studien zu Proverbien 1–9*, 120–121.

[32] *Studien zu Proverbien 1–9*, 121.

[33] "Der religionsgeschichte hintergrund des Prologs zum Johannes-Evangelium," *Eucharisterion Festschrift* Hermann Gunkel N.F. 19 (1923) 1–26.

the content of her analysis of Prov 1:20–33 is the problem which Bultmann's article raises concerning the exact origin (*genaueren Herkunft*) of wisdom. More specifically Kayatz says:

> Die Gattung einer weisheitlichen Lock und Gerichts-predigt kann Bultmann nicht durch frühere ausser-israelitische Texte belegen. Deshalb sind eingehende vergleichende Untersuchungen notwendig zu der Frage, ob das Schelten und Drohen der Weisheit in unserem text genuin weisheitliche oder aber prophetische Redeform ist. Ausserdem ist zu prufen, woher die besstimmenden Motive stammen.[34]

The difficulty in finding a parallel *Gattung* for wisdom's speech *as well as* a source for the wisdom *Motive* form for Kayatz the two poles of analysis for Prov 1:20–33.

By framing her approach along the lines of a clear separation between *Gattung* and *Motive*, we are brought back to the subtitle of Kayatz's book: *eine form- [Gattung] und motivgeschichtliche Untersuchung unter Einbeziehung ägyptischen Vergleichsmaterials.*

The value for Kayatz of returning to Bultmann's 1923 article is twofold: 1) Bultmann's failure to provide an answer for the *Gattung* of the wisdom myth leaves the door open for Kayatz to enter in with her own account; 2) Bultmann's discounting of influence between Prov 1:20–33 and prophetic traditions allows Kayatz to capitalize upon a more or less clear traditio-historical connection between the two. The analysis of the prophetic characteristics in Prov 1:20–33 leads her to conclude that in all likelihood wisdom embodies an earlier form of speech which only later appears in clearer but altered form among the prophets—most especially the deuteronomic sections in Jeremiah. Whatever resemblances that we can detect between wisdom's speech in 1:20–33 and prophetic material are attributed solely to the intimate relation between *Jahwe und Weisheitsgestalt*.[35] The intimacy between YHWH and pre-existent Wisdom results in speech patterns that are notably similar to later prophetic forms.

Her analysis also accords with the Solomonic dating she gives for Proverbs 1–9. Because all the examples of shared prophetic speech patterns are found in exilic traditions, it is inconceivable that Prov 1:20–

---

[34] *Studien zu Proverbien 1–9*, 122. Cf. G. von Rad's comment (*Wisdom in Israel*, 160) concerning Bultmann's argument for a wisdom myth: "Whether there ever was a myth of a searching and disappointed Wisdom, the existence of which has been taken as certain since Bultmann's famous essay . . . has become highly questionable. It leads to disastorous distortions if one interprets texts such as Prov 1.20ff.; Job 28; Sir. 24 on the basis of and with an eye to this 'wisdom myth'."

[35] *Studien zu Proverbien 1–9*, 133.

33 could be influenced by prophetic speech. Thus, what appears to be a case of prophetic influence upon Prov 1:20–33 turns out to be a case of wisdom embodying a speech form which only later re-emerges in altered form in Jeremiah, Deutero-Isaiah, and Trito-Isaiah.[36]

As for Prov 6:1–19, Kayatz is primarily interested in the formal characteristics of vv 6:1–19 and how form is heuristically useful in detecting cross-cultural parallels from Egypt. Kayatz discusses Prov 6:1–19 in the context of her analysis of "Die kasuistisch eingeleiteten Einheiten" and "Die imperativisch eingeleiteten Einheiten" found in Egyptian traditions. The basic characteristic of "Die kasuistisch eingeleiteten Einheiten" is the combination of two clauses introduced by "Wenn" and "dann," respectively. Variations in the form are represented by "Begründung."[37]

After reviewing various Egyptian examples, Kayatz lists Prov 6:1–5 as her first example from the book of Proverbs.[38] Vv 1–5 fit her form critical criteria. V 1 initiates the protasis clause, "if." V 3 represents the apodasis, "then." Kayatz says nothing more about vv 1–5.

As for Prov 6:6–11, Kayatz briefly refers to these verses in her discussion of "Begründung durch Prädikation."[39] The ant, "Die Ameise," functions as the "Begründung durch Prädikation" for the exhortation for the sluggard.[40] Vv 6–11 provide another example for Kayatz of shared forms of expression between Egyptian and Israelite traditions.

In a section entitled "Exkurs: Die Topik der Organe und Glieder," Kayatz makes passing reference to Prov 6:12–15, 16–19. Her interest is primarily in the references to the "heart" and possible connections with an Egyptian motif. Kayatz finds little that is useful.[41] On one other occasion Kayatz mentions vv 12–15 under the subtitle of "Die Prädikation als selbständige Form."[42] The comparisons with Egyptian forms of expression and Prov 6:12–15 prove to be marginally useful for

[36] See pp. 122–133 for examples of *Abwandlung*, "alterations," in prophetic traditions in comparison with Prov 1:20–33. For example, such things as the prophetic speech form marked by *Gerichtsankundigung* and *Anklage*, the combination of the unconditional announcement of judgment in Prov 1:24–31 with the promise in vv 23 and 33, and the motifs of laughing/ mocking, calling/not listening, and seeking/not finding all seem to reflect important "alterations" in Prov 1:20–33. Kayatz concludes that these "alterations" demonstrate that the wisdom traditions in Prov 1:20–33 pre-date the prophetic ones.

[37] *Studien zu Proverbien 1–9*, 26–27.

[38] *Studien zu Proverbien 1–9*, 29–30.

[39] *Studien zu Proverbien 1–9*, 49.

[40] *Studien zu Proverbien 1–9*, 49.

[41] *Studien zu Proverbien 1–9*, 43.

[42] *Studien zu Proverbien 1–9*, 52.

Kayatz. While Kayatz can account for the form critical similarities shared between Hebrew and Egyptian traditions, Kayatz does not raise the question of the larger form critical unity of vv 1–19.

A number of problems can be pointed out concerning her analysis of Proverbs and its relationship to Egyptian traditions. Kayatz confuses the process of *description* of the Egyptian and Israelite traditions with the act of providing *evidence* of adoption or assimilation. In addition, the *einfache Form* is no more than an extrapolation from the Egyptian traditions and an ideal form. Its appearance either in a casuistic or imperative form is so general a speech pattern as to be of little value for the analysis of the traditions. It is also doubtful that we can extract from the biblical traditions a clear presentation of *Jahweglaubens* and *Weisheitgestalt*. Methodologically, the positing of the pair provides Kayatz with an explanation for the similarity between wisdom speech forms and "later" prophetic traditions. But the argument for their place within biblical traditions is never established or described.

Lastly, her argument for the dating of Proverbs 1–9 stands or falls on the presumption of the intense theological endeavors in the period of the Solomonic Enlightenment, providing the functional cause for the evolution of the theological content in Proverbs 1–9.[43] The argument works only if one agrees with her that such a period existed *and* proved to be a crucial intellectual period.

W. McKane: Proverbs 1–9 and the International Form of "Instruction."

W. McKane's approach is eclectic. He appeals to form criticism, traditio-historical phenomena, and examples of didactic material from Egypt in order to demonstrate the formal influences between Proverbs 1–9 and Egyptian Instruction. By surveying carefully Egyptian and Assyrian traditions, McKane posits a formal genre called "Instruction" which is "a clearly demarcated international genre . . . ."[44] The presence

---

[43] See J. Van Seters, *In Search of History, Historiography in the Ancient World and the Origins of Biblical History* (New Haven/London: Yale University Press, 1983) 216–217, who raises questions about the reality of such a historical period and its purported impact upon Israel's traditions.

[44] *Proverbs* 6. McKane divides Proverbs into two large form-critical categories: Instruction and "sentence"(cf. p. 3). McKane is not offering an original form-critical observation at this point. As far as we are aware, H. Gressmann ("Die neugefundene Lehre des Amen-em-ope und die vorexilische Spruchdichtung Israels," *ZAW* 42 [1924] 289–290) is the first scholar to observe the form-critical parallels between the forms "Aussagen und Mahnungen" in the book of Proverbs and Amenemope.

of this international genre in Proverbs allows him to explain the traditio-historical relationship between Proverbs 1–9; 22:17–23:11 (the section purportedly dependent upon Amenemope), and the remaining chapters of Proverbs. He argues that we now have clear evidence of formal and historical links with Egyptian traditions:

> There is the further consideration that 1–9 has the same formal structure as 22.17–23.11. That the latter is formally dependent on *Amenemope* is generally acknowledged, but if this is so, the logic of the form-critical argument in relation to 1–9 collapses. The conclusion to be drawn is that the formal structure of 1–9, 22.17–24.22 and 31.1–9 is that of an international Instruction genre, and that it is not the consequence of a process of form-critical evolution involving the agglomeration of wisdom sentences.[45]

In contrast to the wisdom sentence which "is an observation with an impersonal form which states a truth but neither exhorts nor persuades . . . Instruction commands and exhorts and gives reasons why its directives should be obeyed. These reasons are contained in subordinate clauses of which the most typical is the motive ($k\bar{\imath}$) clause."[46]

McKane further argues that the Instruction genre was adopted from Egyptian educational circles in the time of Solomon where there was a need to train individuals for Solomon's civil service.[47] The problem McKane has, though, with arguing for the adoption of the Instruction model by Israel during the time of Solomon is that the "external examples in 1–9 do not have the character of career advice for officials, so that the argument for its introduction to Israel in the reign of Solomon does involve a process of extrapolation."[48] McKane goes on to say: "In

---

McKane's "Instruction" is formally and functionally comparable to "Mahnungen." Gressmann, however, dates the "Mahnungen" to a post-exilic period(p. 286). In contrast, McKane posits a formal equivalence between Proverbs 1–9 and 22:17–24:22 and places both traditions (i.e., the form Instruction but not necessarily its content) in the Solomonic era in order to circumvent the argument that Proverbs 1–9 is actually a form-critical and traditio-historical outgrowth of the shorter proverbial forms found in Proverbs 10ff. Gressmann argues for such an outgrowth and development(cf. pp. 289–290).

45 *Proverbs*, 6–7. McKane posits a case of direct literary dependence of Prov 22:17–23:11 on Amenemope. As he says: Prov 22:17–23:11 "shows direct literary dependence on the Instruction of Amenemope. . . " (*Proverbs*, 4). "Whatever the precise character of the dependence of this passage on Amenemope, there is little doubt that an appropriation of formal elements of the Egyptian Instruction is involved"(*Proverbs*, 5).

46 *Proverbs*, 3.

47 *Proverbs*, 9.

48 *Proverbs*, 9.

other words, it has to be assumed that the pieces in 1–9 are representative of later stages in the history of the tradition on the Instruction and that we are not able to inspect it at its point of origin,"[49] i.e., we are unable to see what the original *content* was.

The outcome of McKane's argument is that the international form called Instruction has been the constant element throughout the historical development of Proverbs 1–9 as a whole. What has changed in the tradition has been its content. In other words, the form Instruction is the carrier of the content, whatever it may be. As it happens, Proverbs 1–9 is actually a later development in the tradition where the *original* vocational and state-oriented content from the court of Solomon has been wrenched apart from the now vitiated form Instruction.

McKane attributes the cause for the wrenching apart of the original form and content to a gradual theological process whereby the "wise men" refitted the form Instruction as well as the sentence form to the rising influence of "Yahwistic piety" in late pre-exilic Israel. As McKane says: "The history of the tradition of the Instruction is parallel to that of the wisdom sentence; both are eventually integrated into the fabric of Yahwistic piety and become the instruments of its propagation. We may conclude that the Instruction which is originally, in Egypt if not in Israel, a means of educating officials, becomes in Israel a method of generalized mundane instruction and thereafter a way of inculcating Yahwistic piety."[50]

Referring to Prov 1:8–19, our first example, McKane says: "This is Instruction, and its formal correspondence with examples of the same genre from outside the Old Testament [i.e. Egypt] can easily be demonstrated."[51]

McKane's form-critical model of Instruction fits Prov 1:8–19. Besides the presence of a *kî* clause, vv 8,16, the text contains imperatives in vv 10

---

[49] *Proverbs*, 9.

[50] *Proverbs*, 9–10. Concerning the re-application of the literary form Instruction, see R. Knierim, "Old Testament Form Criticism Reconsidered," *Int* 37 (1983) 435–468, where he raises the question, for example, whether we can assuredly speak of "a monolithic conception of genre" and assume "the homogeneity of the typical factors in it"(p. 467). In other words, McKane works with an ideal form of Instruction and does not allow for the possibility that these biblical traditions may have their own unique stylistic features which go beyond any fixed form-critical bounds.

[51] *Proverbs*, 267. See: R. Murphy, *Wisdom Literature: Job, Proverbs, Ruth, Canticles, Ecclesiastes, and Esther* (vol. 13, FOTL. Grand Rapids, Michigan: Eerdmans, 1981) 55: "The genre here [Prov 1:8–19] is Instruction. The admonition in v. 8 (cf. also v. 15), expressed both positively and negatively in antithetical parallelism, serves here as an introduction to the warning. The casuistic style of the warning is a pattern found already in Ptahhotep. . . ."

and 15, where the parent exhorts the son. That the *kî* clause in v 16 is a gloss from Isa 59:7 (an exilic or post-exilic tradition) does not present a serious problem for McKane. The importance of the *kî* clause is its form and not its content.[52]

Following his lead that the form Instruction undergoes an internal transformation and subsequent reinterpretation in order to come in line with "Yahwistic piety," we may be somewhat baffled by his concluding comments for Prov 1:8–19: "There is nothing explicitly Yahwistic in the way in which the concept of retribution is handled in these verses, and there is no overt religious allusion in the entire passage."[!][53] If there is anything remotely "religious" about 1:8–19, it is the fact that "the metaphor of v. 12 derives from a piece of Canaanite mythology . . . ."[54]

McKane also faces a number of difficulties when he tries to interpret Prov 1:20–33, the second lesson in Proverbs, in an international context of Instruction. After offering his analysis of vv 20–33 McKane concludes:

> I would not describe vv. 20–33 as an example of the Instruction genre, although there are a few features which recall the genre, notably the emphasis on attentiveness, the vocabulary and the motive clause in v 32. But there is not a single imperative, which is of the essence of the Instruction, and the formal structure, for the most part, follows prophetic modes of address.[55]

The failure of 1:20–33 to fit into the tightly drawn form-critical description of Instruction is another example of the difficulty McKane has in classifying the traditions along the lines of parallels from Egyptian traditions. We already saw how Prov 1:8–19 reflected the Instructional form but failed to qualify as an example of Yahwistic reinterpretation. In contrast, Prov 1:20–33 fails to fit the mold of the international form of Instruction.

As for the prophetic content and form of wisdom's speech in 1:20–33, he insists that wisdom only "emerges almost as a prophet" and not a

---

[52] *Proverbs*, 268.

[53] *Proverbs*, 271. Cf. p. 8.

[54] *Proverbs*, 269. For evidence of Canaanite mythology, McKane refers to R. T. O'Callaghan, "Echoes of Canaanite Literature in the Psalms," *VT* 4 (1954) 164–176; esp. p. 169. Cf. R. B. Y. Scott, *Proverbs*, 38: "The verse perpetuates ideas and language which can be traced back to the ancient Canaanite myth of Baal and Anath, where the god Mot (death) reigns over the Pit, a land of filth beneath the earth, and *swallows up* Baal and all who 'go down into the earth.'"

[55] *Proverbs*, 277.

full-fledged one.[56] And contrary to other scholars who, according to McKane, interpret wisdom "envisaged as Person within the Godhead in a theological sense," he understands wisdom's function in the market place as representative "of a charismatic wisdom teacher and no more."[57] In other words, what emerges in his analysis of Prov 1:20–33 is the understanding of the teacher who is speaking under the guise of wisdom with only a brief hint of Egyptian influence. The end result of McKane's analysis is that Prov 1:20–33 fits neither fully in the arena of comparative Egyptian studies nor completely in the realm of "Yahwistic religion" as found in the Hebrew Bible. Only by "the mention of the fear of Yahweh" in 1:29 is there "a framework of interpretation for the items of wisdom vocabulary which occur in this passage."[58] At this point, McKane's argument is quite similar to Whybray's earlier argument concerning the theological role played by Prov 1:29. The value of recognizing the central role of 1:29 thus provides a hermeneutical key for reading wisdom in the context of Yahwistic piety.[59]

The outcome of McKane's analysis of 1:20–33 is that it is never clear where he places the text within the traditions. It is not Instruction. It is not prophetic speech. Only by the single reference to the "fear of Yahweh" are we able to imply the larger theological scope of the text. But this larger scope is never developed by McKane.

As for Prov 6:1–19, McKane treats each of the four units in the text individually. We noted the importance that McKane places upon the international form Instruction which is identified by imperatives and by a *kî* clause. Of the verses under consideration only vv 1–5 come close to being formally Instruction.[60] Vv 1–5, however, lack a *kî* clause which does not present a problem for McKane. In its place McKane points to the conditional clause which is a "new formal feature."[61]

Unlike other scholars who treat vv 1–19 as an interpolation, McKane argues that the removal of vv 1–19 would not present a clear connection between 5:23 and 6:20ff. McKane, however, does not elaborate on the interrelationship between the four units in Prov 6:1–19 and the surrounding context. More troublesome is the lack of formal

---

[56] *Proverbs*, 275. "There is no doubt that in v. 22 Wisdom speaks like a wisdom teacher and not like a prophet"(p. 275).

[57] *Proverbs*, 277.

[58] *Proverbs*, 275.

[59] *Proverbs*, 275.

[60] *Proverbs*, 320.

[61] *Proverbs*, 320: "The opening verses (vv. 1–5) are emphatically Instruction and are dominated by imperatives. The only new formal feature in them deserving of comment is the series of conditional clauses preceding the initial imperative and defining the circumstances in which the imperatives are to be heeded. . . ."

characteristics for Instruction: "Yet in this section there is material which is formally different from anything in the earlier chapters and which, because it lacks imperatives, is certainly not Instruction. This is true of vv 12–15, which describe a particular type of malevolence, and of 16–19, an example of a graded numerical saying."[62] McKane also is at a loss to explain vv 6–11. While these verses have the imperative,

> the form is hardly consistent with either parental or scholastic instruction, for there is a significant difference between a 'My son' address, which warns against sloth, and an 'O sluggard' address, which is directed against one confirmed in habits of slothfulness. It is difficult to believe that this would be a normal presupposition in either parental or scholastic instruction.[63]

Even though McKane argues for the contextual unity for 6:1–19, the unit fails to meet his criteria of Instruction. Vv 1–5 are the exception.

Questions can be raised concerning McKane's overall analysis of Proverbs 1–9 when the very first "lesson" in Proverbs meets the form-critical criteria as set up by McKane but then fails to show any evidence whatsoever of Yahwistic influence. If the "wise men" felt in any way obligated to couch the form Instruction with "Yahwistic piety" in order to infuse the international form of Instruction with definitive theological content, would it not make sense that they would use their introductory didactic lesson to establish their own theological credentials? That Prov 1:8–19 does not seem to come close to the process of Yahwistic reinterpretation presents serious problems for McKane's traditio-historical reconstruction of Prov 1:8–19 as well as of other portions of Proverbs 1–9.

Equally problematic is McKane's overriding hypothesis that there was in fact an international form termed "Instruction" which was preserved essentially intact in an ideal form from Solomon's era up to the final editing of the book of Proverbs as a whole. Is it really the case that we have enough evidence at hand to show that a form such as Instruction, which had its home, if not its origin, in court circles, could easily shift to the *Sitz im Leben* of those who espoused a "Yahwistic piety"? Lastly, do we have enough evidence within scripture to draw such clear-cut lines between a monolithic tradition termed "Yahwistic piety," as McKane presents it, and an equally monolithic tradition of courtly wisdom? McKane presupposes far too much concerning the background of the form and content of the traditions to make a

---

[62] *Proverbs*, 320.
[63] *Proverbs*, 320.

convincing argument. Also, Prov 1:8–19; 1:20–33; and 6:1–19 do not fit his theory concerning the international form of Instruction.

SUMMARY.

The discovery of the shared features between portions of Proverbs and Amenemope had a decisive impact on Proverbs research. The interpretations given by Whybray, Kayatz, and McKane indicate well the nature of the impact. Significant for our analysis of Proverbs is the degree of agreement between these scholars concerning the details of how Egyptian didactic traditions help us in our interpretation. On one level, the general theories of Whybray's lesson-book, Kayatz's *einfache Form*, and McKane's international Instruction form explain the literary and historical link with Egyptian wisdom traditions. In each case, those elements within Egyptian didactic literature that can be linked with Israel's sapiential traditions have been altered in order to find a place within Israel's theology. By isolating "alien" elements within Israel's wisdom traditions, Whybray, Kayatz, and McKane have a convenient foil to explain later Yahwistic reinterpretations that portions of Proverbs seem to reflect. The hermeneutic reinterpretation that these scholars detect also has a subtle counterpart. "Israel's religious belief" (Whybray), "Jahwegestalt" (Kayatz), and "Yahwistic piety" (McKane), whatever they are in reality, are not compromised in the reinterpretative combination with the alien wisdom elements but triumph over the foreign influences by setting the standards of theological orthodoxy.

On the level, however, which addresses the details of their general theories of composition, far too many questions are left unanswered on the basis of the models of interpretation. We have already raised a number of questions concerning the analyses of Whybray, Kayatz, and McKane. The most pressing question raised concerns the difficulty of establishing a clear link between Prov 1:8–19; 1:20–33; 6:1–19 and extra-biblical sources based upon comparative models. Using the same traditions, Whybray, Kayatz, and McKane arrive at clearly different interpretations for the interrelationship between Proverbs and Egyptian didactic sources. In face of the difficulties that Whybray, Kayatz, and McKane have in presenting a cogent analysis for Prov 1:8–19; 1:20–33; 6:1–19 and, for that matter, Proverbs 1–9 as a whole, it is time to take a fresh look at the details of the traditions as they appear in the larger context of the Hebrew canon and offer an alternative approach.

A Proposed Approach.

In light of the difficulties scholars have had in providing interpretations for Proverbs 1–9 based upon Egyptian traditions, we are proposing an alternative approach. We will argue that at certain points in Proverbs 1–9 we can find clear evidence of reutilization of traditions from the Joseph story and from portions of Jeremiah. In our analysis we will isolate and describe various redactional techniques that are evident within Proverbs for joining earlier biblical traditions to the book of Proverbs. Primary concern will be given to how the different levels of direct discourse reflect a creative refashioning of earlier speech events and action from Genesis and Jeremiah in order to form new discourse units. Evidence of speech which implies another's speech and action will be found in such phenomena as the transposition of words from another context, the anthological combination of vocabulary adapted to a new sapiential context, key words and phrases, virtual citations, and allusive language all of which imply other scriptural texts and contexts.

As for the dating of Proverbs 1–9, we are in agreement with other scholars who argue that not only is Proverbs 1–9 the latest unit of tradition in the book of Proverbs but that it derives from the period around the end of the exile and the early post-exilic period—i.e., the period when the exiles were returning to Judah and Jerusalem.[64] The

---

[64] The earliest and most detailed argument for dating Proverbs 1–9 to the early post-exilic period that we are aware of is made by C. G. Montefiore, "Notes on the Date and Religious Value of Proverbs," *JQR* 2 (1890) 430–453. He bases his argument for the dating of Proverbs 1–9 to the post-exilic period mainly upon the content of the book (see especially, pp. 439–443). Montefiore lists as evidence for a post-exilic date such things as the unique role played by women, the warnings against involvement with a *nokriyyâ*, "foreign woman," individualism, monogamy, and parallels with earlier prophetic texts, Deuteronomy, and Psalms. C. Camp (*Wisdom and the Feminine*, 233–254) also places the final redaction and content of Proverbs 1–9 in a post-exilic context. Her evidence for dating was presaged by Montefiore's earlier article. See the following scholars who also date Proverbs 1–9 to a post-exilic period: C. H. Toy, *Proverbs* (ICC; Edinburgh: T & T Clark, 1977) xxx; H. Gressmann, "Die neugefundene Lehre des Amen-em-ope und die vorexilische Spruchdictung Israels," 286, 292; A. Robert, "Les attaches littéraires bibliques de Prov. I-IX," *RB* 44 (1935) 502–525; see especially 502–517; B. Gemser, *Sprüche Salomos*, 5, 6; O. Eissfeldt, *The Old Testament: An Introduction*, trans. by P. Ackroyd. (Oxford/New York: Harper and Row,1965), 473; E. Sellin and G. Fohrer, *Introduction to the Old Testament*, 319, 323, 473; H. Ringgren and W. Zimmerli, *Sprüche/Prediger* (Göttingen: Vandenhoeck und Ruprecht, 1980) 8; M. Hengel, *Judaism and Hellenism: Studies in their Encounter in Palestine during the Early Hellenistic Period*, vol 1. (Philadelphia: Fortress Press, 1974) 153. Cf. the following commentators who speak of Proverbs 1–9 as the latest section in the book of Proverbs: E. Bauckman, "Die Proverbien und die Sprüche der Jesu Sirach," 44, 45–46; C. Rylaarsdam, *Revelation in Jewish Wisdom Literature* (Chicago/London: The

evidence for the dating of chapters 1–9 in this period lies in the content of the parents' discourse. The overall interest of the parents is in discouraging the son from getting himself involved with two kinds of people: men who perpetuate "evil" and the $z\bar{a}r\,\hat{a}/nokriyy\hat{a}$, "strange/foreign woman." Like other literature in the post-exilic period such as Ezra and Nehemiah, primary concern is devoted to reestablishing a Jewish community in and around Jerusalem.

In Prov 1:8–19; 2:12–15, 20–22; 4:10–19, reference is made to men who engage in an assortment of violence. In 2:16–19; 5:1–23; 6:20–33; and 7:1–27, the son is warned of the foreign woman who can lead him to ruin. We know that in the period of the return the exiles are faced with "Jewish brethren" who are not only mistreating their own fellow Jews (Neh 5:1–13), but who also have mingled with foreigners in the land of Judah through inter-marriage (Ezra 9; 10), thus presenting the returning exiles with theological and social problems which needed reform. The concentration of the parents' discourse in Proverbs 1–9 upon avoiding the pitfalls of evil men and foreign women has a counterpart in Ezra and Nehemiah.

The books of Ezra and Nehemiah are two examples which record some of the difficulties the returnees had in re-establishing themselves in Judah and Jerusalem. Other books such as Trito-Isaiah, Malachi, Zechariah, Haggai, 1 and 2 Chronicles, reflect the tensions in the period of the return.[65] In the process of our analysis of Proverbs 1–9, we will offer other evidence which supports earlier arguments made by scholars for a post-exilic dating.

By concentrating on the instances of direct discourse within Proverbs 1–9 we are highlighting the unique feature that speech plays within these chapters. While the details of our argument concerning the nature of direct discourse will be developed in the context of our examples, we here indicate the direction that we will take.

University of Chicago Press, 1946) 21; R. B. Y. Scott, *Proverbs*, 15; H. H. Schmid, *Wesen und Geschichte der Weisheit, Eine Untersuchung zur altorientalische und Israelitischen Weisheitsliteratur*, 144; O. Plöger, *Sprüche Salomos*, xxxvi; and R. H. Pfeiffer, *Introduction to the Old Testament* (New York/London: Harper and Row, 1941) 658–659.

[65] For example, see: D. L. Petersen, *Late Israelite Prophecy: Studies in Deutero-Prophetic Literature and in Chronicles* (SBLMS 23, Missoula, Montana: Scholars Press, 1977); P. Ackroyd, *Exile and Restoration, A Study of Hebrew Thought of the Sixth Century B. C.* (Philadelphia: Westminster Press, 1968); W. A. M. Beuken, *Haggai-Sacharja 1–8 Studien zur uberlieferungsgeschichte der Frühnachexilischen Prophetie* (Assen: Van Gorcum and Comp. N. V., 1967); and A. Petitjean, *Les Oracles du Proto-Zacharie, Un programme de restauration pour la communauté juive après l'exil* (Paris: Librairie Lecoffre J. Gabalda, 1965).

Two scholars who are important for our analysis of the speech patterns within Proverbs 1–9 are M. Bakhtin and M. Sternberg.[66] In brief, Bakhtin argues that one of the common features of direct speech is its "double-voiced" characteristic.[67] The speech of one person may covertly imply someone else's speech and action by means of a carefully chosen word, phrase, or an anthology of words.[68] Thus, one hears not only the words of the character who is speaking: one also hears in the background, as it were, the rephrased speech of someone else—hence, "double-voiced discourse."

M. Sternberg also argues for what he calls the "deictic duality of direct speech."[69] Like Bakhtin before him, Sternberg points to the phenomenon of how reported discourse in some cases is actually the combination of "at least two discourse-events": the original speech-event and the speech-event of another. Such a combination of speech within speech is mimetic; i.e., representational of another character in another place and time.[70] The importance of Bakhtin's and Sternberg's analysis of direct discourse is how speech and action is a form of mimetic representation and not reference. Even though Proverbs 1–9, for example, does not overtly refer to any characters in Israel's history (save for Solomon in Prov 1:1), embedded in the various speech patterns in Proverbs 1–9 we can detect historical representations based upon other canonical traditions. A bridge is thus formed between Proverbs and Israel's historical traditions *via* discourse.

The advantage of offering a close analysis of discourse in portions of Proverbs 1–9 lies in the traditio-historical control that we can garner from the texts themselves. We are not dependent upon extra-biblical traditions to provide us with comparative models for interpretation into which Proverbs is made to fit. Instead we take our cues from the numerous internal markings within the traditions of the book of Proverbs which locate it primarily as another member of canonical scripture and not

---

[66] M. Bakhtin, *Problems of Dostoevsky's Poetics*, ed. and trans. by C. Emerson (Theory and History of Literature, vol. 8; Minneapolis: University of Minnesota Press, 1984); *idem*, *The Dialogic Imagination*, ed. by M. Holquist; trans. by C. Emerson and M. Holquist (Austin: University of Texas Press, 1981); M. Sternberg, "Proteus in Quotation Land: Mimesis and the Forms of Reported Discourse," *Poetics Today* 3 (1982) 107–156; "Point of View and the Indirections of Direct Speech," *Language and Style* 15 (1982) 67–117.

[67] *Problems of Dostoevsky's Poetics*, 185.

[68] See: *Problems in Dostoevsky's Poetics*, 185, where Bakhtin speaks of the "twofold direction" of some discourse which directs the hearer's attention to the immediate referent of the speaker and also to "*another's discourse.*"

[69] "Point of View," 111.

[70] "Point of View," 72.

primarily as a wisdom text in an international context. The most obvious sign for the book's intended location within the canon is the role attributed to Solomon in Prov 1:1. Less obvious indicators for Proverbs' location within the canon will be found scattered throughout the compositional forms of discourse units which we will identify in Proverbs 1–9.

Our isolation of discourse units which play upon earlier scriptural traditions will prove to be important because the appeal made to events from Israel's past does more than provide concrete examples for the parents' teachings; the earlier traditions contribute specific content that is addressed further in Proverbs 1–9. As such, a clear play upon traditions from the Torah and the Prophets will be seen to have a direct effect upon our reading of other portions of Proverbs 1–9.[71] The final redactional shape of Proverbs 1–9, with its plays upon traditions from the Torah and the prophets, adds another dimension to the nature of the parents' discourse.

Thus the combination of a cast of characters such as the mother, father, "sinners," wisdom, grandfather, son, "adventuress/loose woman"(RSV), and the "foolish woman," who speak in first person discourse all within the confines of Proverbs 1–9, is more than an aesthetic device; the very content of their speech has the potential of revealing a far richer intertextuality than at first appears. As such, the issues addressed in Proverbs 1–9 do not derive solely from the parents' experience, as many scholars are prone to argue, but rather are linked traditio-historically to earlier biblical traditions. Our awareness of the various ways portions of Proverbs 1–9 play upon earlier traditions will thus go a long way in seeing how the final shape of these chapters helps to situate Proverbs in a larger canonical context.

Our argument concerning the traditio-historical links between portions of Proverbs 1–9 with the Torah and the prophets has an interesting parallel in Ben Sirach. For example, scholars have long recognized that Sirach modelled his book on Proverbs.[72] The obvious

---

[71] The details of our analysis can be found in chaps II, III, and IV.

[72] For example, see S. Schecter and C. Taylor, eds., *The Wisdom of Ben Sira, Portions of the Book of Ecclesiastes*, (Reprint of the Cambridge Editions of 1896 and 1899; Amsterdam: APA-PHILO Press, 1979) where they say: "For B. S. [Ben Sirach], though not entirely devoid of original ideas, was, as is well known, a conscious imitator both as to form and as to matter, his chief model being the Book of Proverbs"(p. 12). See also: C. H. Toy, *Proverbs*, xxiii: "The similarity between *Proverbs* and *Ben Sira* is especially striking. It is not impossible that the similarity is due in part to borrowing;" and A. Robert, "Les attaches littéraires Bibliques de Prov. I–IX," *RB* 44 (1935) 348, where he speaks of the book of Proverbs as the "modéle" for Sirach. Other scholars have noted the similarity between Proverbs and Sirach: E. Schürer, *The*

link between the two resides in the references to wisdom and shared proverbial expressions. However, many scholars are baffled at how easily Sirach links wisdom with Israel's history in contrast to Proverbs' ahistorical format.[73] Proverbs may have been Sirach's model, but Sirach

---

Literature of the Jewish People in the Time of Jesus trans. by P. Christi and S. Taylor; ed. by N. Glatzer (New York: Schocken Books, 1972) 24: "A collection of aphorisms of this sort [as found in the Hebrew Bible] had already found a place among the canonical writings of the Old Testament in the shape of the so-called proverbs of Solomon. We have a collection of a similar character in the book known as *Jesus the Son of Sirach*. . . This book takes that older collection [i.e., Proverbs] as its model, not only as regards the form, but the matter as well, though it contributes a large number of new and original thoughts;" G. W. E. Nickelsburg, *Jewish Literature Between the Bible and the Mishnah* (Philadelphia: Fortress Press, 1981) 59: "It is ben Sira's identification of Wisdom and Torah that we find the heart and dynamic of his thought. The practical sides of his advice notwithstanding, he is concerned for the most part with one's conduct vis-á-vis the Torah and the consequences of that conduct. Although the book of Proverbs identifies the fear of God as the beginning of wisdom, and the author of Psalm 119 extols at great length the joy of the Torah, the Wisdom of Jesus the Son of Sirach is the earliest datable work in our literature that discusses the relationship of Wisdom and Torah in detail and in theory." G. Bickell, "Kritische Bearbeitung der Proverbien," *WZKM* 5 (1891) 79–102; 191–214; 271–299; C. Seligmann, *Das Buch der Weisheit des Jesus Sirach* (Breslau: Druck von Th. Schatzky, 1883) 20; J. K. Gasser, *Das althebräische Spruchbuch und die Sprüche Jesu Ben Sira* (Gütersloh: C. Bertelsmann, 1903) 254; H. Duesberg, *Les Scribes Inspires*, (Desclée De Brouwer: Paris, 1938) 385; T. Middendorp, *Die Stellung Jesu ben Siras zwischen Judentum und Hellenismus* (Leiden: E. J. Brill, 1973) 78; E. G. Bauckmann, "Die Proverbien und die Sprüche des Jesus Sirach," *ZAW* 72 (1960) 33. See G. Sheppard's recent analysis of portions of Sirach which provide him with methodological examples of how post-canonical traditions are linked with earlier traditions from the Torah and prophets in, *Wisdom as a Hermeneutical Construct*, 14–18; 19–71; 72–83. Like earlier scholars, Sheppard speaks of how Sirach "breaks with the older wisdom" in Proverbs by Sirach's combination of wisdom, Torah and the prophets(p.16). B. S. Childs, *Introduction*, 558–559, also speaks of "an important new historical element" which occurs when Sirach combines wisdom and Israel's historical traditions.

[73] See: J. Coert Rylaarsdam, *Revelation in Jewish Wisdom Literature*, 31–32, where he traces the gradual development of wisdom as a "secular movement" within the canon to one that is "nationalized" in Sirach: "We must emphasize that with Ben Sira the Hebrew wisdom movement has taken firm rootage in the particularistic Jewish religious tradition [i.e., its history]. It had begun as a secular movement which could make no use of the too tribalistic religious heritage and relied wholly on man's natural gifts. As time went on, especially in the era recorded by Proverbs, chapters 1–9, the leaders of the movement discovered that religion and its foundations are valid and important in a rational, critical outlook upon the world, and they began to find the deep bases of reason and ethics. Gradually, the wise men were converted to the national religious tradition, which did have a moral interpretation of life that enshrined these bases." Rylaarsdam (p. 35) also states: "Like all other documents that

seemingly breaks stride with Proverbs when he introduces references to events and persons out of Israel's past.[74]

Our analysis of the discourse in Proverbs 1–9 will indicate that within these chapters we can find examples of an earlier traditio-historical process which links the book of Proverbs with the Torah and the Prophets. The differences between Sirach and our examples from Proverbs 1–9 reside more in the nature of historical specificity. By uncovering the traditio-historical undercurrents in portions of Proverbs 1–9 that allude to other texts within scripture, we can at a minimum posit an attempt preceding Sirach which links traditions in Proverbs with traditions from Israel's history. Thus, the overt references to Israel's past made in Sirach are already covertly present in the levels of discourse within Proverbs.

Other support for our argument that portions of Proverbs 1–9 play upon canonical traditions from Israel's history will come from rabbinic commentaries. Indeed, only recently have non-Jewish scholars begun to appreciate the wealth of insight that is available from rabbinic sources. Our appeal to Jewish commentary is one which further complements our goal of describing the interrelationship between Proverbs and earlier biblical traditions by means of paying close attention to the function of discourse in the text.[75] In contrast to biblical scholarship in the last

display pride in the national heritage, the Wisdom of Jesus ben Sira makes much use of the historical records of Israel. This is the first wisdom document that does so." L. Perdue, *Wisdom and Cult: A Critical Analysis of the Views of Cult in the Wisdom Literatures of Israel and the Ancient Near East* (SBLDS 30; Missoula, Montana: Scholars Press, 1977) 227, n. 7: "The absence of theological views involving God as the Lord of Salvation History in wisdom literature before Sirach has always been most perplexing." For similar observations concerning the historical orientation of Sirach in contrast to Proverbs, see: H. Duesberg, *Les Scribes Inspires*, 385; I. L. Seeligmann, "Voraussetzungen der Midrasch-exegese," *VTS* 1 (1953) 177–178; J. Fichtner, *Die altorientalische Weisheit in ihrer israelitische-jüdischen Ausprägung* (BZAW 62; Giessen: Alfred Töpelmann, 1933) 126; G. von Rad, *Wisdom in Israel*, 244.

74 G. E. W. Nickelsburg (*Jewish Literature*, 61) says the following about Sirach's use of traditions from the Torah which approximate examples that we will analyze from Proverbs 1–9: "The focus of ben Sira's covenantal theology is governed first by the fact that he is a teacher of ethics. For this reason, though he takes for granted Israel's covenantal status as God's chosen people (24:12; 46:1), he rarely speaks of the covenant except in the context of Torah. From this same perspective his recitation of Israel's history—a rarity in Israelite wisdom literature—focuses on the right deeds, piety, and obedience of individual Israelites of renown."

75 See J. D. Levenson, *Sinai and Zion: An Entry into the Jewish Bible* (San Francisco: Harper and Row, 1985) who provides an interpretation of the biblical references to Sinai and Zion by combining modern day biblical methodology with medieval rabbinic commentary.

century, rabbinic interpretation is not preoccupied with recovering the earliest traditions within a text for the sake of tracing a text's history. More characteristic of rabbinic interpretation is the understood unity of the traditions whereby later perceived additions in a text are valued for their contributions to the ongoing traditioning process.[76] As such, the clearly defined hermeneutic rules of interpretation, the *middoth*, found within the Talmud and midrashim are understood as the natural outgrowth of similar interpretative commentary found within the Tanakh.[77]

While a description of the various principles of rabbinic interpretation would take us far afield, we can draw attention to M. Fishbane's recent book, *Biblical Interpretation in Ancient Israel*, as an attempt to document the continuity between examples of canonical interpretation, i.e., "inner-biblical exegesis," and postbiblical rabbinic commentary.[78]

Of chief concern for Fishbane is how well he can illustrate that what we know as "scribal comments and corrections," "legal exegesis," "aggadic exegesis," and "mantological exegesis" in the postbiblical period have clear precursors within the Hebrew Bible.[79] Indeed, "inner-biblical exegesis," the general expression used for various forms of interpretation found within the Hebrew Bible, is the seedbed for later rabbinic interpretation. However, one of the difficulties that we face as

---

[76] D. Patte, *Early Jewish Hermeneutic in Palestine* (Missoula, Montana: University of Montana Press, 1975), 19–25, where he discusses the notion of the "unity" of both the oral and written traditions in early Jewish commentary.

[77] For instance, H. L. Strack, *Introduction to the Talmud and Midrash* (New York: Atheneum, 1978) 93: "An effort was made to prove by far the greatest number of the regulations of the 'Oral Law,' in part from the outset and in part at least subsequently, from the written Torah, the Pentateuch, occasionally also from other biblical books. Of these hermeneutics it is to be noted that they very frequently not only appear to be, but really are wide of the mark. Nevertheless they are not, as is often believed, entirely arbitrary, but bound to certain rules *middoth* which one must know in order to form a correct opinion of the talmudic exposition of the Scriptures. In the Haggadah the same rules are employed, but in a still freer manner. . ; so it comes about that in haggadic discussions joined to a Bible word it is quite often a case not of bringing out the sense, but of bringing it in or thoughts loosely connected by means of playing on words or by anything else that will support the memory." See also: M. Mielziner, *Introduction to the Talmud* (New York: Bloch Publishing Company, 1968) 117–189, "Legal Hermeneutucs of the Talmud;" and S. Lieberman, *Hellenism in Jewish Palestine* (New York: The Jewish Theological Seminary, 1962) 46–82, "The Rabbinic Interpretation of Scripture."

[78] M. Fishbane, *Biblical Interpretation in Ancient Israel* (Oxford: Clarendon Press, 1985).

[79] *Biblical Interpretation*, ix-xi.

investigators into the rubrics of interpretation within the Hebrew Bible is the seemingly countless ways that texts borrow, refashion, and reinterpret earlier traditions in contrast to later rabbinic methods. As Fishbane says:

> Moreover, since the Hebrew Bible has an exegetical dimension *in its own right*, and this varies text by text and genre by genre, it also stands to reason that the Hebrew Bible is the repository of a vast store of hermeneutical techniques which long preceded Jewish exegesis. These have yet to be thoroughly investigated and systematized. Of immense interest, then, must be the types of exegetical reasoning that can be found in the received Massoretic text. The interest is not historical alone (in so far as these types are predecessors of rabbinic exegesis), but has an inherent concern with the ways ancient Israelite legists, or prophets, preachers, and scribes, resignified and explained their *traditum*. What were the stylistics of such exegeses, and what the logistics? How, in the diversity of cases, is exegetical technique related to form? Does inner-biblical exegesis manifest explicit or implicit analogies between texts; does it exhibit free or controlled associations among the materials; and does it focus on verbal contexts or isolated words? Or both? And so on.[80]

Fishbane does not so much work backwards from well documented rabbinic techniques of interpretation as he appeals to later techniques in search of heuristic devices for taking a fresh look at portions of scripture. The clearly defined ways of interpreting scripture in rabbinic circles are already present within the Hebrew Bible, albeit buried in the matrices of the texts. The systematizing of biblical interpretation by Fishbane is not intended to be exhaustive but exploratory.

By arguing for some continuity between canonical scripture and post-canonical commentary, Fishbane likewise makes a historical case for the unique diversity of biblical interpretation in contrast to either those who trace biblical interpretation to a single stream of tradition going back to Moses at Sinai, or those who place interpretation in the sphere of the "Alexandrian *oikoumene*."[81] Fishbane argues instead that the seemingly unlimited ways of interpreting scripture reflect the historically diverse communities that contribute to the final form of scripture.[82] Even though no one school of interpretation can account for the diversity of biblical interpretation, one can still account for the varieties of it on the basis of derivative models representative of communities who found their identity within the scriptural traditions.

---

[80] *Biblical Interpretation*, 14.
[81] *Biblical Interpretation*, 19.
[82] *Biblical Interpretation*, 19.

In addition to his appeal to Jewish interpretation, Fishbane tries to add clarity to his work by employing terminology taken from modern day biblical scholarship. Specifically, Fishbane divides the traditions according to the framework of a *traditum*, i.e., the earlier content of a recoverable biblical tradition, and a *traditio*, the later tradition which functions as commentary on an identifiable *traditum*.[83] As Fishbane says:

> This supposition [concerning the complex history of a *traditum*] is, of course, the staple of the historical-philological method, whose primary concern in biblical studies has been to unravel the textual strands and documents of the canonical text, and to reorganize them into modern histories of Israelite religion and institutions. On such large matters no more need be said here. Nevertheless, it will prove beneficial briefly to focus on one branch of modern biblical studies which forms the wider methodological context for the present study and sets the framework within which the early Jewish exegetical dynamic of *traditum* and *traditio* finds its roots and incipient religious dignity.[84]

The major difference that Fishbane sees between his understanding of the traditio-historical process and that of modern day scholars is in the direction of study: "whereas the study of tradition-history moves back from the written sources to the oral traditions which make them up, inner-biblical exegesis starts with the received Scripture and moves forward to the interpretations based on it."[85]

As important as Fishbane's book is for our argument, a number of issues need to be addressed. In a recent review, J. Kugel raises a number of questions concerning the issues of "method" and "definition."[86] He argues that Fishbane's use of the terminology of *traditum* and *traditio* presents a confusing picture of the traditioning process within scripture.[87] As Kugel points out, Fishbane's examples of inner-biblical exegesis are not consistent with his own definition of the characteristcs and function of a *traditum* and *traditio* and the nature of the interrelationship between the two. Again, the difficulty that Fishbane seems to face is in his attempt to offer a systematic analysis of inner-biblical exegesis within scripture which resists such systematizing. As a result, while there are clear cases of a *traditio* being the outgrowth of an

---

[83] See *Biblical Interpretation*, 6, where Fishbane expresses his indebtedness to D. Knight's work, *Rediscovering the Traditions of Israel* (SBLDS 9; Missoula: Scholars Press, 1975).

[84] *Biblical Interpretation*, 6.

[85] *Biblical Interpretation*, 7.

[86] J. Kugel, "The Bible's Earliest Interpreters," *Prooftexts* 7 (1987) 269–283.

[87] Ibid., pp. 273–274.

earlier *traditum*, there are far too many cases, as Kugel points out, which do not fit Fishbane's framework of interpretation.[88]

Instead of substituting terminology to replace Fishbane's use of the pair *traditum/traditio* with a more exacting definition, we will simply speak in general terms of earlier and later traditions as they occur within the canon. As such, we are recognizing the variety of ways that texts allude to, play upon, and represent earlier textual traditions without having to label them as *traditum/traditio*.

In addition, even though we will make use of Jewish commentaries in the analysis of our texts as Fishbane does, we will avoid using rabbinic exegetical terminology. The usefulness of rabbinic sources is in the way they provide confirmation for our own traditio-historical analysis of our examples from Proverbs 1–9. Here again we are in general agreement with Kugel's criticisms of Fishbane's appeal to well established rabbinic exegetical techniques to interpret and classify examples of inner-biblical exegesis.[89] But the success of Fishbane's analyses of biblical exegesis does not stand or fall on how close his examples come to rabbinic exegesis. As Kugel admits, without reference to post-biblical exegetical phenomena Fishbane's book still presents a great number of examples which demonstrate the remarkable inner-biblical relationship of the canonical traditions.[90]

Furthermore, in place of the expression, "inner-biblical *exegesis*," we will substitute "inner-biblical *interpretation*." Although there are cases which Fishbane can point to as "exegesis" (i.e., the interpretation of textual traditions with no regard to later reutilization of traditions), the term tends to gather the variety of ways the traditions play upon each other under the potentially restrictive term of exegesis. The numerous examples of texts that rework, allude to, and reutilize other traditions with primary concern to formulating new textual units, suggest a far broader traditioning process. "Interpretation" functions as a more inclusive description of a process that has many faces, some of which are exegetical. Since part of our goal is to allow the texts under investigation to set the terms of how they can be read, inner-biblical interpretation seems to be a better choice.

---

[88] Ibid., pp. 278–280.
[89] Ibid., pp. 280–283.
[90] Ibid., p. 282.

2

PROV 1:8–19, GENESIS 37, AND INNER-BIBLICAL INTERPRETATION.

TRANSLATION
PROVERBS 1:8–19

8) Hear, my son, your father's
instruction, and reject not
your mother's teaching;
9) for they are a fair garland
for your head, and pendants for your neck.
10) My son, if sinners entice you,
do not go,
11) If they say, "Come with us,
let us lie in wait for blood,
let us wantonly ambush the innocent,
12) like Sheol let us swallow them alive
and whole, like those who down to the Pit;
13) we shall find all precious goods,
we shall fill our houses with spoil;
14) throw in your lot among us, we will
all have one purse."
15) My son, do not walk in the way with them,

hold back your foot from their paths;
16) for their feet run to evil,
and they make haste to shed blood.
17) For in vain is a net spread in
the sight of any bird;
18) but these men lie in wait
for their own blood, they
set an ambush for their own lives.
19) Such are the ways of all who get
gain by violence, it takes away the life of
its possessors.

INTRODUCTION.

In the opening paragraph to the series of articles titled "Les attaches littéraires bibliques de Prov. I-IX," A. Robert clearly distances himself from his contemporaries who were celebrating the newly discovered relationship shared between Egyptian traditions and portions of the book of Proverbs:

> Les brillantes découvertes archéologiques qui ont permis d'éclairer la Ste Bible de l'extérieur ne doivent pas faire oublier que, du moins en matiére doctrinale, elle s'éclaire principalement par elle-meme. C'est cette vérité qu'on voudrait faire toucher du doigt en etudiant les attaches littéraires bibliques de Prov. I-IX.[1]

Robert took the initiative to continue to address the question of "les attaches littéraires bibliques de Prov. I-IX." While expressing his indebtedness to other scholars,[2] Robert tried to forge a clearer

---

[1] *RB* 43 (1934) 42. More recently the following commentators have described the number of ways Proverbs 1–9 reflects similar theological interests and traditions found elsewhere in Israel's biblical traditions: Raymond C. Van Leeuwen, "Liminality and Worldview in Proverbs 1–9," *Semeia* 50 (1990) 111–144; Lennart Boström, *The God of the Sages: The Portrayal of God in the Book of Proverbs* (Coniectanea Biblica, Old Testament Series 29; Stockholm: Almqvist and Wiksell International, 1990); Franz-Josef Steiert, *Die Weisheit Israels—ein Fremdkörper im Alten Testament? Eine Untersuchung zum Buch der Sprüche auf dem Hintergrund der ägyptischen Weisheitslehren* (Freiburger theologische Studien 143; Freiburg: Herder, 1990); and Arndt Meinhold, *Die Sprüche. Teil 1: Sprüche Kapitel 1–15* (Zürcher Bibelkommentare Altes Testament 16.1. Zürich: Theologischer Verlag, 1991).
[2] G. Diettrich, "Die Theoretische Weisheit der Einleitung zum Buch der Sprüche, ihr Spezifischer Inhalt und ihre Entstehung," in *Theologische Studien und Kritiken* (Gotha: Friedrich Andreas Berthes, 1908) 475–512; J. K. Gasser, *Die Bedeutung der Sprüche Jesu*

understanding of the interrelationship between Proverbs 1–9 and other portions of the Hebrew Bible.

Due to the temper of the times as well as doubts about Robert's methodology, his work has often been used as a foil to show the limitations of reading the book of Proverbs in the context of other biblical traditions. Fishbane concludes: "The work of A. Robert, and that of many scholars whom he influenced, is particularly prone to laxity and imprecision . . . despite Robert's often very exact definitions."[3] Fishbane's comments suggest that the problem lies less with Robert's notion of anthological style (i.e., the stringing together of words and phrases from other biblical texts to form a new unit of discourse) than with the use he made of it. Fishbane argues that the methodological claims made by Robert are not confirmed by his sometimes random combination of traditions.[4] We should not be surprised to see that in the context of his own work Fishbane likewise speaks of the "anthological character of the received Hebrew Bible."[5] However, Fishbane pays little attention to Proverbs.[6]

Ben Sira für die datierung des althebräischen Sprüchbuches; F. Delitzsch, *Proverbs*; L. Hackspill, "Etude sur le milieu religieux et intellectual contemporain du N. T.," *RB* 10 (1901) 200–215; and C. G. Montefiore, "Notes upon the Date and Religious Value of the Book of Proverbs," 430–453.

[3] *Biblical Interpretation*, 12, n. 32.

[4] See Fishbane, *Biblical Interpretation*, 288–289: "Thus, in consideration of Robert's own proposition that Prov. 1–9 reflects reutilizations of material in the Book of Deuteronomy, it may be contended that 'wisdom' terms are simultaneously used, altogether independently, by the sage-aphorists who produced the Book of Proverbs, the sage-scribes who, at one point, helped produce the Book of Deuteronomy, and sundry prophets, like Isaiah of Jerusalem. This theoretical possibility does not, of course, invalidate any specific instance of aggadic exegesis in principle, though it does serve as a strict methodological hedge against uncritical assumptions of literary *exegetical* interdependence. It is thus one thing to say that a diverse similarity exists between the language of Jeremiah and Deutero-Isaiah, and it is quite another to assert that this similarity does not so much reflect a direct borrowing or adaptation of a received *traditum* as a common linguistic stream preserved by a particular prophetic school."

[5] *Biblical Interpretation*, 440.

[6] In contrast to Fishbane, F.-J. Steiert, *Die Weisheit Israels*, finds the work of A. Robert helpful in analyzing the interrelationship between the book of Proverbs and other biblical traditions. (See especially pp. 229–238 in *Die Weisheit Israels* for Steiert's comments about Robert's work.) Building upon Robert's insights as to how the book of Proverbs glosses other biblical traditions, Steiert broadens and deepens the scope of biblical influence upon Proverbs by noting examples of "theological influence"(p. 242) and "theological background"(p. 243). Such "influence" and "background" are not accidental but "intentional"(p. 269). Moreover, Steiert points to instances of a didactic tendency common to Proverbs 1–9 and Deuteronomy. And the key to

In the following pages, we will examine evidence of inner-biblical connections between Prov 1:8–19 and other portions of the Hebrew Bible. Specifically, we will argue that Prov 1:8–19 is directly dependent on portions of Genesis 37, the selling of Joseph. By reading Prov 1:8–19 with Genesis 37 in mind, we are obviously not turning to extra-biblical sources to assist us in reading as do, e.g., Whybray, Kayatz, and McKane. By returning to an approach that "hears" portions of the Torah and the Prophets re-echoed within Proverbs itself, our aim is to describe the final stage in the editorial process within the tradition history of the book of Proverbs which utilizes parts of Genesis 37. It has long been recognized that Proverbs as a whole reflects a number of editorial stages which led to its final canonical form.[7] Our analysis for Prov 1:8–19 is another contribution to a fuller understanding of this tradition history.

The following argument is divided into three parts. The first part offers examples of how, at certain levels in the book of Proverbs, scholars have detected traditions which have been editorially worked into Proverbs with the result of establishing a wider canonical context. The examples are not meant to be exhaustive but only representative of the possible interrelatedness of Proverbs, Torah, and the Prophets. The second part will highlight similar editorial stages in Prov 1:8–19. The third part will offer a analysis of Prov 1:8–19 with special attention to the effects achieved by the narrator, who makes use of the direct discourse of both the parents and the "sinners." Such speech patterns and their

---

understanding the interconnectedness of Proverbs with other portions of scripture, according to Steiert, lies in wisdom's understanding of *tôrâ*—*tôrâ* in its sense of moral instruction and *tôrâ* as the developing body of canonical scripture. Thus, Steiert often speaks of how parts of Proverbs "remind" (erinnern) the reader of, say, Deuteronomy or one of the prophets. Some sources in Proverbs are formulated "in the sense of" (im Sinne von) other biblical traditions while others are "like" (gleichen) other biblical sources; or the "color" (Kolorit) of a portion of Proverbs 1–9 is prophetic in spirit leading Steiert to conclude that one has in hand examples of "inner-biblical development"(p. 244), or an "inner-biblical relationship"(p. 227). But like Robert, Steiert overlooks the unique features of direct discourse in Proverbs 1–9.

7 Speaking of the book of Proverbs, R. B. Y. Scott in "Wise and Foolish, Righteous and Wicked," 146, says: "The last-named work gathers together wisdom materials that are widely divergent in literary form, viewpoint and thought content, and—especially in the two sections entitled "Proverbs of Solomon"—in an almost haphazard arrangement. Proverbs is an accumulation of variegated materials old and new, apparently assembled for use as a source-book in a school for youth, and edited by the principal author of the discourses and poems in chapter i-ix." Further on Scott concludes: "The present Book of Proverbs is better seen as the end result of a centuries-long process of composition, supplementing, editing and scribal transmission, a process which has blurred some lines of demarcation between its component parts"(150).

content, we will argue, hold the key to perceiving the underlying relationship Prov 1:8–19 has with portions of Genesis 37.

PROVERBS, TORAH, AND PROPHETS:
EXAMPLES OF EDITORIAL REDACTION.

In two recent analyses of Qoh 12:9–14, G. Sheppard and G. Wilson describe the latest stage in the editorial process of Qoheleth which links together Qoheleth and Proverbs.[8] Their work adds to the continuing discussion of the editorial process which sets the books of Qoheleth and Proverbs within an evolving canonical context.[9] Attention to the details of their arguments will provide us with further evidence for detecting similar editorial techniques within Proverbs.

For example, Sheppard argues that the epilogue of Qoheleth achieves an overall thematizing of the book of Qoheleth.[10] Even though such expressions as *dibrê ḥăkāmîm, mĕšālîm*, and the contrast between "God's commandments" in Qoheleth and the parents' commandments in Proverbs do not lead to an exclusive relationship between Proverbs and Qoheleth, Sheppard still concludes that the "general implications about Qoheleth's prolific activity (vv. 9–10), the public presence of valuable wisdom collections (v. 11), and the warning against making more books (v. 12), probably carry an inclusive reference to Proverbs."[11] Sheppard argues further that there is other evidence within the epilogue which achieves a larger canonical reading for Qoheleth. The clues for Sheppard's analysis are found in Sirach and Baruch. In such places as Sir 1:26–30; 2:16; 43:27; and Baruch 3:9–4:4, Sheppard isolates similar thematic elements and editorial devices in the epilogue of Qoheleth. Most striking is the combination of the "fear of God" and the maintaining of God's commandments, a combination reminiscent of the epilogue of Qoheleth.[12] Sheppard then concludes:

---

[8] G. Sheppard, *Wisdom as a Hermeneutical Construct*, 121–129; G. Wilson, ""The Words of the Wise": The Intent and Significance of Qoheleth 12:9–14."

[9] Earlier scholars who raised the issue of the possible editorial linking of Qoheleth and Proverbs are: F. Hitzig, *Der Prediger Salomos's* (Leipzig: Wedimann'sche Buchhandlung, 1847); D. G. Wildeboer, *Die Fünf Megillot* (Tübingen: J. C. B. Mohr, 1898); and G. A. Barton, *The Book of Ecclesiastes* (ICC; New York: Scribners, 1908).

[10] For a similar discussion of the "thematizing" of the book of Qoheleth see: K. Galling, "Koheleth-Studien," *ZAW* 50 (1932) 276–293; and *Die Fünf Megilloth* (HAT 18; 2nd ed.; Tübingen: J. C. B. Mohr, 1969) 124–125.

[11] *Wisdom as a Hermeneutical Construct*, 123–124.

[12] *Wisdom as a Hermeneutical Construct*, 126.

In sum, only Sirach has exactly the same ideology as Qoh. 12:13–14, a perspective not expressed in the body of Qoheleth itself. It is, therefore, probable that the redactor of Qoh. 12:13–14 either knew of the book of Sirach or shared fully in a similar, pervasive estimate of sacred wisdom. . . . Moreover, this later formulation offers an interpretation of the relationship between biblical wisdom and the commandments of God in the Torah. . . . Qoheleth has been thematized by the epilogue in order to include it fully within a canon conscious definition of sacred wisdom, one that is remarkably close to that of Sirach and Baruch.[13]

Sheppard does not limit the editorial redaction to Qoheleth alone but conjectures that the epilogue joins Qoheleth with the book of Proverbs linking the two to an evolving formation of the canon. Thus the combination of the above factors of common themes, expressions, and editorial devices leads Sheppard to conclude that ". . . the epilogue to Qoheleth would not only thematize that book but apply as well to some larger biblical collection of sacred wisdom. In effect, it would give all of biblical wisdom a singular theological focus in the context of the emerging canon of Scripture."[14]

In his recent analysis of Qoh 12:9–14, G. H. Wilson also describes what seems to be the latest stage in the editorial process of Qoheleth which links Qoheleth and Proverbs.[15] Wilson's central concern is to describe an editorial device that established a literary context between Qoheleth and the book of Proverbs. In Wilson's judgment, 12:9–14 comes from the hand of a later editor.[16] He concurs with the earlier work of Sheppard that the editorial addition has the effect of setting the book of Qoheleth within a larger "scriptural" context.[17] Going beyond Sheppard, Wilson thinks that the epilogue to Qoheleth refers *directly* to the prologue to Proverbs and he concludes "there is sufficient evidence to suggest that the epilogue serves to bind Qoheleth together with Proverbs and provides a canonical key to the interpretation of both."[18]

The importance of Sheppard's and Wilson's work for our analysis is that both of them recognize an attempt within scripture to place both Proverbs and Qoheleth within a larger context, thus achieving what

---

[13] *Wisdom as a Hermeneutical Construct*, 127.
[14] *Wisdom as a Hermeneutical Construct*, 128.
[15] "'The Words of the Wise': The Intent and Significance of Qoheleth 12:9–14."
[16] "The Intent and Significance of Qoheleth 12:9–14," 178.
[17] See: "The Intent and Significance of Qoheleth 12:9–14," 178: "In 12:11, the broad reference of *dibrê ḥăkāmîm*, coupled with the parallel *baʿălê ʾăsuppôt*, seems to indicate a collection of sayings that exceeds the boundaries of Qoheleth alone and suggests the existence of a collection movement to which these verses refer."
[18] "The Intent and Significance of Qoheleth 12:9–14," 179.

Sheppard calls a "canon conscious" redaction.[19] Equally significant, Wilson does not stop with describing what he sees as the editorial attempt to link Proverbs and Qoheleth. He detects a "clear interconnection"[20] in the editorial process between Deuteronomy and Proverbs.[21] Such expressions as "keeping my/his commandments,"[22] the "binding" of the commandments on the body,[23] the numerous references to the heart, walking, lying down, and rising,[24] the references to God as a "father" who disciplines his "son" with love, the connection between possession of the land and righteousness,[25] and the fear of the Lord,[26] offer for Wilson evidence of the implicit connection between Proverbs and Deuteronomy. Wilson's observations are by no means original.[27] But in conjunction with his observations of the editorial process effecting a link between Qoheleth and Proverbs, Wilson is reiterating in part A. Robert's earlier conclusion when Wilson says:

> The common criticism that wisdom shows no concern with Torah and Prophets does not apply to wisdom as redefined by this new canonical context. The canonical editor insists that the "words of the wise[men]" cannot be rightly understood apart from the "commandments of God/YHWH." While this single exhortation by itself might be overlooked, it seems to bring out the *implicit* connections made between Proverbs 1–9 and Deuteronomy, which cannot so easily be dismissed. Where are these "commandments" hammered out but in Torah and Prophets? On the basis

---

[19] *Wisdom as a Hermeneutical Construct*, 128
[20] "The Intent and Significance of Qoheleth 12:9–14," 184.
[21] Ibid., 183.
[22] Ibid., 185.
[23] Ibid., 185–186.
[24] Ibid., 186.
[25] Ibid., 187.
[26] Ibid., 188.
[27] Cf. F. Delitzsch, *Proverbs*, 34: "Who does not hear, to mention only one thing, in i. 7–ix. an echo of the old שְׁמַע (hear), Deut. vi. 4–9, cf. xi. 18–21? The whole poetry of this writer savours of the Book of Deuteronomy. The admonitory addresses in i. 7–ix. are to the Book of Deuteronomy what Deuteronomy is to the Pentateuch. As Deuteronomy seeks to bring home and seal upon the heart of the people the תּוֹרָה of Mosaic law, so do they the תּוֹרָה of the Solomonic proverbs." Note A. Robert's reaction ("Les attaches littéraires bibliques de Prov. I-IX," *RB* 43 [1934] 44) to Delitzsch's comments about Deuteronomy and Proverbs: "Dans son Commentaire sur les Proverbes (1873, p. 29), Delitzsch signale des ressemblances de style entre Deut. vi, 4–9; xi, 18–21, et Prov. iii, 3, vi, 20, 21; vii, 3; il rapproche aussi Prov. xiii, 12 de Deut. viii, 5. Que n'a-t-il exploité cette veine!" See also M. Fishbane's article, "Torah and Tradition," in *Tradition and Theology in the Old Testament* ed. by D. Knight (Philadelphia: Fortress Press, 1977) 275–300; esp. pp. 283–284. Fishbane argues that Prov 6:20–35 reshapes portions of Deut 6:4–9, and 5:6–18.

of this "canonical" statement, Proverbs-Qoheleth can no longer be read simply as practical advice on how to succeed in life, wisdom that could easily pass across national and religious boundaries. They are now inextricably bound up with the Torah and Israel's God, YHWH—his commandments—and cannot be read apart from them.[28]

B. Childs offers another striking example of an editing process within the book of Proverbs which, like Wilson's argument, locates Proverbs in a larger canonical context of "Torah and Prophets." Prov 30:5–6, according to Childs, belongs to "one of the latest stages in the composition of the book of Proverbs. . . ."[29] What is significant about 30:5–6 is that by citing II Sam 22:31 (Prophets) and Deut 4:2 (Torah), 30:5–6 refers its readers to what Childs calls "an authoritative body of scripture."[30] At a minimum, such late editorial additions within the book of Proverbs prove that some late redactors sought to associate directly the book of Proverbs with the larger context of Torah and Prophets.

Similarly, R. B. Y. Scott has addressed the question in what way once unconnected and seemingly "secular" traditions have been embraced by Israel's "religious," i.e., Yahwistic traditions. Scott poses the issue when he states:

It is therefore clear that the Book of Proverbs in its present form is the end result of a long process of compilation. The common denominator of the highly various materials of many origins and periods is that all could be used in one way or another for the purpose of instruction in wisdom. The problem arises as to how such variegated materials without contextual connections can help our understanding the history and nature of Israelite

---

[28] "The Intent and Significance of Qoheleth 12:9–14," 192.

[29] *Introduction to the Old Testament*, 556.

[30] *Introduction to the Old Testament*, 556. "It registers the point that the proverbs which originally derived from man's reflection on human experience of the world and society had become understood as divine words to man which functioned as sacred scripture along with the rest of Israel's received traditions"(556). Cf. F. Delitzsch, *Proverbs*, 278; and J. K. Gasser, "Die Bedeutung der Sprüche Jesu Ben Sira," 183: "Prov. 30, 4: מִי עָלָה־שָׁמַיִם וַיֵּרַד, Diese Frage, welche die Beschrankheit das natürlichen menschlichen Erkennens betont, hat, soweit es sich um den Ausdruck handelt, eine auffallende, dem Zusammenhang von Deut. 30, 11–14 angehörige Parallele." For Prov 30:6 Gasser notes the striking similarity between it and Deut 4:2 and 13:1: "Prov 30, 6ª אַל תּוֹסְףְ עַל דְּבָרָיו klingt deutlich an den Geist und die Form der Ermahnungen Deut. 4, 2; 13, 1 an und setzt in anscheinendem Widerspruch zu dem soeben Bemerkten eine gewisse Bekanntschaft mit dem Inhalt des Deuteronomiums und *eo ipso* die Priorität des letzteren gegenüber Prov. 30, 6 voraus"(184).

wisdom. In particular—to what extent and in what way was this wisdom "religious," and in what respects and to what degree was it "secular"?[31]

Scott builds upon W. McKane's earlier argument concerning the presence or absence of religious terminology which serves as the determining factor for the demarcation of collections within the book of Proverbs. Scott continues McKane's study by dividing a group of seven sayings which appear scattered throughout Proverbs 10–29. The first division includes *"Folk sayings . . . representing not moral instruction but adult comments," "Folk sayings . . . which embody moral instruction* of the home or community but *not in terms of formal instruction in wisdom," "Teaching proverbs,"* and sayings pertain to *"training for professional service in government."* Scott finds "no positive religious note" in them.[32] The remaining sections demonstrate a contrast between the *"ṣaddîq"/"rāšāᶜ," "ḥākām"/"kĕsîl"* and *"ᵓĕwîl;"* groups of sayings which speak of Yahweh's presence; and, lastly, sayings which employ the phrase "fear of the Lord."[33] Scott finds striking an internal editing process which functions in bringing once unrelated secular traditions into a larger biblical context. Such a process likewise has bearing on other Yahwistic traditions outside the book of Proverbs. Thus Scott concludes: "Evidence of duplicate or variant couplets and half-couplets and of real differences between types of sayings points to the origins of the corpus of wisdom sayings through a process of accumulation, supplementing and editorial modification over a long period of time."[34]

The studies of Sheppard, Wilson, Childs, and R. B. Y. Scott, illustrate the potential inner-biblical connections between Proverbs, Torah and the Prophets. The usefulness of the above scholars' work is that we see how the editorializing of portions of Proverbs has refashioned the traditions in such a way that once unrelated texts now achieve a larger "canon conscious" context of Torah and Prophets. As for Prov 1:8–19, there seems to be evidence of similar editing.

---

[31] "Wise and Foolish, Righteous and Wicked," 147.
[32] "Wise and Foolish, Righteous and Wicked," 156–159.
[33] "Wise and Foolish, Righteous and Wicked," 160–164.
[34] "Wise and Foolish, Righteous and Wicked," 164.

PROV 1:8–19 AND EVIDENCE OF
EDITORIAL REDACTION.

Some evidence of late editorial contributions occurs in Prov 1:8–19. Except for the presence of the particle *kî* and the absence of *nāqî*, "innocent," in Prov 1:16, there is a striking similarity between Isa 59:7 and Prov 1:16:

> Isa 59:7: *raglêhem lāraʿ yārūṣû wîmahărû lišpok dām nāqî*
> Prov 1:16: *kî raglêhem lāraʿ yārûṣû wîmahărû lišpok dām.*

Virtually every scholar who has paid close attention to Prov 1:16 recognizes it as a gloss from Isa 59:7.[35] The basis for treating Prov 1:16 as a gloss from Isa 59:7 is dependent on a commonly understood practice of comparing the MT with its versions. In laying down methodological criteria for the identification of glosses, Fishbane says:

> Scribal comments may also be isolated by comparing parallel texts *within* the MT, or *between* the text of the MT and its versions (for example, the LXX or Samar.), to show their degree of variance from each other.[36]

Another methodological criterion used by Fishbane to isolate glosses is that of "disruptive features in the MT."[37] Scholars such as C. H. Toy and W. O. E. Oesterley both argue that 1:16 disrupts the otherwise smooth flow between v 15 and v 17.[38] Under such circumstances, there is

---

[35] R. N. Whybray (*Proverbs*, 39) says that because "it is absent from the best MSS of LXX (except A)," some scholars treat 1:16 as an unwanted interpolation. Whybray (*Proverbs*, 39) offers his own estimation as to why the verse was added: "V. 16 is an interpolation taken from Isa. 59.7a and inserted here, perhaps to provide a more religious reason for the avoidance of sin." Also, W. O. E. Oesterley, *Proverbs*, 9; C. H. Toy, *Proverbs*, 13, 17, 20; H. Wiesmann, "Das Buch der Sprüche," 141; A. Müller, *Proverbs*, 34. The following scholars also see Prov 1:16 as a gloss from Isa 59:7 but add that as a gloss the verse contributes to the parent's lesson: A. J. Baumgartner, *Proverbes*, 33: "Le v. 16 n'a nullement l'apparence d'être une importation d'És. LIX; il a sa place bien marquee dans l'enchaînement des idees; il se rattache logiquement a ce qui precede (au רגלך du v. 15 repond le רגליהם du v. 16) et a ce qui suit (au דם du v. 16 repond le דמם du v. 17). Refuser a ce v. l'authenticité, se serait détruire de partie pris l'ordre qui règne dans l'ensemble." See also: F. Delitzsch, *Proverbs*, 64–65; B. Gemser, *Sprüche Salomos*, 20; A. Barucq, *Proverbes*, 50.

[36] *Biblical Interpretation*, 43. Cf. also p. 291. See pp. 50, 61, for two examples where Fishbane isolates a scribal annotation in the MT on the basis of a comparison with the LXX where a portion of the MT is absent. Cf. J. Weingreen, "Rabbinic-Type Glosses in the Old Testament," *JSS*, 2 (1957) 149–162.

[37] *Biblical Interpretation*, 43.

[38] C. H. Toy, *Proverbs*, 17; W. O. E. Oesterley, *Proverbs*, 9.

strong reason to agree with scholars who interpret Prov 1:16 as a gloss. The presence of the gloss from Isa 59:7 suggests that we have another example of an attempt to place the Proverbial traditions in a larger inner-biblical context.

The gloss in Prov 1:16 is not the only example of an interrelationship between Proverbs and Isaiah. The presence of what Childs calls a "summary-appraisal form" in Prov 1:19 indicates that Prov 1:8–19 probably derives from an editorial process similar to that found in the book of Isaiah.[39] After analyzing three examples of the summary-appraisal form in Isa 14:26–27, 17:14b, and 28:29, Childs concludes that each represents a later editorial addition. The function of such a form is to act in an independent but summary role for the unit to which it is attached.[40]

The presence of the summary-appraisal form in Prov 1:19 serves a similar function. Childs states this about 1:19: "The verse generalizes on the fate of all who act in such wickedness. The lesson which he [the parent] draws is not in the form of a warning directed to the wicked, but rather a general didactic statement which seeks to find a universal element."[41] This is the only example of such a form in the book of Proverbs.

After noting other examples of the summary-appraisal form scattered about in a "wisdom psalm" and sections from Job and Qoheleth, Childs concludes tentatively that "Isaiah is dependent on a traditional form which had its setting within a Hebrew school of wisdom."[42] He does not give an exact date to any of the wisdom sources cited. He assumes that the example from Proverbs pre-dates the Isaiah traditions where the similar form appears. Also, he does not mention the resemblance between Isa 59:7 and Prov 1:16.

The dating of the summary-appraisal form as well as its life setting has been recently reconsidered by G. Sheppard.[43] Sheppard points out that each of the examples of the summary-appraisal form in Isaiah appears to come from the time of a late seventh-century redaction and *not* from eighth-century Isaiah of Jerusalem as Childs argues.[44] In view of

---

[39] *Isaiah and the Assyrian Crisis*, 132. See also: G. Sheppard, "The Anti-Assyrian Redaction and the Canonical Context of Isaiah 1–39," *JBL* 104 (1985) 193–206.

[40] *Isaiah and the Assyrian Crisis*, 130. Cf. also, F. Delitzsch, *Proverbs*, 66–67.

[41] *Isaiah and the Assyrian Crisis*, 132.

[42] *Isaiah and the Assyrian Crisis*, 136.

[43] "The Canonical Context of Isaiah 1–39," 193–216.

[44] The period of redaction has been fixed by H. Barth and titled the "Assur-Redaction." See: H. Barth, *Die Jesaja-Worte in der Josiazeit: Israel und Assur als Thema einer produktiven Neuinterpretation des Jesajaüberlieferung* (WMANT 48; Neukirchen-Vluyn: Neukirchener, 1977).

the citation from Isa 59:7 in Prov 1:16 and the fact that Prov 1:19 is the only example of a summary-appraisal form in Proverbs, it is more likely that the editor of Prov 1:8–19 stood within a familiar editorial tradition and employed a well-known technique.[45]

To understand the final editorial shape of Prov 1:8–19 as an example of the reutilization of older editorial devices does not lessen the importance of Childs' observation concerning the universalizing effect of the summary-appraisal form. If anything, knowing what we do about the function of the summary-appraisal form elsewhere, we can surmise that Prov 1:8–19 is not anchored traditio-historically to the narrow confines of a "wisdom" school in association with the book of Proverbs, but reflects a wider editorial activity belonging to a broad range of biblical traditions.

We have already seen that the most obvious reference pointing to other biblical traditions is the gloss found in Prov 1:16. The editor of the text does not highlight Prov 1:16 by means of attributing the words to Isaiah but places them in the mouth of the parent. Prov 1:16 is treated as a gloss and Prov 1:19 as a summary-appraisal form only on the basis of an insight into the esoteric technique of ancient editors. Such observations are claims about the aesthetic skills and standards of editors. Also decisive for our analysis of Prov 1:8–19 is the strategy of speaking by means of direct discourse of the parent and the ḥaṭṭāʾîm, "sinners." As the initial didactic lesson in the book of Proverbs, the parent in Prov 1:8–19 does not string together proverbial maxims as is done in Proverbs 10–31. Instead, the parent assumes the role of controlling the flow of the lesson by citing the first person speech of others. As we shall see, the occurrence of direct discourse is one of the dominant literary characteristics of Proverbs 1–9 in contrast to Proverbs 10–31.[46] Being aware of the role that discourse plays in Proverbs 1–9 as a

---

[45] G. Sheppard draws a similar conclusion: "The similarities in form and function of these occurrences suggest that the summary-appraisal form likely belongs to the repertoire of stylistic editorial devices employed by the AR [Assur Redaction] to help create a new literary context from older oracular material. Therefore, its sapiential tone might reflect its life setting within the scribal schools rather than indicate wisdom influence on the eighth-century prophet"("Redaction and Context of Isaiah 1–39," 209–210).

[46] Carol Newsom ("Woman and the Discourse of Patriarchal Wisdom: A Study of Proverbs 1–9," in *Gender and Difference in Ancient Israel*, ed. Peggy L. Day [Minneapolis: Fortress Press, 1989] 142–160) has made a strong case for the centrality that speech plays in Proverbs 1–9. The core of Newsom's analysis is that Proverbs 1–9 is "virtually all talk," that is, discourse(p. 142). But such discourse reveals a "narrow social dimension" of language in that the "privileged axis of communication is that from father to son"(p.142).

whole requires a different level of reader competence which goes beyond
attention to the mere form of the traditions.

PROV 1:8-19 AND THE ROLE OF DIRECT DISCOURSE
IN INNER-BIBLICAL INTERPRETATION.

McKane's formal identification, for example, of "Instruction" as
being made up of a motive clause and the imperative[47] is applicable to
Prov 1:8-19. However, McKane and others fail to note that Prov 1:8-19 is
also one of the many examples of *direct speech* which occur in Proverbs 1–
9. Prov 1:8-19 contains not only the words of the parent in 1:10, 15-19,
but the words of the sinners in vv 11-14, albeit re-stated through the
mouth of the parent. This combination of direct speech presents a dense
embedding of speech within speech. The narrator quotes the parent who,
in turn quotes the sinners. The parent also paraphrases the words of the
sinners and includes a gloss from Isa 59:7 in Prov 1:16.[48]

Alongside this example of direct discourse in 1:8-19 we can list other
examples. In 1:20-33 *ḥokmâ*, "wisdom," speaks. But *ḥokmâ* does not begin
to speak in direct discourse until v 22. The speech of *ḥokmâ* is framed by
the introduction of the narrator in vv 20-21, just as the parent's words
are framed by an introduction in 1:8-9. The parent again speaks in 2:1–
22; 3:1-35. In 4:4ff the grandfather speaks. The son, whom the parent
addresses throughout Proverbs 1-9, speaks in 5:12-14. The parent speaks
in 6:1-19, 20-35; 7:1-13, 21-27. The adulteress speaks in 7:14-20 as well as
the foolish woman in 9:16-17. And *ḥokmâ* speaks again in 8:4ff and 9:4ff.
Even the *miṣwâ*, "commandment," and *tôrâ*, "teaching,"(RSV) have the
power of speech in 6:22. But in each case "speech" is mediated through
the voice of the parent who in turn adds to the verbal montage by

---

[47] *Proverbs*, 3.

[48] Such a verbal montage is characteristic of direct discourse. See: M. Sternberg,
"Proteus in Quotation Land," 110. Also, G. Savran, "The Character as Narrator in
Biblical Narrative," *Prooftexts: A Journal of Jewish Literary History* 5 (1985) 1-17, speaks
of the "omniscient narrator" who maps out "his" strategy by the way the characters
speak, the content of their words, when they speak, and the like. "The greatest part of
Biblical narrative is presented to the reader by a single type of narrator—
undramatized, omniscient, and reliable. Whether we speak of the narrator, or
narrators of Genesis, of Judges, or of Samuel, the position of the narrator vis-a-vis his
characters is always the same. Like some transcendent deity he creates the world of
his characters, manipulates their words and actions, and penetrates to their deepest
feelings without actually becoming part of that world"(p. 1). I wish to thank Prof. E.
Greenstein of the Jewish Theological Seminary, New York City, for bringing these
two articles to my attention.

quoting and/or paraphrasing others. As it is, Proverbs 1–9 is a densely packed collection of direct discourse. Thus, while the form *Mahnreden* ("Instruction" for McKane) may be the identifiable feature which differentiates Proverbs 1–9 from Proverbs 10–31, it necessarily includes this feature of direct discourse. Because the language and discourse style in the older collection of Proverbs 10–31 is so similar to that in Proverbs 1–9, their editorial complementarity deserves more recognition than scholars have conventionally recognized.[49]

M. BAKHTIN AND M. STERNBERG:
DOUBLE-VOICED DISCOURSE
AND INNER-BIBLICAL INTERPRETATION.

The presence of so many examples of direct discourse in Proverbs 1–9 as well as the strong interest in direct discourse in Proverbs 10ff provides us with another possible way of detecting the inner-biblical connections between Prov 1:8–19, Proverbs as a whole, and other portions of the Hebrew Bible. While some scholars have recognized the presence of other's words and have relegated their importance to that of

---

[49] See Prov 20:9, 14, 22, 25; 23:7; 24:12, 24, 29; 25:7; 26:13, 19; 28:24; 30:1–4, 9, 15–16, 20 for examples of direct discourse in Proverbs 10–31 which are marked by a *verbum dicendi*. W. McKane ("Functions of Language," 167) notes, however, that even though there are few examples of direct discourse, one of the major themes in Prov 10–30 concerns language and speech: "The area covered is chapters 10–30 of the book of *Proverbs* and I estimate that about 19% of these sentences are concerned with the functions of language and the objectives of discourse." As striking as the amount of examples of direct speech is in Proverbs 1–9 in contrast to Proverbs 10–31, A. N. Aletti ("Seduction et Parole en Proverbes I-IX," *VT* 27 [1977] 129–144) is the only scholar we are aware of who has addressed the phenomenon of direct speech in Proverbs in any detail. But his analysis is narrowly focused. Aletti examines Prov 1:22–33; 7:14–20; and 1:11–14. His interest in the incidences of direct speech center around *discours humain* in contrast to that of the sage. After noting how the words of the wise often duplicate the seductive words of the adulteress and sinner, Aletti comments: "La seduction rend le discours du sage suspect. Si la parole trompeuse se met a employer les memes expressions que la parole vrai, comment distinguer et choisir entre les deux?"(pp. 140–141) Aletti concludes that the difference between the two lies in their origin. The sage's word originates with Yahweh. The others' words do not. As much as Aletti attempts to address the issue of the presence of examples of direct speech patterns in Proverbs 1–9, his contribution is more of a description of some of the speech patterns which are highlighted by a theological description of wisdom. He fails to raise the question of the strategy of the narrator who chooses to present his/her position through the direct discourse of such a cast of speakers as sinners, father, mother, grandfather, son, adulteress, foolish woman, and wisdom and what relationship direct speech has with other portions of the Hebrew Bible.

the artistic freedom of the wise to create speech,[50] recent analyses of direct speech by M. Bakhtin and M. Sternberg can help in unravelling the subtle inner-biblical connections that direct speech can achieve.

For Bakhtin, the significance of direct speech is that a dialogic relationship is achieved whenever we are confronted with what he terms "embodied speech." For example, Bakhtin provides the following example:

> "Life is good." "Life is not good." We have before us two judgments, possessing specific logical form and specific content oriented semantically toward a referential object. . . . Between these two judgments there exists a specific logical relationship: one is the negation of the other. But between them there are not and cannot be any dialogic relationships; they do not argue with one another in any way (although they can provide the referential material and logical basis for argument). Both these judgments must be embodied, if a dialogic relationship is to arise between them and toward them. Thus, both these judgments can, as thesis and antithesis, be united in a single utterance of a single subject, expressing his unified dialectical position on a given question. In such a case no dialogic relationships arise. But if these two judgments are separated into two different utterances by two different subjects, then dialogic relationships do arise.[51]

Bakhtin argues that the most common form of a dialogic relationship is represented in the *"direct speech of characters,"*[52] and the common trait of such direct speech (i.e., quoted speech) is that it is "double-voiced."[53]

---

[50] Cf. B. Gemser, *Sprüche Salomos*, 20, where he says this about the sinners' words in Prov 1:11–14. "Der Weise führt nicht etwa die Worte der Frevlar an, sondern macht von sich aus die Schlechtigkeit diesen Leute kenntlich;" and J. Crenshaw's "imagined speech" in *Old Testament Form Criticism*, ed. by J. Hayes (Austin: Trinity University Press, 1975) 255–256.

[51] *Problems of Dostoevsky's Poetics*, 183.

[52] "By far the most typical and widespread form of represented objectified discourse is the *direct speech of characters*." (*Problems of Dostoevsky's Poetics*, p. 186)

[53] *Problems of Dostoevsky's Poetics*, p. 185. See also: M. Bakhtin, *The Dialogic Imagination: Four Essays*, esp. pp. 259–422, "Discourse in The Novel," where he speaks of "double-voiced discourse;" and J. Kristeva, *Desire in Language: A Semiotic Approach to Literature and Art* ed. by L. S. Roudiez; trans. by T. Gora, A. Jardine, and L. S. Roudiez (New York: Columbia University Press, 1980). At one point Kristeva says the following about the inferential characteristics of "novelistic speech" which approximates Bakhtin's analysis of double-voiced discourse: "It [novelistic speech] unveils the writer as principal actor in the speech play that ensues and, at the same time, binds together two modes of the novelistic utterance, *narration* and *citation*, into the single speech of he who is both *subject* of the book (the author) and object of the spectacle (actor), since, within novelistic nondisjunction, the message is both

By taking the authorial strategy of quoting one or more characters, real or hypothetical, in a juxtaposed verbal exchange, the narrator projects not only the overt referent of the speakers, but the narrator also covertly implies, by means of a single word, a web of word combinations, common themes, and the like, the discourse of another person.[54]

Bakhtin substantiates his observations about the referential and representational characteristics of double-voiced discourse by providing numerous examples from Dostoevsky's writings. What is important for our argument, and, as we shall see, is confirmed in principle in M. Sternberg's observations, is that direct speech does not necessarily function as an isolated incident of someone's speech but can have intertextual links which connect the verbal and thematic position of one speaker in one time and place with the direct speech of another speaker whom the narrator quotes. Such discourse of someone else is not cited directly but, as Bakhtin argues, is only "implied" in the web of intertextual associations of quoted speech. And its implication can be detected not only in a well chosen word or words, but by the structure of the implied speech as well. Speaking of double-voiced discourse which inherently contains a "hidden polemic" against the implied speech of another, Bakhtin says:

> In a hidden polemic the author's discourse is directed toward its own referential object, as in any other discourse, but at the same time every statement about the object is constructed in such a way that, apart from its referential meaning, a polemical blow is struck at the other's discourse on the same theme, at the other's statement about the same object. A word, directed toward its referential object, clashes with another's word within the very object itself. The other's discourse is not itself reproduced, it is merely implied. . . One word acutely senses alongside it someone else's word

---

discourse and representation. The author-actor's utterance unfolds, divides, and faces in two directions: first, towards a referential utterance, *narration*—the speech assumed by he who inscribes himself as actor-author; and second toward textual premises, *citation*—speech attributed to an other and whose authority he who inscribes himself as actor-author acknowledges. These two orientations intertwine in such a way as to merge."(p. 45)

54 "All these phenomena, despite very real differences among them, share one common trait: discourse in them has a twofold direction—it is directed both toward the referential object of speech, as in ordinary discourse, and toward *another's discourse*, toward *someone else's speech*"(*Problems of Dostoevsky's Poetics*, p. 185). For a recent attempt to employ Bakhtin's observations concerning double-voiced discourse, see: R. Polzin, *Moses and the Deuteronomist, A Literary Study of the Deuteronomic History*.

speaking about the same object, and this awareness determines its structure.[55]

Bakhtin's observations concerning "double-voiced discourse" were made in the 1920's and were based upon examples from Dostoevsky. Bakhtin does not address in any detail the issue of the source or sources from which an author draws for generating double-voiced discourse. Even so, the presence of the implied speech of someone else which double-voiced discourse can achieve has a bearing on the use of direct speech in, for instance, Prov 1:8-19. In these verses we have the embodied speech of the sinners and the parent, who use basically similar terminology. Their quoted words likewise "clash" concerning the same referential object. Yet the source for their words, that is, the lexical and thematic "speech" matrix which not only helped to generate 1:8-19 but which is implied by 1:8-19 is not found in the book of Proverbs itself. We are not saying that Prov 1:8-19 is unconnected to other portions of the book of Proverbs, but rather that there is no direct speech elsewhere in Proverbs which, according to Bakhtin's rubrics, Prov 1:8-19 could "imply."

In two recent articles, Meir Sternberg addresses many of the same issues considered by Bakhtin.[56] In addition to added detail and scope of his work, Sternberg discusses a contemporary theoretical issue, foreshadowed in part by Bakhtin, concerning the matter of the substantive accuracy and independence of quoted speech with its purported original.[57] For Sternberg, reported discourse, like Bakhtin's

---

[55] *Problem of Dostoevsky's Poetics*, 195-196.

[56] "Proteus in Quotation Land: Mimesis and the Forms of Reported Discourse," and "Point of View and the Indirections of Direct Speech."

[57] See "Proteus in Quotation Land," 127 and "Point of View," 73, for two places where Sternberg makes mention of Bakhtin. For Sternberg, Bakhtin does not fully take into account the fact that a quoted speech by the narrator has a controlling effect on the form and content of the "original" utterance. The reporter, according to Sternberg, envelopes the quoted words of another with a new set of potential effects by the very fact that he or she has manipulated someone else's words into another context. Bakhtin, again according to Sternberg, allows for the original utterance sometimes to gain the upper hand over the discourse of the reported speech. Sternberg's depiction of Bakhtin, however, is not altogether accurate. For example, Bakhtin, *The Dialogic Imagination*, 340, clearly states that the reframed speech of another is *always* refracted through its new authorial context: "The following must be kept in mind: that the speech of another, once enclosed in a context, is—no matter how accurately transmitted—always subject to certain semantic changes. The context embracing another's word is responsible for its dialogized background, whose influence can be very great. Given the appropriate methods for framing, one may bring about fundamental changes even in another's utterance accurately quoted."

double-voiced discourse, "brings together at least two discourse-events: that in which things were originally expressed (said, thought, experienced), by one subject (speaker, writer, reflector) and that in which they are cited by another."[58] As a result, quotation represents two discourse events which, as Sternberg says, "enter into representational ('mimetic') relations."[59] Sternberg notes that one has to recognize degrees of correspondence between an original discourse and its quoted counterpart all on account of the artificial yoking together of once independent and unrelated discourse events.[60] In no way can the quoted discourse replace the original nor must one suppose that the quoted discourse was intended to offer a word-for-word duplication of the original.[61] The reason for inter-textual ambiguity between the original and the quoted version is that quotation is a form of mimetic representation and not reference. Reported discourse thus represents not only the words of someone else but also the manipulative hand of the narrator who, for whatever thematic, lexical, or literary reasons, freely plays with the discourse of another in order to form a new but inter-related discourse-event.[62] Moreover, a quote is situated contextually, chronologically, and thematically as an "*inset*" that rests in an authorial "*frame*," thus generating not only other meanings but other points of view which go beyond the original discourse. The result of authorial "interference" with the original message is to effect a literary "montage."[63]

Thus, the center of focus for Sternberg's analysis of direct discourse is not the isolation of the inset and the frame, nor the attempt to determine literary accuracy, character identity, or social matrix of the

---

[58] "Proteus in Quotation Land," 107.

[59] "Proteus in Quotation Land," 107

[60] See "Point of View," 72.

[61] See "Proteus in Quotation Land," 108: "What is cited in the subject's name is one thing; what that subject originally said or thought is another. The relations these two things hold are (in semantic terms) those between signifier and signified or (mimetically speaking) between image and object. So, however specific the representation and whatever its linguistic form, it cannot exhaust—let alone replace—the original act of discourse or expression, which is and remains a unique event. No mimetic bond, no mode or amount of quotation, can in the least affect its independent status (including, of course, the fictional equivalent of such independence within the created world)." Cf.: "Point of View," 68–69; 75.

[62] "Point of View," 68–69.

[63] See "Point of View," 69, where Sternberg addresses the issue of how a reporter exercises "control and manipulation" over someone else's speech for his/her own purposes.

original discourse. Sternberg rather focuses on the text, the reader and the communicative matrix initiated by the collated inset and frame.[64]

Sternberg argues that even if one can pinpoint the deictic independence of direct discourse which implies an original discourse one cannot conclude that the same utterance ("inset") is communicatively independent or inviolable.[65] As Sternberg says: "From the fact that the inset is deictically independent of the frame, it does not follow that the inset enjoys the communicative independence or inviolability distinctive of any normal speech-event, including the very one it represents. For once framed, an utterance becomes penetrable, manipulable, and hence essentially ambiguous out of context, even in all that concerns deictic features."[66] As a result, the inset is shifted to another communicative context by means of its frame with the result that there is a "deictic duality of direct speech:"

> The necessary and sufficient condition of direct speech is, then, not the literal congruence between inset and original, but the basic deictic incongruence between inset and frame. Even in the absence of any other more or less distinctive (typological, syntactic, semantic) marks, where we fail to make sense of an utterance in terms of a single deictic center, we hypothesize two (or more) originating and/or refracting perspectives combined within a double-centered reported speech.[67]

The hypothesizing of "two (or more) originating and/or refracting perspectives" leaves the door open for the reader to make his or her own communicative contribution to the indices of direct speech in the form of intra- and inter-textual linkages. For Sternberg, it is unimportant whether the original discourse is at hand in order to check the accuracy of the reported speech. Important is the "perspectival shift"[68] to other (con)texts that is achieved in the reader or hearer who recognizes the potential in reported speech to imply the speech of another.

The value of Sternberg's and Bakhtin's analysis of direct speech is that they allow us to enter into the inner-biblical complex of Prov 1:8–19 through the dialogic angle of the quoted words of the characters with the

---

[64] For references to the "communicative structure" of direct and indirect speech, see: "Point of View," 69, 111; "Proteus in Quotation Land," 147, 152. As for Sternberg's comments concerning the "larger role" played by the reader which underlies his work, see: "Proteus in Quotation Land," 110. See also his opening comments concerning the "direct speech fallacy" in "Point of View," 67–69.

[65] "Point of View," 110.

[66] "Point of View," 111.

[67] "Point of View," 111.

[68] "Point of View," 113.

possibility of discovering a far richer inter-textuality which has escaped modern interpreters of the book of Proverbs. More directly, if Sternberg's observation that "direct speech presupposes three distinct components: frame, inset, and the original utterance that serves as object of orientation,"[69] then we can broaden our scope of investigation to see if in fact we can find such an original utterance that serves as object of orientation. Such a possibility has its best example in Genesis 37.

PROV 1:8–19 AND GENESIS 37: A CASE OF
INNER-BIBLICAL INTERPRETATION.

Genesis 37:12–36 is the account of Joseph's search for his brothers and their attempt to be rid of Joseph by selling him to the Ishmaelites/Midianites.[70] Remembering Sternberg's and Bakhtin's argument that direct discourse has the potential of representing (*not* referring to) the discourse of someone else by means of selected words and phrases, we can see how Prov 1:8–19 has portions of Genesis 37 in view as an example of what Fishbane calls "'texts-in-the-mind.'"[71]

We list first the shared lexical features and expressions between Prov 1:10–19 and Genesis 37:

| 1. | *ʾal tōbēʾ* | "do not go"[72] | Prov 1:10 |

---

[69] "Point of View," 113.

[70] For a recent attempt to interpret the Joseph story which takes into account the inconsistencies in the narrative, see: E. L. Greenstein, "An Equivocal Reading of the Sale of Joseph," in *Literary Interpretations of Biblical Narratives*, vol 2, edited by K. R. R. Gros Louis. (Nashville: Abingdon, 1982) 114–125.

[71] Speaking of the aggadic exegete as a "latecomer on the stage of Israelite culture" who is conditioned by the "theological *traditum* and its literary fund," Fishbane says: "From this point, confirmed by the biblical evidence, it is justified to observe that the purveyors and creators of aggadic exegesis appear to live with 'texts-in-the-mind'— that is, with texts (or traditions) which provide the imaginative matrix for evaluating the present, for conceiving of the future, for organizing reality (the inchoate, the negative, the possible), and even for providing the shared symbols and language of communication. With aggadic *traditio* the world of Israelite culture is thus one which talks and thinks, which imagines and reflects, and which builds and rejects *through* the traditions"(*Biblical Interpretation*, 435).

[72] There is a question concerning how to translate *tōbēʾ*, "consent" (RSV). The LXX reads *boulethḗs* meaning "consent." As scholars have generally recognized, if the LXX is a direct translation of our received Hebrew text, the Hebrew should read *tʾbh*. See: A Barucq (*Le Livre des Proverbes* [Paris: J. Gabalda et Cie, 1964] 50): "LXX μη δε (sic) βουληθῆς supposant la lecture תאבה . . . ." Cf. C. H. Toy, *A Critical and Exegetical Commentary on the Book of Proverbs*. ICC. Edinburgh: T & T Clark, (1977) 19; W.

	wayyābō'	"and he [Joseph] went	Gen 37:14
2.	*lĕkâ 'ittānû*	"come with us"	Prov 1:11
	weʿattâ lĕkû	"come now"	Gen 37:20, cf. vv 13–14, 27
3.	*dām*	"blood"	Prov 1:11, 16, 18
	dām	"blood"	Gen 37:22, 26, 31
4.	*kĕyôrĕdê (bôr)*	"as those going down (to the pit)" where "pit" is parallel to "Sheol"	Prov 1:12
	'ērēd. . .(Sheol)	"I will go down (. . . to Sheol)" *bôr*, "pit"	Gen 37:35, cf. v 25 cf. Gen 37:20, 24, 28, 29
5.	*lāraʿ*	"for evil"	Prov 1:16
	rāʿâ (ḥayyâ)	"evil (beast)"	Gen 37:20
6.	*lišpok dām*	"to shed blood"	Prov 1:16
	'al tišpĕkû dām	"shed no blood"	Gen 37:22
7.	*'orḥôt*	"paths," "ways"	Prov 1:19
	'orḥat	"caravans"	Gen 37:25
8.	*bāṣaʿ + dām*	"ill-gotten gain" + "blood"	Prov 1:19

Nowack, *Die Sprüche Salomo's*, erklart von E. Bertheau in Kurzgefasstes exegetisches Handbuch zum Alten Testament. Leipzig: Verlag von S. Hirzel (1893) 4; and A. Baumgartner, *Proverbes*, 31. The problem in analyzing *tb'* as if its root were *'bh* is that of explaining adequately both the elision of the *h* and the transposition of the *'* and the *b*. Toy argues that "the ℵ is the writing of an Aram. [Aramaic] scribe for ח, the initial ℵ of the stem being omitted because it was unpronounced." C. H. Toy, *Proverbs*, 19. See W. Gesenius, *Hebrew Grammar* (ed. E. Kautzsch; Oxford: Clarendon, 1910) pars. 68h, 75hh. Hereafter cited as *GKC*. While such a grammatical process is possible, in the context of vv 1–10 it does not seem to be the most probable explanation. Granted, the lexical equivalent of *t'bh* is found in some sixty Greek manuscripts. But in the broader context of our pericope there is reason to read the root of *tb'* as *bô'*, "to go," thus translating the text as "do not go" in contrast to the RSV, "do not consent." The point of the warning to the son concerns the actual going and joining league with the sinners. The synonymous verb *hlk* appears in vv 11 and 15 and there is equally strong imagery concerning "pathways" and physical movement. Similarly, the root *bô'* is used elsewhere in the Hebrew Bible in the sense of entering into specific relations with someone. W. Gesenius, *A Hebrew and English Lexicon of the Old Testament* (trans. E. Robinson; eds. F. Brown, S. R. Driver, C. A. Briggs; Oxford: Clarendon, 1968) 98. Cf. Gen 49:6; Jos 23:7, 12. Hereafter, cited as *BDB*. To read *tb'* as the second person, masculine verb of *bô'*, as we are suggesting, one need not then explain the elision of the *h*, and the transposition of the *'* and *b*. The only change involved would be that of the pointing, which is easier to explain when we recall the distance between the writing of the consonantal text and its subsequent pointing. Thus, we propose the following reading for Prov 1:10: "My son, if sinners entice you, do not go."

	bāṣaʿ + *dām*	"ill-gotten gain" + "blood"	Gen 37:26
9.	*nepeš*	"life"	Prov 1:19
	nepeš	"life" Note the similar connection made between *dām*, "blood" and *nepeš* "life" in Gen 37:21–22 and Prov 1:18 & 19.	Gen 37:21

It is noteworthy that even though the expression *bṣʿ*, "ill-gotten gain," "profit," occurs elsewhere in the Book of Proverbs,[73] it appears only two times in the Torah: here in Gen 37:26 and Ex 18:21. The Exodus citation does not have any of the other shared lexical and thematic features that we find in Genesis. As an important word in the parent's concluding discourse, the expression *bṣʿ* serves as one of the key terms which the editor uses to forge a link with Proverbs and the Genesis 37 episode of the selling of Joseph.[74]

---

[73] See: Prov 15:27; 28:16.

[74] See: M. Bakhtin, *Problems of Dostoevsky's Poetics*, 195–196, where he argues that a word can serve to link different discourse units together. Additionally, the use of a key term which links a *traditio* to a *traditum* is a common aggadic technique called *"lemmatic deduction or inference"*(M. Fishbane, *Biblical Interpretation*, 419). Fishbane explains lemmatic deduction in this way: "By this procedure, a particular *traditum* is first cited, summarized, or posited before an addressee, and then a conclusion is either deduced or inferred from the topos as a whole or specific terms contained therein"(*Biblical Interpretation*, 419). Fishbane uses Hag 2:11–14 as one example of lemmatic deduction. The key term in Hag 2:11–14, according to Fishbane's analysis is *ṭāmēʾ*, "impure." By focusing on *ṭāmēʾ*, the prophet draws further inferences concerning what is pure and impure on the basis of an earlier but more ·limited *traditum*. Fishbane concludes: "Indeed, the prophet has not only imputed a state of impurity comparable to corpse defilement to the people, without evidence, but has furthermore gone on to deduce from it the impurity of all sanctified and also (*a fortiori*) of all non-sanctified obejcts (*sic*) with which the Israelite might come in contact. The key term ('impure'), used in the lemma (v. 13) and its application (v. 14), provides the formal exegetical nexus between the premise and the deduction"(p. 420). The key term also links the *traditum* to its *traditio*. Elsewhere, Fishbane also notes the use by Haggai of the expression *kēn* in Hag 2:11–14(p. 297–298). Within Hag 2:13–14 *kēn* signifies the analogical correlation between earlier specific situations of ritual impurity and the current state of impurity because the Temple has not been rebuilt. The example from Hag 2:11–14 and Fishbane's analysis of the verses lends further credence to our contention that the expression *bṣʿ*, "ill-gotten gain, profit," serves as a key term which bridges the traditio-historical gap between Prov 1:10–19 and Genesis 37. *bṣʿ*, "ill-gotten gain," appears in v 19, the verse which Childs calls the summary appraisal form. As Childs argues, the summary appraisal form achieves a broader application of the parent's teaching. Childs' analysis of Prov 1:19 is remarkably similar to Fishbane's analysis of earlier aggadic reutilization of traditions.

In addition to these above shared expressions and words, there is the imagery of "devouring/consuming" in both Genesis 37 and Prov 1:10–19. In Gen 37:20 the brothers say: *wĕʿattâ lĕkû wĕnahargēhû wĕnašlikēhû bĕʾaḥad habbōrôt wĕʾāmarnû ḥayyâ rāʿâ ʾakālātĕhû,* "Come now, let us kill him and throw him into one of the pits; then we shall say that a wild beast has devoured him. . . ." Similar imagery of "devouring/ consuming" is alluded to in Prov 1:12 in conjunction with the parallel phrase *šĕʾôl,* "Sheol," *bôr,* "pit," and *ḥayyîm,* "living:" *niblāʿēm kišʾôl ḥayyîm ûtĕmîmîm kĕyôrĕdê bôr,* "like Sheol let us swallow them alive and whole, like those who go down to the Pit."

Added to the imagery of devouring/consuming is that of the "profit" motive. In the Genesis account there is no "profit," *bṣʿ,* as Judah says, in slaying Joseph. The sale of Joseph to the Ishmaelites/Midianites reaps them a profit of twenty shekels and an unspoken portion of the inheritance since the favored son of Jacob is "dead."

The profit motive also plays a part in "lying in wait for blood" in Prov 1:10–19. There, the outcome is *hôn yāqār,* "precious goods," *šālāl,* houses filled with "spoil," and *kîs ʾeḥād,* a "common purse." In Prov 1:19 the combination *ʾorḥôt,* "paths"/"ways," and *bṣʿ,* "profit/ill-gotten gain," may be a word play on *ʾorḥat,* "caravan," and *bṣʿ,* "profit/ill-gotten gain," in Gen 37:25–26. What sparks Judah's rhetorical query in Gen 37:26, *mah beṣaʿ kî nahărōg ʾet ʾāḥînû wekissînû ʾet dāmô,* "What profit (*bṣʿ*) is it if we slay our brother and conceal his blood?" (*dm*) is the sight of the *ʾōrḥat yišmĕʿēʾlîm* "caravan/way of the Ishamaelites," going down (*yrd*) to Egypt. By selling Joseph to the caravaneers Judah not only gets rid of Joseph (he takes his life, *nepeš,* away, Gen 37:21; cf. Prov 1:19), but also adds to their wealth (cf. the reference to *kîs ʾeḥād* in Prov 1:14).[75] But the outcome of Judah's profit-motivated act is the ironic reversal of fortune for himself, his brothers, their father, and Joseph. The very deed of selling Joseph into slavery, thus dividing the family and covering up their own treachery, actually initiates a series of events which result both in uncovering the brothers' deceitfulness and in bringing the family

---

The use of the particle *kēn* which introduces v 19 serves to give a universal tone to the parent's words while at the same time reutilizing the specific content of Genesis 37.

[75] J. S. Ackerman "Joseph, Judah, and Jacob," *Literary Interpretations of Biblical Narratives,* vol 2 edited by K. R. R. Gros Louis (Nashville: Abingdon, 1982) 103, notes the profit motive in Judah's words: "The text makes no mention that Judah's interest is to rescue Joseph. Instead Judah piously speaks of not laying a hand on a brother; but the effect of his suggestion is not so different from murder: Joseph will be removed from their midst and reduced to slavery. In many ways biblical law equates selling a person into slavery with murder. Judah wants the same results as his other brothers, but he seeks profit from the deed (37:26–27)."

together again.[76] A similar reversal is verbally plotted by the parents' words in Prov 1:10–19.[77] The reasons are not given nor are any details provided as to the factors leading to the reversal. It is as if the narrator/parent is appealing to the son's and reader's common knowledge of the lesson.[78] Those who engage in plotting to get gain by violent means actually lay the groundwork for their own demise.

In addition to the similar imagery and shared expressions, the emphasis placed on speech stands out. The narrator introduces the parents' speech by commanding the son to listen, *šmᶜ*, Prov 1:8. The direct discourse of the "sinners'" speech in conjunction with the parents' words adds to the emerging importance given to correct listening and speech. Implied in the parents' discourse is the son's welfare. Even though the parents' discourse adopts some of the "sinners'" terminology, only by heeding the parents' words will the son avoid destruction.

In the Genesis episode, the different speeches first by the brothers at large (37:19–20), then of Reuben (37:21–22), and lastly of Judah (37:26–27) determine the fate of Joseph as well as his brothers. For example, after the brothers speak in 37:19–20, plotting Joseph's death, Gen 37:21–22 reads: *wayyišmaᶜ rĕʾûben wayyaṣṣīlēhû miyyādām wayyōʾmer lōʾ nakkennû napeš wayyōʾmer ʾălēhem rĕʾûben ʾal tišpĕkû dām hašlîkû ʾōtô ʾel habbôr hazzeh ʾăšer bammidbār wĕyād ʾal tišlĕḥû bô lĕmaᶜan haṣṣîl ʾōtô miyyādām lahăšîbô ʾel ʾābîw*, "But when Reuben heard it [the brothers' words], he delivered him

---

[76] Cf. H. C. White's recent interpretation of the Joseph story: "The Joseph Story: A Narrative which 'Consumes' its Content," *Semeia*, 31 (1985) 49–69. As for the expression *bṣᶜ*, White says (p. 64): "Judah, then, seeing the opportunity this caravan [i.e., the Ishmaelites/Midianites] presents, offers his proposal to sell Joseph into slavery and avoid responsibility for his death, 'for,' he adds with more than a hint of cynicism, 'he is our brother, our flesh' (37:27). There was also a new factor which had not been a part of the brother's (*sic*) thinking up until this point, i.e., silver. Not only would the sale of Joseph rid them of him bloodlessly, but would actually produce a 'profit' (בֶּצַע). Joseph in their midst would be replaced by silver in their coffers, an appealing prospect indeed! Thanks to the timely appearance of the Ishmaelites, a third possibility has thus arisen that has the virtues of both the previous proposals while lacking their respective disadvantages. Within the possibilities presented by these circumstance, a dialogical process has developed which carries the brothers away from the ultimately self-destructive system of rivalry toward an open unknown end."

[77] Even though the opening discourse is attributed to the mother and father (v. 8), C. Newsom ("Woman and the Discourse of Patriarchal Wisdom," p. 144) argues that the father is the only one who speaks. The mother's words are silenced.

[78] E. Greenstein, "An Equivocal Reading of the Sale of Joseph," 307, also notes the latent theme of ironic reversal in Gen 37ff: "Briefly stated, a theme running through the entire story, *most intensely perhaps in chap. 37*, is the dialectic between what is and what will be, reality and destiny . . . "(emphasis added).

[Joseph] out of their hands, saying, 'Let us not take his life.' And Reuben said to them, 'Shed no blood; cast him into this pit here in the wilderness, but lay no hand upon him'—that he might rescue him out of their hand, to restore him to his father."

In vv 21–22 what Reuben "says" temporarily saves Joseph from the proposed fate as "said" by the brothers in 37:19–20. Moreover, by heeding Reuben's words, the brothers temporarily refrain from engaging in bloodshed. Reuben uses some of the same terminology of the brothers to convince them as the parent adopts the "sinners'" words in Prov 1:8–19. The brothers in Gen 37:20 say: wĕnašlikēhû bĕʾaḥad habbōrôt, "and we shall cast him into one of the pits," while Reuben says in Gen 37:22: hašlîkû ʾōtô ʾel habbôr hazzeh, "cast him into this pit."

When Judah makes his case before his brothers while Reuben is absent, Gen 37:27 concludes: wayyišmĕʿû ʾeḥāyw "his brothers listened (to him)," in contrast to Reuben's attempts to get his brothers to heed his words in vv 21–22. Over and above the strategy of Reuben to save Joseph in order to regain favor before his father Jacob,[79] later in the Joseph story Reuben reminds his brothers of their mistake in not listening to his words in Gen 37:21. After the brothers admit their guilt in regard to Joseph in Gen 42:21, Reuben says in v 22: wayyaʿan rĕʾûbēn ʾōtām lēʾmōr hălôʾ ʾāmartî ʾălêkem lēʾmōr ʾal teḥeṭʾû bayyeled wĕlôʾ šĕmaʿtem wĕgam dāmô hinnēh nidrāš, And Reuben answered them, "Did I not tell you not to sin against the lad? But you would not listen. So now there comes a reckoning for his blood."[80] Aside from the fact that there is no record of Reuben ever expressing such a warning, the emphatic position of dāmô, "his blood," in the phrase dāmô hinnēh nidrāš, drives home the ironic twist in the story of Joseph and his brothers which has a complementary counterpart in Prov 1:8–19 as a whole. The metaphorical shedding of Joseph's blood ends up, in the brothers' eyes, in the potential shedding of their own blood.[81] By failing to listen to Reuben's words the brothers initiate a series of events which leads to their own "destruction." The expression dāmô, "his blood," thus has the potential of linking the events in Genesis 42 with the earlier discussion concerning Joseph's life, i.e., dām, "blood," in Genesis 37.

---

[79] See J. Goldin, "The Youngest Son or Where Does Genesis 38 Belong," JBL 96 (1977) 40, where he points out that Reuben's attempt to save Joseph was in reality an attempt to regain the favor of their father, Jacob.

[80] M. Sternberg ("Point of View," 76–77) speaks of the "verbally pinpointed" nature of "blood," "require" and how these two terms link Reuben's words with other portions of the book of Genesis.

[81] See J. S. Ackerman, "Joseph, Judah, and Jacob," 90.

Earlier we noted Sternberg's argument that "reported discourse yokes together two (or more) speech-events that are by nature removed from each other in time and place and state of affairs, in the identity of the participants, in their characters, outlooks, interpersonal relations, goals, milieus, languages or dialects."[82] We now are in a position to recognize a traditio-historical connection between Prov 1:8–19 and Genesis 37 by means of the incidence of direct speech in Prov 1:8–19. By appealing to Sternberg's observations concerning deictic duality of direct speech, we are also in the realm of deciphering what Fishbane refers to as the *traditum* and the subsequent *traditio* which it serves.[83] The goal of such an analysis is to propose an inner-biblical reading serving portions of Proverbs by means of traditions drawn from Genesis 37.

We will see later how this introductory didactic lesson from Prov 1:8–19 in many ways lays out the preparatory groundwork for themes which re-echo in Proverbs 1–9. The hermeneutic move of planting the traditio-historical identity within Genesis, on the one hand, and in the book of Proverbs, on the other hand, facilitates a hearing of the traditions which fluctuated within the history of Israel's memory. Such a strategy is played out to the attentive reader or hearer who recognizes the rephrased words of the older sections of Proverbs in the mouth of the implied speakers from Genesis 37, i.e. from Torah. The voice of the parents within the Proverbs tradition, combines the speech of the *ḥaṭṭāʾîm*, "sinners," in 1:18, a citation from Isaiah 59:7, and the rephrased words from Genesis 37. Hence, "Torah" is assumed to imply knowledge of "Proverbs," and "Proverbs" implies knowledge of the words of "Torah." An exchange of theology, point view, and traditions takes

---

[82] "Point of View," 72.

[83] Even though Fishbane does not speak in terms of such things as the "deictic duality of direct speech" as Sternberg does, there are places in Fishbane's work where he speaks of "*implicit* or virtual citation" of the content of another tradition which can involve direct and indirect discourse: "Aside from the few instances of *explicit* citation or referral, the vast majority of cases of aggadic exegesis in the Hebrew Bible involve *implicit* or virtual citations. In these cases, it is not by virtue of objective criteria that one may identify aggadic exegesis, but rather by a close comparison of the language of a given text with other, earlier Scriptural dicta or topoi. Where such a text (the putative *traditio*) is dominated by these dicta or topoi (the putative *traditum*), and uses them in new and transformed ways, the likelihood of aggadic exegesis is strong. In other words, the identification of aggadic exegesis where external objective criteria are lacking is proportionally increased to the extent that multiple and sustained lexical linkages between two texts can be recognized, and where the second text (the putative *traditio*) uses a segment of the first (the putative *traditum*) in a lexically reorganized and typically rethematized way"(*Biblical Interpretation*, 285).

place. The authority of the parents' words, as framed by the narrator, in Prov 1:8–19 is not derived solely from their own *experience*, but is now fixed within the "biblical" traditions which they imply.[84] The freedom which the tradent exercises over the previous traditions from Genesis is not grounds for laying claim to an uncontrollable flux of traditions during the period when Proverbs 1–9 was finally being shaped. Rather, it is another indication of the traditio-historical process found in many parts of scripture whereby earlier traditions are recontextualized. Speaking of typology as a form of linking the past, present, and future, Fishbane asserts:

> Many other images were employed typologically, ranging from the creation itself to historical personages and their exploits in *illud tempus*, in order to convey or assert the fundamental continuity linking contemporary Israel in crisis with Israel of sacred memory. Here. . . aggadic exegesis serves to link the past with the present and future, only now the *traditio* is regarded as a reactualization of the *traditum*, and not its replacement; and the *traditum* does not serve as the backdrop and foil for a discontinuous *traditio*, but is rather the screen upon which nationalized hope and renewal is contextualized, even imagined.[85]

---

[84] See R. Van Leeuwen, "Liminality and Worldview in Proverbs 1–9," where he argues that Proverbs 1–9 is "primarily concerned to inculcate a particular Yahwistic worldview"(p.113), a worldview not derived from experience but found elsewhere within scripture. For Van Leeuwen, Prov 1:10–19 provides an example of a negative object lesson of "sinners" who violate the orders of God's creation. See: L. Boström, *The God of the Sages Proverbs*, who describes a common core of traditions and motifs concerning creation, order, justice, and individual ethics that link Proverbs with the sovereign God depicted elsewhere in the Bible. Prov 1:8–19 provides Boström with an example of what he calls "character-consequence relationship," a relationship that operates not mechanically but rather involves at times an intimate relationship with Yahweh(p. 114). Also, A. Meinhold, *Die Sprüche*, is aware of the broad international context of wisdom that is evident in the book of Proverbs. Even in terms of the overall pattern of Tun-Ergehen-Zusammenhang (deed-result relationship), a concept found in non-biblical wisdom traditions, the book of Proverbs reflects a similar theological interest. Yet for Meinhold the larger and more decisive factor of "JHWH-Glaubens"—Yahwistic faith—determines the true theological character of Proverbs(p. 38). "JHWH-Glaubens" is an all inclusive term for the divinely created order, an order which likewise embraces creation and the social order. According to Meinhold, "JHWH-Glaubens" implies other biblical traditions. Prov 1:8–19 provides Meinhold with an example of the outcome of those who violate "JHWH-Glaubens." Interestingly, Meinhold notes the unique feature of quoted speech and twice he refers to the Joseph story in his analysis of Prov 1:8–19(pp. 53–54).

[85] *Biblical Interpretation*, 413.

Such a recontextualization of Genesis 37 lends itself to an inner-biblical understanding of Prov 1:8–19 as well as to other thematically and lexically resonant portions of Proverbs. The fact, moreover, that Prov 1:8–19 is presented in a hypothetical framework, "If sinners entice you. . . ," "If they say. . ." (Prov 1:10, 11), placing any outcome in a future context, does not hinder the argument presented here for the imaginative reuse of portions of Genesis 37. If anything, the future oriented nature of direct discourse in Prov 1:8–19 lends credence to the observation made above by Fishbane that "the *traditio* is regarded as a reactualization of the *traditum*"[86] linking past, present and future. Such hypothetical, future oriented discourse Sternberg calls "preproductive discourse:"

> All these double-framed structures of report are Janus-faced in temporal orientation. One of their faces, that of the global frame occupied by narrator and reader, is turned, as usual to a past speech-event. . . ; whereas the other, that of the local frame with its different speaker and addressee, is turned to the future. . . , envisaging a speech-event that has not yet come into being. Thus oriented to the future, these quotations-within-quotations are not categorical but modally qualified; not retrospective but prospective, predictive, directive; not *re*productive but, so to speak, *pre*productive.[87]

An awareness of "preproductive speech" can go a long way in helping us to understand better the use of Israel's historical traditions not only for Prov 1:8–19 but also for 1:20–33 and 6:1–19 as well. In contrast to the reported discourse of historical accounts in, for example, Genesis and Exodus, which has allowed scholars to offer accounts of Israel's early history, the discourse structure of portions of Proverbs, we are arguing, is not any less historically oriented. That is to say, just because portions of Proverbs do not report history the way an account in Genesis does, does not mean that Proverbs is therefore ahistorical or that it does not reflect an awareness of Israel's historical traditions. At a minimum it means that Proverbs is "history" only oriented in another way. It is not referential but representational by means of direct discourse.

Our awareness of the play upon portions of Genesis represents a limited understanding of the nature of the parents' discourse in 1:8–19. The backward glance at events from the Joseph story serves the dual purpose of fixing the parents' discourse in the realm of scriptural tradition (i.e, Torah) while at the same time providing an authoritative platform for the future oriented nature of his/her discourse (i.e., Proverbs). Thus, our analysis of the traditio-historical background of

---

[86] *Biblical Interpretation*, 413.
[87] "Proteus in Quotation Land," 138.

Prov 1:8–19 provides evidence of inner-biblical interpretation which looks back on an earlier historical event in order to address concerns in the parents' historical period of time.

PROV 1:8–19, GENESIS 37, AND RABBINIC COMMENTARY.

An indication of how double-framed structures of reported discourse have had an effect upon later readers of 1:8–19 is evidenced by the medieval Rabbinic commentary, *Midrash Mishle*.[88] While it is the case that the darshan (tradent) isolates a number of other contexts within the Hebrew Bible in commenting upon Prov 1:8–19 in *MM*, there is evidence of a sustained commentary upon the direct discourse of the sinners and the account of the selling of Joseph in Genesis 37. For example, for Prov 1:11, *MM* reads, *ʾm yʾmrw lkh ʾtnw nʾrbh ldm nspnh lnqy hnm. d"ʾ nspnh lqny hnm ʾylw ʾhyw sl ywsp shyw mspyn wōmrîn, ʾymty ygyʿ hqs wnhrgnw*,[89] "If they say: 'Come with us, let us lie in wait for blood, let us lurk for the innocent without cause.'" (Prov. 1:11) Another interpretation: "Let us lurk for the innocent without cause: (ibid.) This refers to Joseph's brothers who were looking [for an opportunity] saying: When will the time come that we may kill him?"[90]

Preceding this interpretation for 1:11, an interpretation is given for Prov 1:10 by referring to Ps 56:6 and perhaps Proverbs 13.[91] The midrash on Prov 1:11 stands as a proof text for the darshan's comments on 1:10 as well as a transition for the expanded comments on Prov 1:8–14. The key to the midrash for Prov 1:11 lies in the word *dām*, "blood:" *whyth skynh*

---

[88] S. Buber, *Midrasch Mischlé: Samlung agadischen Auslegung der Sprüche Salomonis* (Wilna: Druck v. Wittwe & Gebr. Romm., 1883.) Two other sources, *Yalqut Shimoni*, Saloniki and J. ibn Nachmias, *Kommentar zu den Sprüchen Salomos* (Berlin: Schriften des Vereins Mekize Nirdamim, 1911) quote *Midrasch Mishlé* with some minor changes. Cf. also B. L. Visotzky, *Midrash Mishle: A Critical Edition Based on Manuscripts and Early Editions with an Introduction and Annotated English Translation of Chapters One through Ten*, Two Volumes. Unpublished Dissertation, Jewish Theological Seminary, 1982. While our interest here is not in offering a detailed history of Jewish interpretation of the selected portions of Proverbs, it should be noted, however, that *Midrash Mishle* is not the only work which comments on Proverbs. B. Visotzky's dissertation offers the most complete and up to date text analysis of *Midrash Mishle* along with cross references to other Rabbinic works from which *Midrash Mishle* drew. See, for example, the "Index of Primary Sources," 139–149. (Hereafter, *Midrash Mishle* = *MM*.)

[89] B. Visotzky, *Midrash Mishle: A Critical Edition*, 2. 331.

[90] B. Visotzky, *Midrash Mishle: A Critical Edition*, 1. 189–190.

[91] See B. Visotzky, *Midrash Mishle: A Critical Edition*, 1. 188, where he discusses the possible connection with Proverbs 13.

mshqh ʿlyhm wˀwmrt, ˀwy lkm mdmw sl sdyq hzh,[92] "And the Shechina laughed at them and said: Woe to you for the blood of this righteous one."[93] J. ibn Nachmias identifies Joseph as the "righteous one:" *wbmdrs mtprs prsh zw ʿl ywsp hsdyq shwrydwhw ˀhyw lbwr wmkrwhw lysmˁlym bˀsrym ksp,* "In the midrash this portion is explicated as referring to Joseph the righteous one whom his brothers put into the pit and then sold him to the Ishmaelites for twenty pieces of silver"(my translation).[94] *MM* likewise expands its references to Genesis, weaving into its comments the paraphrased words of Reuben and Judah from Gen 37:21 and 37:27 in *MM*'s comments for Prov 1:11: *lkk nˀmˀ nspnh lnqy hnm, wmkwlm lˀ rsh lhsylw ˀlˀ rˀwbn, snˀ wysmʿ rˀwbn wysylhw mydm (brˀsyt lz:kˀ) ˀmˀ lhn bˀw wntn lkm ʿysh, ˀmrw lw mh ʿsh ˀth nwtn lnw, ˀm lhm nslyk ˀwtw lbwr kshwˀ hy, wydynw ˀl thy bw,*[95]

> Thus it says, "Let us lurk for the innocent without cause. . ." And of all of them, only Reuben wanted to save him, as it is said, "But when Reuben heard it, he tried to save him from them." (Gen. 37:21) He said to them: Come here, and I'll give you a piece of advice. They said to him: What

---

[92] B. Visotzky, *Midrash Mishle: A Critical Edition,* 2. 331.

[93] B. Visotzky, *Midrash Mishle: A Critical Edition,* 1. 190–191. Visotzky also notes that "God refers to blood they wish to spill." (p. 191)

[94] *Kommentar zu den Sprüchen Salomos,* 3. In Wisdom of Solomon 10:13, Joseph is alluded to and is identified as *ho dikaios,* "the righteous one." What is also interesting in this brief allusion to Joseph's plight is the combination of *ho lakkos,* "the pit," *he hamartia,* "sin," *sygkatabaino,* "to descend," and the "turn-about" theme where Joseph is rescued and "those who accused him she showed to be false:" *aute prathenta dikaion ouk egkatelipen, alla ech hamatias errysato auton· sygkatebē autō eis lakkon, kai hen desmois ouk aphēken auton, heōs ēnegken autō skēptra basileias kai echousian tyrannountōn autou pseudeis te edeiche tous momēsamenous auton, kai edōken autō doxan aiōnion,* "When a righteous man was sold she ("wisdom") did not abandon him, but delivered him from sin. She descended with him into the pit and when he was in prison she did not leave him until she brought him the scepter of a kingdom and authority over his masters. Those who accused him she showed to be false, and she gave him honor everlasting."(my translation) See also, G. E. Nickelsburg, Jr., *Resurrection, Immortality, and Eternal Life in Intertestamental Judaism* (Cambridge/London: Harvard University Press, 1972) 48–58, where he treats Genesis 37 as an example of a story of the "persecution and exaltation of the righteous man." The significance of Nickelsburg's work is the fact that the use made of the Joseph story in later literature indicates the continuing vitality of the story of the selling of Joseph and how it has been utilized in another context.

[95] B. Visotzky, *Midrash Mishle: A Critical Edition,* 2. 331.

advice would you give us? He said to them, Let's throw him into the pit alive, "but let us not do away with him ourselves." (Gen. 37:27)[96]

In Prov 1:12 *MM* associates *blʿ*, "swallowing up," *bôr*, "pit," with Joseph: *nblʿm ksʾwl hyym, zh ywsp wywrd lbwr kshwh hy. wtmymym kywrdy bwr, syrd lbwr btwmw, wlʾ hyh ywdʿ mh hyw ʿwsyn lw*,[97]

> "Let us swallow them up alive as the grave. . . This refers to Joseph who descended into the pit while alive. "And whole, as those that go down to the pit."(ibid.) For he descended into the pit in innocence, and did not know what they were doing to him."[98]

The following references to *hôn yāqār*, "precious goods," *nemalleʾ batênû šālāl*, "we shall fill our houses with spoil," are linked to Joseph in *MM*: *kl hwn yqr nmṣʾ nmlʾ btynw sll kl hwn yqr nmṣʾ. zh mkyrtw sl ywsp smkrw bn shwʾ yqyr lʾbyn. nmṣʾ. snmṣʾ mhyyh lpnyhm. nmlʾ btynw sll. smylʾw btyhm ksp wzhb mʾwsrwtyw sl ywsp*,[99]

> "We shall find all precious substance, we shall fill our houses with spoil."(Prov. 1:13) "We shall find all precious substance"(ibid.) This refers to the sale of Joseph, for they sold a son who was precious to his father. "We shall find"(ibid.) He was found to be a life saver before them. "We shall fill our houses with spoil"(ibid.) They filled their houses with silver and gold from the treasuries of Joseph.[100]

Interestingly, at the point where the sinners' discourse ends in Prov 1:14, *MM* diverges from its sustained comments on the Joseph story and

---

[96] B. Visotzky, *Midrash Mishle: A Critical Edition*, 1. 191, speaks of the "odd paraphrase of Reuben's speech" in *MM*.

[97] B. Visotzky, *Midrash Mishle: A Critical Edition*, 2. 331.

[98] B. Visotzky, *Midrash Mishle: A Critical Edition*, 1. 191: "*Let us swallow*—This citation of Prov 1:12 continues the allegorical interpretation of Prov. 1:11–14 as referring to Joseph and his brothers."

[99] B. Visotzky, *Midrash Mishle: A Critical Edition*, 2. 335.

[100] B. Visotzky, *Midrash Mishle: A Critical Edition*, 1. 194. See Buber's *MM* where it expands its references to later portions of Genesis: *kl hwn nmṣ' nml' btynw sll. zw mkyrtw sl ywsp, shyh bn yqyr l'byw, sn'mr ky bn zqwnym hw' lw (br'syt lz:g), nmṣ' mhyh lpnyhm, dktyb ky lmhyh slhny 'lhym lpnykm (br'syt mh:h): nml' btynw sll. sml'w btyhm ksp wzhb m'wsrwtyw sl ywsp,* "'We shall find all precious goods, we shall fill our houses with spoil.' This refers to the sale of Joseph who was a precious son to his father; as it says, 'for he was a son of his old age to him.'(Gen 37:3) 'We shall find,' he was life before them; as it is written 'God sent me before you to preserve life'(Gen 45:5): 'Let us fill our houses with spoil.' They filled their houses with silver and gold from the treasuries of Joseph."(my translation)

its relationship to Prov 1:10ff and instead offers comments concerning, idol worship, the "evil-tongued," and bribe taking.[101]

The importance of *MM* is that in its comments on Prov 1:10ff it "hears," as it were, the speech of the brothers from Genesis 37 through the direct discourse section in Prov 1:10–14. Such hearing bears out Bakhtin's and Sternberg's argument concerning the representational quality of direct speech as well as Fishbane's observations which highlight the vital and dynamic interrelation between a given *traditum* and a subsequent *traditio*.

The general consensus among scholars that the book of Proverbs as a whole lacks any reference to events or personages in Israel's history represents a narrow reading of the traditions.[102] We know from the citations within the book of Proverbs itself that editors have identified the traditions with Solomon (Prov 1:1; 10:1) and Hezekiah (Prov 25:1). The contents of Proverbs 8 can certainly be identified with the kind of creation terminology found in Genesis 1.[103] Similarly, we should not be surprised to find traditions within Proverbs which remind us of, but do not necessarily refer explicitly to other portions of the canon. What we are proposing, then, is that reference is not solely a matter of naming. Reference can be made by a literary form of representation as in the case of Prov 1:8–19. And such instances do not merely represent the traditio-historical source by means of exegesis, but provide interpretation in service to a later textual tradition—its needs, agenda, context, theology, point of view, and traditions. Hence, one can acknowledge the argument that portions, if not all, of Proverbs 1–9 stand as the "Introduction" to the remaining chapters of the book of Proverbs without getting involved in

---

[101] B. Visotzky, *Midrash Mishle: A Critical Edition*, 1. 199–202.

[102] C. Camp's recent assessment of the lack of a traditio-historical relationship between Proverbs and Torah in *Wisdom and the Feminine*, 234, exemplifies a common perception of the book of Proverbs: "This failure of the book of Proverbs to reflect explicitly on the Torah may provide another clue to its dating as well. The Proverbs poems are clearly concerned to offer a theological legitimation of Wisdom. Why then was there no effort made to connect this tradition with the Torah - unless the presence of the latter had not been felt; i.e., unless the book of Proverbs had already received its essential shape prior to the time that Ezra brought the book of the law back to Judah? On the other hand, if the rather striking theological perspective expressed in Prov 1–9 had been known to and respected by the exilic editors of the Torah, one might expect to see more traces of it there than are apparent. We might then conclude that this theology was either unknown or unacceptable to these editors, its creation or its rehabilitation awaiting a later day."

[103] See: G. Landes, "Creation Tradition in Proverbs 8:22–31 and Genesis 1," in *A Light Unto My Path: Old Testament Studies in Honor of Jacob M. Myers*, ed. H. Bream, R. Heim, and C. Moore (Philadelphia: Temple University, 1974) 279–293.

the knotty problems of deciding which section post- or predated other sections. In its present context, Prov 1:8-19, provides the initial didactic lesson of the Proverbs of Solomon and belongs to the introductory section of the book. As an Introduction, it serves both to prepare the reader for the context of the book and to signify that this book belongs to a larger, implicit inter-text of scripture.

3

PROV 1:20–33, JEREMIAH 7, 20, AND INNER-BIBLICAL INTERPRETATION.

TRANSLATION.
PROV 1:20–33

20) Wisdom cries aloud in the street;
in the squares she raises her voice;
21) on the top of the walls she cries out;
at the entrance of the city gates she speaks:
22) "How long, O simple ones, will you love simplicity?
As long as babblers delight in babbling?
As long as fools hate knowledge?
23) If you turn to my reproof, behold, then
I will pour out my thoughts to you;
I will make my words known to you.
24) 'Because I called and you refused
to listen, I have stretched out my
hand and no one has heeded,
25) and you have ignored all my counsel
and would have none of my reproof,
26) I also will laugh at your calamity;
I will mock when panic strikes you,

27) when panic strikes you like a storm,
and your calamity comes like a whirlwind,
when distress and anguish come upon you.'
28) Then they will call upon me, but I
will not answer; they will seek me diligently
but will not find me.
29) Because they hated knowledge and did
not choose the fear of the Lord,
30) and would have none of my counsel, and
despised all my reproof,
31) therefore they shall eat the
fruit of their way and be sated
with their devices.
32) For the simple are killed by their
turning away, and the complacence of
fools destroys them;
33) but he who listens to me will dwell
secure and will be at ease, without
dread of evil."

INTRODUCTION

In our analysis of Prov 1:8–19 we saw how the verses imply portions of the Joseph story found in Genesis 37. Our next example for analysis is Prov 1:20–33. Even though some scholars argue that vv 20–33 lack any connection whatsoever to 1:8–19, we are prepared to account for the juxtaposition of these verses on the basis of similar editorial techniques and a similar reutilization of direct discourse.[1] Where Prov 1:8–19 refashions discourse from Genesis 37 with a combined gloss from Isa 59:7, the narrator in Prov 1:20–33 combines different levels of prophetic speech in order to form another unit of discourse.

Our appeal to prophetic tradition as the backdrop for Prov 1:20–33 is not new. Scholars have long recognized strong resemblances between Prov 1:20–33 and prophetic speech.[2] A. Robert offered his own

---

[1] See: C. H. Toy, *Proverbs*, 20: "The section [Prov 1:20–33] is independent, having no immediate connection with the preceding or the succeeding context." Cf. also, W. McKane, *Proverbs*, 268–273; R. B. Y. Scott, *Proverbs*, 39; C. Camp, *Wisdom and the Feminine*, 200.

[2] B. Gemser, *Sprüche Salomos*, 23: "Gattungsgeschichte gehört der Abschnitt zu den jüngeren Formen der Weisheitsliteratur, wobei lyrische und prophetische Stilformen endringen . . . . Er hat die Form eines prophetischen Schelt- oder Drohwortes. . . ; besonders sind Berührungen mit den Stilformen Jeremias und des Deuteronomiums

assessment of the prophetic traditions which resurface with Prov 1:20–33.[3] Because Robert's analysis of Prov 1:20–33 combines so many prophetic traditions, it is difficult to grasp a controlled reutilization of the traditions. Rather, we are left with a confusing list of prophetic cross-references with no attention to form or to recurring patterns of speech.[4]

There is one point, however, where Robert argues how portions of Jeremiah 7 and Isaiah 65 and 66 stand out in Prov 1:24–33. Robert says:

> Outre ces ressemblances générales avec la littérature prophétique, il faut signaler des contacts très précis, qui se constatent non seulement dans les versets 24, 25 [Prov 1:24–25], mais dans toute la fin de la pièce, et qui, par conséquent, aident à en comprende le développement. Ces passages parallèles sont Jer. vii, 24, 26, 27 et Is. lxv, 2, 12; lxvi, 3, 4.[5]

Further, Robert narrows his focus and concentrates on the striking similarity between Prov 1:20–33 and Jeremiah 7:

---

vorhanden (עַד־מָתַי 22, יַעַן 24, מְשׁוּבָה 32, שָׁכֵן בֶּטַח 33; zu 24ff. Jer 7:24–28 und zu der Schadenfreude 26 Jes 66:3f . . . ;" R. Murphy, *Wisdom Literature*, 55: "This [Prov 1:20–33] is a unique genre, which can be best termed a SPEECH of personified wisdom; the only parallels are Proverbs 8–9 and Sirach 24. The motifs show that Wisdom speaks in the guise of a prophet. . . ;" W. O. E. Oesterley, *Proverbs*,10: "The general tone of this section recalls the utterances of the prophets; like the prophets of old, Wisdom goes out into the broad places of the city with denunciation and the prophecy of doom." Cf. also: C. Kayatz, *Studien zu Proverbien 1–9*, 120; C. H. Toy, *Proverbs*, 22, 26, 27; A. Barucq, *Le Livre des Proverbes*, 53; O. Plöger, *Sprüche Salomos*, 18–19; W. Frankenberg, *Die Sprüche*, 24.

3 "Les attaches littéraires bibliques de Prov I-IX," 43 (1934) 172–181.

4 See C. Kayatz's comments concerning A. Robert's anthological style (i.e., the stringing together of words and phrases drawn from various places within the Hebrew Bible) as it pertains to Prov 1:20–33: "So zwingen die mancherlei sprachlichen und inhaltlichen Anklänge, die A. Robert (Les Attaches Littéraires Bibliques De Prov. I-IX in Revue Biblique 1934/1935) insbesondere zwischen Prov. 1–9 und Jer., DT.- und Trito-Jesaja (neben vielen anderen prophetischen und weiteren alttestamentlichen Stellen) aufzeigt, nicht dazu, eine Abhängigkeit unserer Sammlung von ihnen anzunehmen. Abgesehen davon, dass manche der angeführten Analogien zu sehr allgemeiner Natur sind, als dass sie wirkliche Schlüsse erlaubten, sind viele von ihnen sicher aus der gemeinsamen Teilhabe an älteren Traditionen zu verstehen. Robert bringt ja selbst auch viele ältere Belege. Vor allem aber hat sich ja die Herkunft der wesentlichen Motive der Weisheitspredigt in Prov. 1,20ff aus viel älteren Texten als Jer. (in der dtr. Schlicht), DT.- und Trito-Jesaja aufzeigen lassen, so dass diese späteren Texte durchaus nicht vorausgesetzt werden müssen"(*Studien zu Proverbien 1–9*, n. 3, 128–129).

5 "Les attaches littéraires bibliques de Prov. I-IX," 177.

Les Prophète est pourtant invité à crier vers eux וְקָרָאתָ אֲלֵיהֶם, sans esperer aucune response וְלֹא יַעֲנוּכָה (Prov. [1:] 28, mais avec situation renversee). Comme on le voit, les ressemblances de vocabulaire sont peu nombreuses, mais la parenté de pensée est frappante, d'autant plus que Jérémie vient d'affirmer (vv. 21, 22) [Jer 7:21–22] l'estime très modérée qu'il professe pour le culte, et que tout-a-l'heure (32ss.) il va, en conséquence des reproches, annoncer le châtiment.[6]

In the following pages we will argue that the similarities between Prov 1:20–33 and portions of Jeremiah offer us more than a vague hint into the inner-biblical connection between wisdom and prophecy. Even though Robert observes that "les ressemblances de vocabulaire [i.e., between Prov 1:20–33 and Jeremiah 7] sont peu nombreuses," additional factors indicate a level of editing which employs specific prophetic speech forms and content from Jeremiah in service to a sapiential context.[7] More specifically, the combination of vocabulary, stock prophetic speech, and compositional devices in Prov 1:20–33 reflect the common biblical explanation of the sixth century destruction of Judah and Jerusalem. By examining how such a pivotal event in Judah's history was reported in these traditions, we can glimpse again how once unconnected traditions are editorially brought together in order to achieve a new interpretation.

To uncover the editorial reutilization of traditions within Prov 1:20–33, we will first of all consider the difficulties scholars have with translating and interpreting Prov 1:22–23. As part of our analysis of vv 22–23, we will describe a common editorial device for introducing reported discourse. After coming to terms with these difficulties, we will turn to a fresh examination of wisdom's discourse for vv 20–33. As we will see, Bakhtin's "double-voiced discourse" and Sternberg's "deictic duality of direct speech" will again assist us in our detecting inner-biblical interpretation by clarifying the dense array of speech patterns in Prov 1:20–33.

---

[6] "Les attaches littéraires bibliques de Prov. I-IX," 178.

[7] F.-J. Steiert, *Die Weisheit Israels*, 259–270, concurs with Robert's description of the prophetic elements in Prov 1:20–33. Steiert argues that that parallels between wisdom's prophetic form and content and other traditions are not accidental. Rather, the connections he detects are "intentional"(p. 269). These verses also provide Steiert with further evidence to contrast the book of Proverbs with Egyptian traditions. Influenced by Robert, Steiert concludes that wisdom is portrayed as a "Etre divin"(*sic*, p. 270).

PROV 1:22–23: PROBLEMS IN
TRANSLATION AND INTERPRETATION.

For Prov 1:22 the text reads: *ʿad mātay pĕtāyim tĕʾēhăbû petî wĕlēṣîm lāṣôn ḥāmĕdû lāhem ûkĕsîlîm yiśnĕʾû dāʿat*, which the RSV translates as, "How long, O simple ones, will you love being simple? How long will scoffers delight in their scoffing and fools hate knowledge?"

A number of problems in v 22 need to be addressed for they determine how we view the overall nature of wisdom's speech. For example, the MT shifts from the second person plural in 1:22a to the third person plural in 1:22bc and then back to the second person plural in 1:23. The verbs *ḥāmĕdû*, "they desire," and *tĕʾēhăbû*, "you will love" present another problem. In context with *ʿad mātay*, "How long?" and *tĕʾēhăbû* "you will love," we expect the imperfect form of *hmd* and not the perfect.[8] Some scholars find the vocalization of *tĕʾēhăbû* to be unsatisfactory. Toy argues that "the final letter of the stem is omitted because not pronounced—תֶּאֱהָבוּ Qal = תֶּאֱהָבוּ."[9] GKC notes that "תֶּאֱהָבוּ Pr 1:22 is to be explained from the endeavour to avoid too great an accumulation of short sounds by the insertion of a long vowel. . ."[10]

To overcome the problems in v 22, scholars have offered a variety of interpretations. Toy, for instance, deletes 1:22b on the grounds that it is a "scribal addition."[11] He translates 1:22 as "How long, ye dullards, will ye love ignorance, and fools hate knowledge?"[12] But he does not explain the shift to the third person in the second stich, "and fools hate knowledge."

J. A. Emerton offers another interpretation. He concludes that 1:22bc is "a separate proverb, which has been displaced from its original position. . . ."[13] Emerton translates vv 22a and 23a as, "How long, ye

---

[8] W. Nowack, *Sprüche Salomo's*, 8; C. H. Toy, *Proverbs*, 30.

[9] *Proverbs*, 30. So also, A. Müller and E. Kautzsch, *The Book of Proverbs*, 34.

[10] GKC par. 63m. For a similar analysis, see also: W. Nowack, *Sprüche Salomo's*, 8; D. G. Wildeboer, *Die Sprüche*, 5; B. Gemser, *Sprüche Salomos*, 22; F. Delitzsch, *Proverbs*, 70. Such diffculties led A. Baumgartner (*Proverbes*, 34) to conclude that "Le texte hébreu est difficile a découvrir dans le v. de LXX."

[11] *Proverbs*, 24. Toy supports his argument by first pointing out that v 32, which is a "résumé of the preceding statement," makes mention of *pĕtāyim*, "simple ones," and *kĕsîlîm*, "fools," but leaves out *lēṣîm*, "scoffers"(p. 24). The absense of *lēṣîm* in v 32, he argues, indirectly indicates the secondary nature of *lēṣîm lāṣôn* in v 22. He goes on to argue that because "Wisdom is here dealing with the unwise" who "are urged to listen to instruction"(p. 24), wisdom's address does not pertain to *lēṣîm*. Toy finds support for his analysis by noting that the LXX does not mention *lēṣîm*, "scoffers."

[12] *Proverbs*, 20. A. Müller and E. Kautzsch, *The Book of Proverbs*, 34, follow Toy's reading.

[13] "A Note on the Hebrew Text of Proverbs i. 22–3." *JTS* NS 19 (1968) 611.

simple ones, will ye love simplicity? When will you turn to my reproof?" thus deleting 22bc altogether.[14]

A more recent attempt to provide a reading for 1:22 has been offered by R. E. Murphy.[15] He tries to overcome the textual problems in 1:22 by arguing that the plural verb *tāšûbû*, "turn," in v 23 has as its antecedents the *pĕtāyim*, *lēṣîm*, and *kĕsîlîm* in v 22. Thus, "all three classes of individuals are put on the same level."[16] The difficulty with Murphy's analysis is that if such a leveling is in fact present in 1:22, then this is the only place in Proverbs where it occurs. Moreover, he does not explain the change in person between v 22a and 22bc. But there is a way around these problems in 1:22 which complements, in part, Murphy's attempt to offer an interpretation which values the integrity of the MT.

Murphy detects, for instance, the importance placed upon "hearing" within 1:20–33.[17] Support for his textual retention of the MT for 1:22 can be found in an earlier article by H. N. Richardson.[18] In attempting to provide a definition for the root *lîṣ* which appears seventeen times in various forms in the book of Proverbs, Richardson concludes that "the verb 'talk freely or big' and the noun 'babbler' seem to satisfy the sense

---

[14] "A Note on the Hebrew Text of Proverbs i.22–3," 614. Emerton offers three reasons for the correction he has made: 1) the shift in person between 22a, 22b and c; 2) the presence of the perfect *ḥāmĕdû* between two imperfects; and 3) because vv 22–23 have three lines each where two lines are, for Emerton, "normal"(p. 16). A similar analysis and translation was offered earlier by C. Steuernagel ("Die Sprüche," in *Die heilige Schrift des Alten Testaments*, ed. by E. Kautzsch, vol. 2 [Tübingen: J. C. Mohr, 1910] 252) and W. O. E. Oesterley (*Proverbs*, 11). Referring approvingly to Steuernagel's work, Oesterley says: "Steuernagel would omit the two last lines of the verse [v 22bc]; their form certainly suggests that they are a copyist's addition. As the next verse has three lines instead of the usual two, he takes the first line of *v.* 23 as belonging to *v.* 22, and reads: 'How long will ye love simplicity, And turn from my reproof?' This has much to commend it"(p. 11). So also, M. Gilbert, "Le Discours menaçant de Sagesse en Proverbes 1,20–33," in *Storia e tradizioni di Israele* (Brescia: Paideia Editrice, 1991) pp. 106, 108, treats Prov 1:22b/c as a gloss, thus eliminating the problem of third person plural discourse in a context that is clearly addressed to "you," second person plural.

[15] "Wisdom's Song: Proverbs 1:20–33," *CBQ* 48 (1986) 456–460.

[16] "Wisdom's Song," 457. See: P. Trible, "Wisdom Builds a Poem, The Architecture of Proverbs 1:20–33," *JBL* 94 (1975) 511–512. F.-J. Steiert, *Die Weisheit Israels*, 262, also treats the *pĕtāyim*, *lēṣîm*, and *kĕsîlîm* as equals.

[17] "Wisdom's Song," 459–460. Cf. P. Trible, "Wisdom Builds a Poem," 511; H. Ringgren and W. Zimmerli, *Sprüche/Prediger*, *übersetzt und erklärt* (Göttingen: Vandenhoeck & Ruprecht, 1980) 16; and W. Nowack, *Sprüche Salomo's*, 8, for similar observations concerning "hearing."

[18] "Some Notes on לִיץ and its Derivatives," *VT* 5 (1955) 163–179.

of the context best."[19] A further characteristic of a "babbler," as Richardson shows, is that a "babbler" does not "listen." Such an observation fits well into the context of wisdom's complaint in Prov 1:20–33 that even though she "cries aloud," "raises her voice," and "cries out," her potential hearers "refused to listen"(v 24, RSV; cf. v 33).

We can build on the work of Murphy and Richardson which concentrates on the importance placed upon hearing. For instance, scholars have long recognized a difference between the portrayal of the *pĕtāyim* over against other references to the *lēṣîm* and *kĕsîlîm* in Proverbs.[20] In brief, a difference is maintained between *pĕtāyim*, "simple ones," and *lēṣîm*, "babblers" (using Richardson's translation), on the basis of "hearing." For example, 13:1 reads, *bēn ḥākām mûsar ʾāb welēṣ lōʾ šāmaʿ gĕʿārâ* "A wise son hears his father's instruction, but a scoffer/babbler does not listen to rebuke." Here the *lēṣ*, "scoffer/babbler," is likened as

---

[19] "Some Notes on ליץ," 179.

[20] W. O. E. Oesterley (*Proverbs*, lxxxv) observes the potential that the *pĕtî* has and the contrast that the book of Proverbs makes between the *pĕtāyim*, and the *lēṣîm* and *kĕsîlîm*: "Three points regarding this type of 'fool' come out here: he is without experience, he is one who is young, and he is thought of as teachable. As the most hopeful type one can understand that the *Pethi* is the most frequently occuring term for 'fool' in *Proverbs*. . . ." Oesterley continues: "So that this type of 'fool' is the man of weak character with no will of his own; he is by no means a hardened sinner, for he is teachable; and in the right hands may be made to go right. He was the kind of young man with whom the Wisdom writers were especially concerned." For the *kĕsîl*, Oesterley says that Proverbs presents the *kĕsîl* as "always morally bad"(p. lxxxvi). And of the *lēṣ*: "But perhaps the most objectionable type of all is that known under the name of *Letz* ('scorner'), for he is as much an enemy to God and to man as to himself"(p. lxxxvii). See also, A. Robert, "Les attaches littéraires bibliques de Prov. I-IX," *RB* 43 (1934) 173: "On sait que les simples פְּתָאיִם se distinguent des "railleurs" צְלִים [*sic* לֵצִים] et des insensés כְּסִילִים en ce que leurs écarts de conduite procèdent, non pas de la méchanceté, mais de la légèreté ou d'une ignorance involontaire. Au contraire, railleurs et insenses sont intentionnellement et obstinément attachés au mal: il ne sont pas susceptibles de conversion. . . ." More recently, B. Lang, *Wisdom and the Book of Proverbs*, 15, makes a similar distinction between *pĕtî* and *lēṣ*. See also J. Crenshaw, *Old Testament Wisdom, An Introduction*, 81, where he sees a clear differentiation made within Proverbs between the *pĕtî* and all other less desireable people. After listing eight expressions which generally designate the "fool," Crenshaw says this: "Naturally, not all of these were beyond help. The *pethi*, for example, presented a real challenge, inasmuch as he or she could readily be influenced for good or ill. Like an inexperienced young girl, whose vulnerability offered a rare opportunity for preying individuals, the *pethi* could easily be swayed. For the rest, the wise had nothing but contempt." That contempt, according to Crenshaw, extends to the *lēṣ*, "scoffer," and *kĕsîl*, "fool." A. Meinhold, *Die Sprüche*, 59–60, also is aware of the sharp contrast drawn between the "simple ones" in v. 22a, and the "scoffers" and "fools," in v. 22b/c.

one who does not listen as in 1:23–24, 33. In 1:22, *pĕtāyim tĕʾĕhăbû pĕtî*, "the simple ones love simpleness," being linked in 1:23 to *tāšûbû lĕtôkaḥtî*, "turn to my reproof," suggests that a remedy for "simpleness" consists in turning to wisdom.

A similar thought is conveyed by 15:12, but this time the *lēṣ*, "scoffer/babbler," is portrayed as one who refuses to be "reproved" and who does not seek the wise: *lôʾ yeʾĕhab lēṣ hôkēaḥ ʾel ḥăkāmîm lōʾ yēlēk*, "A scoffer/babbler does not like to be reproved; he will not go to the wise." The reference of "not going to the wise"(plural) and reference to *ykḥ*, "reproof," in 15:12 is a characteristic of the *lēṣ* which strikes a similar chord with 1:20–33. In 19:25 the *pĕtāyim* are taught to learn from the treatment accorded the *lēṣîm*: *lēṣ takkeh ûpetî yaʿrîm wĕhôkîaḥ lĕnābôn yābîn dáʿat*, "Strike a scoffer/babbler, and the simple will learn prudence, reprove a man of understanding and he will gain knowledge"[21](my translation); so also 21:11: *baʿanāš lēṣ yeḥkam petî ûbĕhaśkîl lĕhākām yiqqaḥ dáʿat*, "When a scoffer/babbler is punished, the simple become wise; when a wise man is instructed he gains knowledge"(RSV).[22]

In contrast to examples where the *pĕtāyim*, "simple ones" are portrayed as being able to learn from the *lēṣîm*, "babblers," there are no examples where the *lēṣîm* can learn from the ways of the *pĕtāyim*. The effect of these examples from Proverbs is twofold: 1) the *lēṣîm* are characterized as those who are not prone "to listen;" 2) in two examples (19:25; 21:11) the *pĕtāyim* are differentiated from the *lēṣîm* with the indication that the *pĕtāyim* can learn from the ways of *lēṣîm* while the *lēṣîm* remain unreprovable.

As a result, even though the change in person between 1:22a and b/c in the MT may represent an editorial addition to v 22, evidence of such

---

[21] For Prov 19:25 C. H. Toy says: "The morally ignorant man [*pĕtî*, "simple one"], says the proverb, is warned when bad men [*lēṣîm*, "scoffers/babblers"] are punished—it is an intelligible object-lesson"(*Proverbs*, 380). W. O. E. Oesterley, *Proverbs*, 163, makes a similar observation: "The verse sets in contrast the ways in which the foolish and the sensible man, respectively, acquire knowledge. The former requires something in the shape of a warning; there must be some tragic object-lesson before he will be deterred from following his evil course. . . This is one of a number of passages which show that though the Wisdom writers have a profound contempt for 'fools' in general they recognize that there are many such whose case is not hopeless. The remedy may require to be severe, whether by way of warning in seeing the plight of others, as in this verse. . ." Cf. F. Delitzsch, *Proverbs*, 34–35.

[22] For 21:11 C. H. Toy says: "The punishment of the bad man is a warning to the morally untrained"(*Proverbs*, 402). Again, W. O. E Oesterley (*Proverbs*, 179) agrees with Toy: "The simple-minded man learns both from the adversity of the scorner, by taking warning from him, and by prosperity of the wise, by encouragement ('he receiveth knowledge')." Cf. F. Delitzsch, *Proverbs*, 70.

an addition sets in sharper focus the words of wisdom and the object of wisdom's speech. As such 1:22 is another example of instructing the *pětāyim* by alluding to the ways of the *lēṣîm*. F. Delitzsch's comment that, "Intentionally, Wisdom addresses *only* the פְּתָיִם, to whom she expects to find soonest access"[23] (emphasis added), is certainly a viable way to interpret 1:22.

Contrary to Murphy's analysis which places the *pětāyim*, *lēṣîm*, and *kěsîlîm* all on the same level, and contrary to Toy's and Emerton's radical excising of portions of vv 22–23, wisdom is addressing the *pětāyim*, the "simple ones," by recalling the ways of the "babblers" and "fools." While some scholars attribute the shift in voice in 1:22a & b/c to the awkward hand of a later redactor, the same shift can be read as a stylistic feature drawing the readers' and "simple ones'" attention to the perennial ways of the *lēṣîm* and the *kěsîlîm*. A similar address is made in 1:10 where the root *pth* appears in relationship to the words of the sinners as quoted by the parent: *běnî ʾim yěpattûkā ḥaṭṭāʾîm*, "My son, if sinners entice/persuade you . . . ," presupposing that the addressee is "persuadable," "enticeable," "simple," in differentiation from the *ḥaṭṭāʾîm*, "sinners." The text implies that the *ḥaṭṭāʾîm* are beyond help.

As for the parallel reference to the *kěsîlîm*, "fools," in 1:22c, the "fools," like the "babblers," are consistently portrayed in Proverbs as those who do not listen and who do not accept reproof. While there are numerous examples pertaining to the ways of the fool and fools,[24] let it suffice here to note just one. In 14:6–7 the "scoffer/ babbler" and the "fool" are mentioned together: (6) *biqqeš lēṣ ḥokmâ wāʾayin wědaʿat lěnābôn nāqāl*; (7) *lēk minneged lěʾîš kěsîl ûbal yādaʿtā śiptê dāʿat*, (6) "A scoffer/babbler seeks wisdom in vain, but knowledge is easy for a man of understanding. (7) Leave the presence of a fool, for there you do not come to know words of (literally: "lips of") knowledge"(my translation). The associations made in 14:6–7 between "the babbler," "wisdom," "the fool," and "knowledge" offer an inviting parallel reading for 1:22bc. As 1:22c records that *ûkěsîlîm yiśneʾû dāʿat*, "and fools hate knowledge," 14:7 records that *dāʿat*, "knowledge," does not reside with the *kesîl*, the "fool."(cf. 1:23,29)

In sum, we know of no references in the book of Proverbs which suggest that the *lēṣîm*, "babblers," or *kěsîlîm*, "fools," are able to be anything other than babblers and fools in contrast to the *pětāyim* who are

---

[23] *Proverbs*, 70.
[24] For example: Prov 3:26,35; 8:5; 9:13; 10:1,18,23; 12:23; 13:19,20; 14:7,8,24,33; 15:27,14; 17:10,12,16,21,24,25; 18:2,6,7; 19:1,10,13,29; 23:9; 26:1,3,4,5,6,7,8,9,10,11,12; 28:26; 29:11. See W. Richter, *Recht und Ethos*, 176: "Eine entsprechende Aussage findet sich Spr. 18,2 (mit Gegenhaltung) und verallgemeinert Spr 1,22c."

potentially "reprovable." In addition, the book of Proverbs is addressed to the "simple" according to Prov 1:4. The *lēṣîm* and *kĕsîlîm* are not mentioned. The radical emendations in v 22 as made by Toy and Emerton are unnecessary once one reads the verse in the larger context of the book of Proverbs.

Thus, the translation that we are offering plays upon the comparative disjunction between the *pĕtāyim*, "simple ones," on the one hand, and the *lēṣîm*, "babblers," *kĕsîlîm*, "fools," on the other hand. Reading the initial *waw* in v 22bc as a "comparative *waw*,"[25] Prov 1:22 can be translated as:

> How long, O simple ones, will you love simplicity?
> As [long as] babblers delight in babbling?
> As [long as] fools hate knowledge?[26]

Our translation of 1:22 also has an important bearing upon the interpretation given below for vv 24–33 and for the shift in voice from the second person plural in 1:24–27 to the third person plural in 1:28–31. For example, commentators offer a variety of interpretations for Prov 1:23. The text reads, *tāšûbû lĕtôkaḥtî hinnēh ʾabbîʿâ lākem rûḥî ʾôdîʿâ dĕbāray ʾetkem*, "Give heed to my reproof; behold I will pour out my thoughts to you; I will make my words known to you" (RSV).

---

25 R. Williams, *Hebrew Syntax: An Outline*, 2nd edition (Toronto and Buffalo: University of Toronto Press: 1976) 71. See D. Steuernagel, "Die Sprüche," in *Die Heilige Schrift des Alten Testaments*, ed. E. Kautzsch (Tübingen: Verlag von J. C. B. Mohr, 1910) 252, who sets 1:22b in comparative contrast with 1:22a as we are doing:

> Wie lange wollt ihr Einfältigen Einfalt lieben
> und [wie lange wollen] die Spötter Luft zum
> Spötten haben,
> und die Toren Erkenntnis hassen?

Steuernagel puts v 22bc in bold face indicating that stichoi b and c break the rhythm of the verse. Steuernagel, however, does not elaborate on his interpretation of the text.

26 Cf. the following translations:

> How long, ye simple, will ye love simplicity?
> And scorners delight in scorning,
> And fools hate knowledge? (F. Delitzsch, *Proverbs*, 69)

> How long, you simpletons, will you prefer ignorance?
> The insolent ones delight in the insolence?
> The brazen hate knowledge? (R. B. Y. Scott, *Proverbs*, 34)

> How long, untutored youths, will you love immaturity!
> Scoffers are infatuated with scoffing,
> and fools hate knowledge. (W. McKane, *Proverbs*, 212)

The only outstanding problem in 1:23 is the phrase *tāšûbû lětôkaḥtî*, "Give heed to my reproof"(RSV).[27] The problem is not in the analysis of the words but in the syntactical arrangement of the clause.[28] For example, Toy drops altogether the phrase *tāšûbû lětôkaḥtî, "turn to my admonition."* Such a phrase, according to Toy, "only introduces confusion, since v. 24ff assume that they [the hearers in v 22] have not turned."[29] But there is no textual basis for such a change.

R. E. Murphy offers another interpretation. He argues that *ʿad mātay*, "how long," v 22, governs *tāšûbû*, "turn," v 23a.[30] For Murphy, it is inconsequential whether or not v 22bc is omitted. More important for Murphy is that along with the combination of *ʿad mātay* and *tāšûbû*, the *lě* of *lětôkaḥtî* is to be read "as a dative of specification," meaning "with respect to."[31]

---

[27] R. E. Murphy, "Wisdom's Song," 457: "The first two words, *tāšûbû lětôkaḥtî*, are the *crux*." The RSV's rendering of *tāšûbû* as an imperative is highly improbable. See: Toy, *Proverbs*, 30, where he states that *tāšûbû* cannot be an imperative.

[28] M. Dahood, *Proverbs and Northwest Semitic Philology* (Roma: Ponticium Institutum Biblicum, 1963) 6: "The chief dispute here concerns the nature of the first clause: is it conditional or no?"

[29] *Proverbs*, 25. CF. also, *Proverbs*, 21: "The interpretation of the paragraph depends in part on the view taken of the relation between v. 22. 23 and the following verses. If the former are held to contain an exhortation to repentance (v. 23a), they can hardly be closely connected with the latter, since they presume that the call of Wisdom has been rejected, and the discourse should state, after v. 23, the repellant answer of the persons addressed; *as the text stands, v. 24–31 constitute a separate discourse which states the result of disobedience.* Unity of thought may be gained by omitting v. 23a, and taking the whole piece as minatory, the connection being: you have turned a deaf ear to me long enough (v. 22), I have lost patience and will tell you my decision (v. 23): because you have refused, etc. (v. 24–31)"(emphasis added). See also W. Zimmerli, "The Structure of Old Testament Wisdom," n. 18, p. 203, in *SAIW* who also comments on the peculiar turn that takes place with Prov 1:24; H. Ringgren, *Word and Wisdom*, 96, for a similar conclusion for vv 22–23: "It is a reproach for disobedience and aversion to listening to her message;" and J. A. Emerton, "A Note on the Hebrew Text of Proverbs i. 22–3," 609, who concludes: "Verses 22 and 23 of Prov. i contain the opening words of an address by the personified figure of wisdom to the simple. The verses that follow do not, as in viii. 44ff. and ix, 4ff., invite them to receive instruction, but speak of the disaster that is to befall them because of their refusal to pay heed to wisdom." See: L. Boström, *The God of the Sages*, 149, for a similar conclusion.

[30] "Wisdom's Song," 457.

[31] "Wisdom's Song," 457. Murphy's analysis is dependent upon P. Volz's idiosyncratic analysis and reading of Prov 1:20–33 in "Weisheit," *Die Schriften des Alten Testaments*, III/2 (Göttingen: Vandenhoeck & Ruprecht, 1911) 143–144. Volz translates 1:22–23 as:

    22) Wie lange, ihr Einfaltigen, liebet ihr Einfalt,

Murphy translates *tāšûbû lĕtôkaḥtî* as "turn aside from my reproof,"[32] the opposite of the RSV. Like Toy before him, Murphy's text critical analysis of 1:23a is largely predetermined by his interpretation of the meaning of "Wisdom's" speech in vv 24–33.[33] There are no manifest *text-critical* problems in 1:23. Moreover, there is good reason to read 1:23a as the protasis of a conditional sentence.[34] The presence, also, of *hinnēh* between the protasis and apodasis is not problematic. Indeed, *hinnēh*, as an interjection, emphasizes wisdom's delight if and when *pĕtāyim* "turn."[35]

We are translating Prov 1:23 as follows:

> If you turn to my reproof, behold, [then] I will pour out my thoughts to you;
> I will make my words known to you.

Such a reading likewise complements our analysis and translation of v 22a, *ᶜad mātay pĕtāyim tĕᵊēhăbû petî*, "How long, O simple ones, will you love being simple?" The question as posed suggests a potential response in the present or future from the *pĕtāyim*, "simple ones." The response motif is present again in 1:33. V 23a records the potential reaction of wisdom to such a "turn." As we have seen from other examples in the book of Proverbs, such an option is not available to "babblers" and "fools."

---

gefallt euch Spott, ihr Spotter,
hasset ihr Toren Erkentnis,
23) kommt nicht zu meiner Predigt!
[space = pause]
Nun lass ich meinem Zorn den Lauf,
ich kunde euch den Spruch. . . .(p. 143)

---

[32] "Wisdom's Song," 459. As Murphy says: ". . . *tāšûbû* in v 23 is not an invitation to repent, but part of Wisdom's indictment"(p. 459).

[33] Also, M. Gilbert, "Le Discours menaçant de Sagesse," 107–108, combines Prov 1:22a with Prov 1:23. He treats v 22b/c as a gloss. As for the peculiar combination of second and third person speech in vv. 24–31, Gilbert concludes that these verses refer to the same group of people, only spoken of from two different perspectives, first "you," then "they"(pp. 113–115). Prov 1:26–27 speaks of the first moment of punishment while the following verses describe an even worse punishment that ensues.

[34] See: GKC, par. 159b; 159w.

[35] GKC 105b: An interjection such as *hinnēh* is "used to emphasize a demand, warning, or entreaty, and *always* placed after the expression to which it belongs"(emphasis added). See R. Murphy, "Wisdom's Song," 457–458: "The rest of v 23 is introduced by *hinnēh*. . . The *hinnēh* calls attention to something new, and is hardly to be understood as introducing the apodosis of a conditional clause (*pace* NEB)."

Our translation of vv 22–23 lays the basic groundwork for a new reading of vv 24ff. Because the potential salvation or destruction of the pĕtāyim is directly related to "hearing," the words which follow vv 22–23 take on special significance. Wisdom's call to turn (tāšûbû) to her "words," dĕbārîm, presupposes speech and hearing. Thus to read tāšûbû as a conditional form serves more than an invitation to hear. The invitation to turn lays the onus of responsibility solely upon the pĕtāyim.

The invitation also raises the question of wisdom's authority. What is the basis for wisdom's invitation to hear its word with the subsequent promise of security without dread of evil, mippaḥad rāʿâ, as stated in v 33? Contrary to the argument that v 24 initiates a section judging the failure of the pĕtāyim in v 22 to respond or to hear, we are prepared to argue that starting with v 24, the pĕtāyim and the reader are presented a reappropriated and refashioned judgment speech against a previous generation's failure to hear a similar word of warning and repentance. Thus by drawing upon a familiar prophetic tradition and by framing the diction in Prov 1:20–33 in such a way as to represent not only the event but similar prophetic words of warning to an earlier generation which went unheeded, the narrator through ḥokmâ lays claim to an authoritatively verifiable scriptural tradition. Thus, Toy's earlier observation about vv 24–31 being a "separate discourse" bears repeating because it may be closer to the intention of the tradition than he realized: "... as the text stands, v. 24–31 constitute a separate discourse which states the result of disobedience."[36] It is the nature of the separate discourse in vv 24–31 that now needs closer investigation and clarification.

PROV 1:20–33 AND THE
IDENTIFICATION OF QUOTED SPEECH.

In an article titled, "The Identification of Quotations in Biblical Literature,"[37] M. Fox builds upon R. Gordis' earlier work on quotations in biblical and extra biblical literature.[38] The importance of identifying quotations within scripture leads Fox to argue that our understanding of a text may be literally reversed.[39]

---

[36] C. H. Toy, *Proverbs*, 21.

[37] ZAW, 92 (1980) 416–431.

[38] R. Gordis, "Quotations in Wisdom Literature," JQR 30 (1939–1940) 123–147; "Quotations as Literary Usage in Biblical, Oriental and Rabbinic Literature," HUCA 22 (1949) 157–219.

[39] As Fox says ("Quotations in Biblical Literature," 416): "Identifying certain words as a quotation may have considerable significance for the understanding of a

He offers this definition of quotation:

> Quotations are words that either (1) are taken from another source but used as the speaker's words or (2) are meant to be understood as belonging to a person other than the primary speaker, regardless of their actual source, and only repeated by him.[40]

He argues that to understand quotations as he is defining them improves Gordis' earlier definition.[41] Fox differentiates "between quotations from another source spoken in the speaker's voice as his own thoughts, and quotations that have to be recognized as spoken by another voice in order to be understood (let us call the latter *attributed* quotations)."[42]

---

passage; it may at times even reverse our understanding of the author's intention." One may want to argue with Fox's presupposition that an "author's intentions" are conveyed by the isolation of quotations. There are a number of cases (see examples below) where Fox assumes we can know what the author intends by what the author values as important. Value derives from what the author directly quotes. Such a narrow understanding of quotation fails to see the communicative network of inner biblical associations that can be made either by direct quotation or by a strategy of paraphrasing someone else's words.

[40] "Quotations in Biblical Literature," 417.

[41] R. Gordis ("Quotations as a Literary Usage," 166) defines quotation as follows: "... *words which do not reflect the present sentiments of the author of the literary composition in which they are found, but have been introduced by the author to convey the standpoint of another person or situation*. These quotations include, but are not limited to, citations of previously existing literature, whether written or oral." Fox's main complaint with Gordis' definition is the uncontrolled freedom Gordis exercises when it comes to employing transition phrases in the text where they are simply implied. Such a tactic has the advantage of clarifying otherwise difficult passages. The disadvantage of Gordis' definition is that in far too many places Gordis simply harmonizes traditions by the use of a *verbum dicendi*. Fox, in contrast, proposes some basic guidelines for identifying quotations. As Fox says ("Quotations in Biblical Literature," 419): "What follows is not an attempt to present a formula that can mechanically and unmistakably identify quotations, but an attempt to discover some guidelines more definite and verfiable than the commentator's sense that the content of a passage would be more appropriate in the mouth of another speaker."

[42] "Quotations in Biblical Literature," 420. Because Fox limits the scope of his work only to Qoheleth and Job, one may allow him his differentiation between "quotations from another source" and "*attributed* quotations," as if they represent two different authorial strategies. But Fox never explains the phenomenon of why some quotations "*have to be* recognized as spoken by another in order to be understood"—his definition for attributed quotations—and others do not. Surely his reasoning that "the more important for the meaning of a passage it is for the reader to understand that certain words are quoted, the more clearly the writer must show him what they are," ("Quotations in Biblical Literature," 421) presupposes on Fox's part privy

Most useful for our analysis is how he isolates possible examples of quotation which are not marked by a *verbum dicendi*; i.e., verb forms of *ʾmr* or *dbr*. For instance, Fox cites Ps 55:22–23 as an example of how a quotation is indicated by the nominals *pîw*, "his mouth," and *děbāryw*, "his words:"

> Smoother than cream were the speeches of his mouth, But his heart was war:
> His words were softer than oil,
> Yet were they keen-edged swords,
> As he said,
> "Cast thy lot upon the Lord and He will maintain thee;
> He will never permit the righteous to stumble."[43]

The expression "*As he said,*" is absent in the Hebrew. Only on account of *pîw*, "his mouth," and *děbāryw*, "his words," are we able to supply the clarifying expression "*As he said,*" thus setting off the words of the enemy more clearly.[44]

Equally significant for our analysis of Prov 1:20–33 is that Fox allows for a change in perspective or content as further indicators of possible quotation.[45] Within Prov 1:23–24 there is strong evidence of the introduction of another level of discourse which is marked both by nominals indicating speech and by a clear change in perspective.

In Prov 1:22–23, for example, *ḥokmâ* follows its question in v 22 with the following words: *tāšûbû lětôkaḥtî hinnēh ʾabbîʿâ lākem rûḥî ʾôdîʿâ děbāray ʾetkem*, "If you turn to my reproof behold I will pour out my thoughts to you, I will make known my words to you." In v 23c the expression is: *ʾôdîʿâ děbāray ʾetkem*, "I will make known my words to you." The effect of v 23, like the effect achieved by the combination of *pîw*, and *děbāryw* in Ps 55:22, is to introduce wisdom's words in 24–31 in the form of a quotation; i.e., the expression prefaces a portion of the text which signals to the reader/listener that what follows are words spoken in another context

---

knowledge to what the writer values as important and unimportant. In exchange for Gordis' freedom of supplying transition phrases, Fox posits a rigid definition of quotation. The rigidity of Fox's definition becomes especially evident on pp 426–427 where he finds some cases which appear in the gray area between quotation and paraphrase. As we shall see, M. Bakhtin's M. Sternberg's description of reported and reporting discourse is heuristically a more productive way of reading a text for it takes into account how one text appropriates vocabulary, expressions, and form from another text while not necessarily following rigid lines of quotation.

[43] "Quotations in Biblical Literature," 422.

[44] See "Quotations in Biblical Literature," 421–426 for other examples.

[45] "Quotations in Biblical Literature," 423.

and time. To read vv 24–31 as words drawn from another context and time likewise overcomes the tension set up by the sequence of speech and hearing in vv 22–31. The change in perspective and point of view that scholars have indicated after 1:23 is also taken into account in our proposed reading. The content shifts because wisdom, according to the text, is resurrecting words from the past.

Similarly, the parallel expression *rûḥî*, "my spirit" is taken as synonymous for *dĕbāray* "my words." G. Boström's argument that the mention of *rûaḥ* in Prov 1:23 as rooted in *ruaḥ Spekulation*[46] is an example of the lengths to which scholars have gone to explain the presence of *rûaḥ* while ignoring parallel expression for speech found elsewhere in other biblical traditions.[47] A more compelling case can be made, however, for understanding the paired expression *rûḥî* and *dĕbāray* as a circumlocution for speech. Toy and Delitzsch say as much when they interpret the combination as synonymous expressions for speech.[48]

In addition, the expression *ʾabbîʿâ*, "I will pour forth," in Prov 1:23 allows us to argue further that in v 23 *ḥokmâ* is calling attention to the significance of the words starting with v 24. The root *nbʿ* is translated by *BDB* as "flow, spring, bubble up."[49] A common use of the verb is "usually of speech, *pour forth, emit, belch forth*. . . .[50] *BDB* lists Prov 15:2, 28; Pss 59:8; 78:2; 94:4; 119:171 as examples.[51]

Because the combination of *dĕbāray*, "my words," *rûḥî*, "my spirit," and *ʾabbîʿâ*, "I will pour forth," functions in Prov 1:23 as an introduction to wisdom's words in the form of a quotation, we are in a better position

---

[46] G. Boström, *Proverbiastudien, Die Weisheit und Das Freunde Weib in Spr. 1–9* (Lund: C. W. K. Gleerup, 1935) 31.

[47] As G. Boström says (*Proverbiastudien*, 31): "Es ist charakteristisch, dass die Propheten hier als eine Einheit behandelt werden, als Träger der Offenbarung von Jahve, von seiner *ruaḥ* inspiriert. Wenn nun die Predigt der Weisheit zweifellos nach der "der Propheten" geformt ist, so scheint *die Weisheit in diesem Punkte ganz einfach eine Nachfolgerin der ruaḥ* zu sein, da die Verbindung zwischen dieser letzteren und den Propheten offenbar typischen ist. Die beiden Gestalten sind ja sehr nahe verwandt, wechsel oft miteinander und bekommen teilweise genau die gleichen Funktionen zuerteilt. Beide spielen bei der Erschaffung der Welt eine Rolle (Gen. 1; Spr. 8; B.S. 24:3; bei Judith 16:15 ist es der Geist, der "baut", usf.), beide haben die Geschichte Israels geführt (vgl. Jes. 63:10, 14 und Weis. 1:18), beide sollen auch die Propheten inspiriert haben."

[48] C. H. Toy, *Proverbs*, 24: "The *words* (here = *decision*) and the *mind* are stated in the following address (v. 24–27)." F. Delitzsch, *Proverbs*, 71: "Wisdom appears here as the fountain of the words of salvation for men."

[49] *BDB*, 615.

[50] *BDB*, 615.

[51] Cf. A. Robert's translation of *ʾabbîʿâ* ("Les attaches littéraires bibliques de Prov I-IX," 175): "אַבִּיעָה רוּחִי signifierait simplement: je vais vous manifester ma pensée."

to understand the import of the words starting in v 24. As the narrator introduces wisdom's words in vv 20–21 by calling attention to wisdom's forthcoming direct discourse through the use of *verba dicendi* and nominals related to speech, wisdom adds depth to Prov 1:20–33 by supplying an additional level of discourse starting with v 24. The positive word which ends Prov 1:20–33 returns to wisdom's invitation to hear and learn as stated in vv 22–23.

THE DIFFERENT LAYERS OF
SPEECH IN PROV 1:20–33.

The effect of reading v 24ff as a quotation opens up the possibility that the second person plural pronoun "you" in vv 24–27 need not necessarily refer to those mentioned in v 22, but to another group of people who are outside the scope of the immediate text in terms of time, reference, and place. While current translations do not provide quotation marks for the speech starting with v 24, we are arguing that the circumlocutions for speech found in v 23 suggest as much.

The shift to the third person plural "they" for the first time in vv 28–31 does not diminish the direct speech nature of the reported speech in vv 24–27. The shift from "you" to "they" is further confirmation that whatever "distance" scholars have noted in the text, it is between the quoted speech in vv 24–27 and the subsequent review of the effect of that speech in vv 28–31. By looking back on her earlier words and by shifting to the third person plural "they," the reader stands alongside *ḥokmâ*, as it were, joining in her reproof of those (i.e., "you" in vv 24–27) who failed to heed her plea. As we shall see, there are numerous examples in prophetic speech where second person plural direct discourse is immediately followed by third person plural speech which refers back to a previous discourse event.[52] The appearance of a combination of speech patterns that is duplicated in prophetic discourse is further evidence that Prov 1:20–33 represents editorial techniques which are found in other portions of scripture.

One of the difficulties we face in viewing Prov 1:24–27 as a quotation is that there is not a clear change in characters as we have in Prov 1:8–19. In Prov 1:8–19 the speakers are clearly identified and demarcated by name (i.e., parents, son, sinners) and speech content. In Prov 1:20–33 it is *ḥokmâ* herself who is the controlling voice throughout. Yet even though

---

[52] See C. Westermann, *Basic Forms of Prophetic Speech*, 152, 170–171 for his discussion of the phenomenon of first or second person speech followed by third person speech in prophetic literature. Cf. Jer 7:21–26 and Zech 1:2–6; 7:8–14 for examples.

ḥokmâ alone speaks, her speech represents a combination of speech within speech, just as Prov 1:8–19 is characterized by a similar if not identical layering of speech of narrator, parents, and sinners. The difference between Prov 1:8–19 and 1:20–33 has more to do with the presence or absence of clear deictic indicators of direct speech than it has to do with the presence of direct speech itself. Indeed, wisdom is the only speaker throughout; but a speaker who assumes different character roles by staging various levels of discourse within the text.

In addition, the foregrounding of her speech as a quotation in vv 24–27 indicates more than a subtle surface level strategy on the part of the narrator who speaks through *ḥokmâ*. As direct discourse, the reader is alerted to the special weight that attaches to wisdom's discourse which would not necessarily be achieved had wisdom assumed a less direct style of speech. The distance that is achieved by recalling her words as a quotation is an invitation to attentive readers to bridge the distance by means of potentially significant words and phrases.[53] Distance (i.e., *via* quotation) invites participation (i.e., reader response). Moreover, the offering of her words as a quotation presupposes a level of potential familiarity on the part of the readers not only with the content of her speech but with the circumstances that her speech represents.

As a quotation, vv 24–27 thus function as the inset within the framework of vv 20–23, 28–33 whose content is noticeably incongruent with its surroundings. As we saw earlier, Toy's comment that vv 24–31, as they stand, seemingly clash in content and point of view with the surrounding verses is but one of many examples of scholars who have recognized the awkward nature of vv 24ff but who have taken the route of emending the text.[54] But such incongruence, we are arguing, is not a

---

[53] M. Sternberg ("Point of View," 111) says the following about how direct discourse achieves levels of distance depending on how close or far the inset matches its frame: "Thus, while a normal speech-event is always spatiotemporally unique, the reported speech-event can be variously deconcretized along either referential dimension or both so as to stand for a whole range of deictic contexts: the inset will then . . . retain its deictic distinctiveness vis-a-vis the frame in a considerably modified and attenuated form. . . . [T]he situational matrix of the original utterance is liable to temporal misdating and spatial displacement—to be distanced from or brought closer to the frame's here-and-now, according to the reporter's powers to recall and deliberate designs."

[54] R. Murphy's recent comment about vv 24–32 best sums up what many scholars have said about the peculiar context of these verses: "The tenor of Lady Wisdom's words in vv 24–32 shows that an invitation to listen to her reproof (as some would understand v 23) does not make sense.[!] One does not issue an invitation to heed a reproof by describing past infidelity (vv 24–25), which is the reason for the statement of joy in the actual destruction of those addressed (vv 26–27), and finally by a

negative attribute of the text but rather underscores the "double-centered deictic structure" of direct speech.

Because the inset quotation in Prov 1:24–27 takes its orientation from the spatiotemporally self-contained speech event it represents, we are then reminded of the inter-textual potential that direct speech has in linking text and reader to the broader intertext of scripture. We are likewise reminded that direct discourse can represent "two (or more) originating and/or refracting perspectives combined within a double-centered reported speech. . . ."[55]

In the case of Prov 1:8–19 we detected a clear play on portions of the discourse found in Genesis 37 through the direct discourse of the sinners and parents. Thematic echoes also found in later portions of the Joseph narrative played upon the discourse of the brothers in Genesis 37. Woven into Prov 1:8–19 was a gloss from Isa 59:7.

As for Prov 1:20–33, we are arguing for a similar reutilization of earlier direct discourse from a given tradition. Like Prov 1:8–19, Prov 1:20–33 represents a clearly definable speech-event tied to a moment in Judah's history. The discourse upon which Prov 1:20–33 itself relies derives from portions of Jeremiah 7 and 20—two texts which clearly preserve the people's refusal to hear/listen to Jeremiah's word. The reappearance of portions of Jeremiah 7 and 20 in Prov 1:20–33 forms a new discourse event which combines once separate prophetic speech in a sapiential context. As such, Prov 1:20–33 represents a verbal montage of prophetic direct discourse.

Recently, R. Murphy recognized the "literary creation" that marks Prov 1:20–33:

> Such speech is a literary creation, and presumably composed by a sage, precisely to undergird the authority of the instructions. Wisdom's authority is in fact put on the same level as that of the prophets. The intention is to persuade the listener to follow instruction.[56]

If persuasion is achieved by couching discourse in a prophetic mode, one wonders why the sages did not "undergird" other sections of Proverbs with similar prophetic forms of speech. Because Prov 1:20–33 is the *only* example of sustained prophetic discourse in the book of Proverbs we may look for other reasons to explain the presence of

---

justification of the destruction (vv 28–32)" ("Wisdom's Song," 460). M. Gilbert, "Le discours menaçent de Sagesse," 105–108, also reasons that the verb *tašûbû* cannot be translated as an invitation to repent. If it were, there would be an irreconcilable contradiction between vv 22–23 and vv 24–33.

55 M. Sternberg, "Point of View," 111.

56 *Wisdom Literature,* 55.

prophetic speech. The sages more likely did not tap the prophetic traditions solely because they were authoritative but primarily because there were historical and theological elements in the speech-events from Jeremiah 7 and 20 which lent themselves to the redactor's immediate needs. As such, the clues to unraveling the traditio-historical components of Prov 1:20–33 have their best representatives in the direct discourse in vv 24–27 and vv 28–31.

P. Trible's Analysis of the Structure of Prov 1:20–33.

In an article analyzing the literary and rhetorical features of Prov 1:20–33, P. Trible notes how vv 24–30 "forms the core of the poem."[57] Her analysis of the structure of vv 24–30 helps to locate the impetus for wisdom's speech. According to Trible, v 24 introduces us to the "Reason" for wisdom's direct discourse.[58]

> yaʿan qārāʾtî wattĕmāʾēnû "Because I called and you refused to listen,
> nāṭîtî yādî wĕʾên maqšîb I have stretched out my hand and no one has heeded."

That wisdom's main complaint centers in the people's failure to heed her call (qrʾ) is further expanded upon in v 25.[59] Following vv 24–25 is the "Announcement" of wisdom's pending laughter and mocking as her reaction to the people's calamity. Significantly, when the people respond to wisdom as a result of their distress, wisdom's refusal to respond in vv 28–30 picks up similar terminology found in vv 24–25, but now in a reverse combination.

The structure of vv 24–30 thus indicates the importance of the verb qrʾ by the fact that it initiates both the "Reason" in v 24 and the "Announcement" in v 28. Wisdom calls (qrʾ) and the people refuse to listen (mʾn, ʾyn mqšyb) in v 24. The people call (qrʾ) and wisdom does not

---

57 "Wisdom Builds a Poem," 512. Trible does not count v 31 as part of the poem's "core." As Trible recognizes, v 31 does not fit her chiastic schema because v 23, the corresponding verse to v 31 in her analysis, does not have the requisite "signal word" and "verbal similarities:" "'C' (vs. 31): A Summary of natural retribution, this verse corresponds to vs. 23, which is a preface to the central section. Yet these two lines have no verbal similarities; they differ in length; and neither one commences with a signal word. Together they are perhaps the rhetorical equivalent of synthetic parallelism, aiding the movement of thought."(p. 517)
58 "Wisdom Builds a Poem," 512.
59 "Wisdom Builds a Poem," 513.

answer (ʿnh) in v 28.[60] In addition, the particles yʿn, "because" in v 24 and
ʾz, "then" in v 28 clearly signal motive and consequence.[61]

Trible's primary interest is in providing an analysis and description
of the literary and rhetorical features of Prov 1:20–33. As she admits,
even though the text may have a "history," we do not have enough data
to recover the text's past.[62] Trible's literary analysis, however, is useful
for initiating a probe into the inner-biblical background of 1:20–33 by the
very fact that her rhetorical study serves to isolate key terms and themes
of which the verb qrʾ and the complementary theme of calling and not
hearing are central. We can build on her work to the extent that the
theme of calling and not hearing that is connected to wisdom's discourse
leads to a number of other significant parallels within the speech-events
in the Jeremianic corpus of traditions.

Preliminary Observations Concerning the
Similarities Between Proverbs 1:20–33 and
Jeremiah 7 as Seen by Contemporary Commentators.

B. Gemser earlier recognized a number of corresponding words and
expressions that Proverbs 1:20–33 shares with Jeremiah. He lists ʿad
mātay, Prov 1:22; yaʿan, Prov 1:24; mĕšûbâ, Prov 1:32; šākēn beṭaḥ, Prov 1:33
as resembling Jeremianic "Stilformen."[63] Gemser then calls attention to

---

[60] See C. H. Toy, Proverbs, 27, for his description of how portions of vv 28–31
"answer" earlier verses: "The correspondence with the preceding paragraph is close,
with inversion of the order of thought: v. 28 answers to v. 26. 27, and v. 29. 30 to v.
24. 25; the conclusion is repeated in v. 31."

[61] "Wisdom Builds a Poem," 515.

[62] "Wisdom Builds a Poem," 510.

[63] Sprüche Salomos, 23. Gemser also mentions Isa 66:3f. Gemser is dependent on A.
Robert's work, "Les attaches littéraires Bibliques de Prov. I-IX," 172–181, for the
above expressions. Actually the two variations of the refrain appear in Isa 65:12 as:
yaʿan qārāʾtî wĕlōʾ ʿănîtem dibbartî wĕlōʾ šemaʿtem, "because, when I called, you did not
answer, when I spoke, you did not listen; and in 66:4 as: yaʿan qārāʾtî wĕʾên ʿôneh
dibbartî wĕlōʾ šāmēʿû "because, when I called, no one answered, when I spoke, they
did not listen." C. Westermann (Isaiah 40–66, A Commentary [Philadelphia:
Westminster, 1969] 405, 414) remarks that both instances of the refrain are additions
to the text and certainly of Deuteronomic origin. Westermann says: "The language is
manifestly Deuteronomic, and the allegation a perfectly general one. 65.12, too, has
the feel of an addition. In both places rehearsals during worship of such words as
these against cultic malpractices may have been responsible for their addition. They
are stereotyped, and represent something like a refrain in them"(p. 414). Even though
the refrain in Isa 65:12 and 66:4 appears in a cultic context somewhat like Jeremiah
7:13, 28; 35:17, there are no other similarities between them. In addition, there are no

the similarity between Prov 1:24ff (the verse where wisdom's speech shifts to a quotation) and Jer 7:24-28 without adding specific details.

The context of Jeremiah's words in vv 24-28 relates to forbidden cultic practices as found in vv 16-20 and vv 30-34. As part of Jeremiah's message, Yahweh through Jeremiah reflects on the current cultic practices of Jeremiah's generation by recounting the continuing recalcitrance of the people from the time of the Exodus to the present day in 7:21-26. Such recounting is achieved in part by combining second person plural and third person plural speech in vv 21-26. Gemser does not explain why he limits his comparisons between Jer 7:24-28 and Prov 1:24ff, or why 7:24-28 seems to represent a unit.

The recent work by C. Holladay, C. D. Isbell, and M. Jackson contributes to the ongoing analysis of the complex traditio-historical composition not only of Jer 7:21-28 but of Jeremiah 7 as a whole.[64] Their work is useful because it highlights the rhetorical devices utilized by editors to join together otherwise independent units of tradition.

Holladay argues, for example, that Jeremiah 7 can be broken down into five blocks of tradition which have been arranged according to a chronological order. The blocks are: 7:1-12; 13-15; 16-20; 21-29; and 30-34.[65] In an earlier work, Holladay found an organizing principle for all of Jer 7:1-34 and an explanation for its proximity to 6:16ff in such catchwords as ʿmd, 7:2, 6:16; šmʿ, 7:16, 6:18; ʾbwt wbnym 7:18, 22, 25, 26, 30, 31, 6:21; and ʾbd, 7:28, 6:21.[66]

---

detectable similarities between the Isaiah references and Prov 1:20-33. Westermann's observation that the Isaiah traditions are manifestly Deuteronomic may represent the shared circle of traditions out of which the traditions arose both for the texts from Jeremiah and Isaiah. Recently, Louis Stulman (*The Prose Sermons of the Book of Jeremiah, A Redescription of the Correspondences with Deuteronomistic Literature in the Light of Recent Text-critical Research* [Atlanta: Scholars Press, 1986] 44) places the expression qrʾ wlʾ ʿnh as resembling deuteronomistic expressions but not attested in the deuteronomic traditions. Further on (p. 110), he treats Jer 35:17 as a gloss from Jer 7:13. Earlier, W. Thiel, *Die deuteronimistische Redaktion von Jeremia 1-25* (Neukirchen-Vluyn: Neukirchener Verlag, 1973) 133, made the same observation. For Prov 1:24-25 R. Murphy (*Wisdom Literature*, 55) lists Isa 65:12; 66:4 and Jer 7:23-27 as having similar content.

[64] C. Holladay, *Jeremiah*, 234-270; C. D. Isbell and M. Jackson, "Rhetorical Criticism and Jeremiah VII 1-VIIII 3," *VT* 30 (1980) 20-26. As for the evidence of deuteronomic editing of Jeremiah 7 see: W. Thiel, *Die deuteronimistische Redaktion von Jeremia 1-25*, 103-134.

[65] *Jeremiah*, 252.

[66] *The Architecture of Jeremiah 1-20* (Lewisburg, Pennsylvania: Bucknell University Press, 1976) 104. Cf. also Holladay's recent commentary, *Jeremiah*, 252, where he summarizes his earlier work by saying: "In an earlier publication I . . . proposed essentially that 7:1-34 was united by the word "place" (מָקוֹם: 7:3, 6, 7, 12, 14, 20, 32),

The analysis of C. Isbell and M. Jackson substantiates further the internal structure of 7:1–34 by means of select vocabulary. Like Holladay, they isolate five units of tradition.[67] In their analysis of 7:21–28 they argue that the expression which links together these verses is the verb *šmᶜ*, "to hear:"

> Our fusion of *vv.* 27–28 with 21–26 is based upon the structural link provided by the verb *šmᶜ*. The central idea of *vv.* 21–25 is that the people had not "listened" (*lōʾ šāmĕᶜû*, *v.* 24) to Yahweh in the past. Accordingly, it should come as no great surprise that they will not "listen" (*lōʾ yišmĕᶜû*) to the prophet of Yahweh either (*v.* 27). In fact, the most accurate designation of the people which can be given by the prophet is simply, "this is the nation which has not listened (*lōʾ šāmĕᶜû*) to Yahweh its God" (*v.* 28).[68]

Further on Isbell and Jackson again indicate the important role that the "thematic word" *šmᶜ* plays in the context of Jer 7:1–28:

> The thematic word, *šmᶜ*, noted above as the major theme of section III, must be tied in closely with the appearances of the same word in section I (*vv.* 2, 13) and in section II (*v.* 16). In fact, the specific phrase *dbr wlʾ šmᶜ wqrʾ wlʾ ᶜnh* (spoke but no hearing, called but no answer) is found in both sections I (*v.* 13) and III (*v.* 27).[69]

---

by pronouns ("they," v 4; "you," plural, v 8; "you," singular, v 16; "they," vv 17, 19); and by "fathers" (vv 18, 22, 25, 26) and "children" (vv 18, 30, 31)." In his subsequent commentary on Jeremiah, Holladay has revised his analysis of 7:1–34 and substitutes a chronological interpretation of the five units for an analysis based on catchwords. The obvious advantage to a chronological analysis is that it suits Holladay's larger theme concerning the compositional ordering of the scrolls. Holladay, however, never explains why a chronological interpretation and one based on catchwords are mutually exclusive to the extent that we have to choose between one or the other. Holladay's initial rhetorical analysis of 7:1–34 is useful for it helps to account for the connection of the five units by means of their lexical and thematic content. Interestingly, Holladay seems to allow for a catchword arrangement on the subtheme of "fathers" and "children" in vv 16–20 (see: *Jeremiah*, 252).

[67] The units which Isbell and Jackson ("Rhetorical Criticism and Jeremiah VII 1 - VIII 3," 21) isolate are the following:

    I. The temple sermon with literary introduction, 7:1–15

    II. The cult of the queen of the heavens, 7:16–20

    III. The lessons from the past, 7:21–28

    IV. The dirge over Tophet, 7:29–34

    V. Astral worship, 8:1–3

[68] "Rhetorical Criticism and Jeremiah VII 1– VIII 3," 22.

[69] "Rhetorical criticism and Jeremiah VII 1– VIII 3," 24.

The linking of once unconnected traditions forms a rhetorical unit for 7:1–28 based in part on hearing. The importance of the word *šmʿ* and other expressions relating to speech and hearing is found throughout much of Jeremiah 7 to such an extent that we can see how the theme aids not only in holding chapter 7 together but in providing a thematic center for Jeremiah's temple sermon.

According to Holladay, 7:28 functions as a summary-appraisal for vv 1–27.[70] We should take note how v 28 likewise recalls the lexical contrast between speaking/calling and not-hearing that characterizes Jeremiah 7. Jeremiah's call to hear (*šmʿ*) God's word (*dbr*) leads to potential dwelling (*škn*) in security/trust (*bṭḥ*). The people, however, trust (*bṭḥ*) in deceptive words (*dbry šqr*) which lead to potential destruction as happened to Shiloh and its inhabitants.

In addition, scholars have recognized the importance of the repeated refrain in 7:13 and 7:27 for the thematic structure of Jeremiah 7.

7:13	7:27
wāʾădabber ʾălêkem haškēm	*wĕdibbartā ʾălêhem ʾet kol*
wĕdabbēr wĕlōʾ šemaʿtem wāʾeqrāʾ	*haddĕbārîm hāʾēlleh wĕlōʾ*
ʾetkem wĕlōʾ ʾănîtem	*yišmĕʿû ʾēleykā wĕqārāʾtā*
	ʾălêhem wĕlōʾ yaʿănûkâ
And when I spoke to you persistently you did not listen, and when I called you, you did not answer.	So you shall speak all these words to them, but they will not listen to you. You shall call to them, but they will not answer you.

Holladay argues that 7:13 is a later addition affixed during the time of the second scroll in 601–600.[71] As an addition, its function is to clarify

---

[70] See: W. Holladay: *Jeremiah*, 259: "Verse 28 is a summary-appraisal. . . ; it is a form that appears to have its origin in wisdom circles. It functions here as a concluding judgment on the people: Yahweh has excluded all possibility of hope—it is almost an epitaph on the career of the people." R. P. Carroll (*Jeremiah*, 218) refers to 7:28 as an "editorial comment" which links the previous units together on the theme of not listening to Yahweh's and Jeremiah's words: "An editorial comment [v 28] provides for the delivery of 'all these words' (presumably 21–26 if not the previous two units) and the reactions of the people to them. . . . The people will not listen to the speaker (Jeremiah as in v. 1?), but then as they have not listened to Yahweh (v. 13), why should the messenger receive any different response? The unit is shaped by v. 13 and demonstrates its truth by having the speaker ignored."

[71] See *Jeremiah*, 3–6. Holladay argues that 7:1–12 is part of the "first scroll" which he dates to 605. The addition of vv 13–15 reflect for Holladay the "crucial change in Jrm's perception" that occurred as a direct result of the burning of the first scroll by

the reason for the "forthcoming destruction:" "The verse . . . introduces a description of the human action that is the reason for the forthcoming divine action. . . . That divine action is set forth in vv 14–15."[72] Holladay offers the following divisions for 7:1–15:

> Through v 7 the words are clearly warning, an appeal to repentance. Verses 8–12 makes accusations of present behavior and mention Shiloh as an example of what Yahweh did in the past. Verses 13–15 announce punishment *because the people have not listened.*[73](emphasis added)

Holladay also concludes that 7:27, as a later addition, is modeled on 7:13. He dates vv 21–28 to 594.[74] V 27 functions in the same manner as v 13.

Carroll isolates two charges that are made against the community in Jeremiah 7: (1) the confusion of substituting false cultic practices for ethical conduct; and (2) the rejection of the divine word. Jer 7:13 summarizes the second charge and it represents a deuteronomistic addition.[75] In contrast to Holladay, Carroll dates 7:13 to a post-587 period and attributes the varieties of tradition in Jeremiah 7 not to Jeremiah's change in self-understanding but to later redactors who are looking back upon the destruction of Jerusalem.[76] The thematic refrain of

---

Jehoiakim. No longer is there a chance for repentance. According to Holladay, the change in content in Jeremiah's message is a direct result of Jeremiah's initiative. While our interest is not primarily in the book of Jeremiah and the reconstruction of the redactional layers in the text, a question can be raised, however briefly, about Holladay's interpretation of Jeremiah's role in initiating alterations in his message all on the basis of a change in Jeremiah's "perception" and "self-understanding."(p. 5) If such is the case, then it seems that Holladay attributes to Jeremiah a role in the original content of the material which stands in contrast to Jeremiah's call in chapter 1 as well as to Jeremiah's poignant words in Jeremiah 20:7ff. It goes without saying that the interpretation of Jeremiah's *perception* of his role as messenger plays a crucial part in Holladay's arranging and dating of the traditions. By doing so Holladay can link subtle changes in Jeremiah's message to Jeremiah himself and not to a later editorial hand. The dating of the traditions associated with Jeremiah then are more easily anchored to specific events and periods. There are places, however, where the interpretation and arrangement of the traditions according to very specific dates appears to be strained.

72 *Jeremiah*, 239.

73 *Jeremiah*, 238.

74 *Jeremiah*, 258, 259, 349.

75 *Jeremiah*, 210: "The Deuteronomistic theme of the sending of the divine word and its continual rejection by the people occurs in v. 13. Throughout its history the deity has sent that word via the prophets . . . , but that word has not been heard."

76 E. W. Nicholson (*Preaching to the Exiles: A Study of the Prose Tradition in the Book of Jeremiah* [Oxford: Basil Blackwell, 1970] 70), like Carroll, sees the final redaction of Jer

speaking/not hearing, and calling/not answering sums up the period leading up to the destruction of Jerusalem and the temple.[77] Like Holladay, Carroll argues that 7:27 is modelled after 7:13.[78]

The difficulty of dating 7:13 and 27 is overshadowed by the clear reference to the destruction of Judah and Jerusalem that both Carroll and Holladay recognize in Jeremiah 7. Thus, whether one reads 7:13, 27, and their respective units as a pre-587 prophecy or as a post-587 *vaticinium ex eventu* "prophecy," does not diminish their theological and historical importance for understanding the traditions. As Shiloh was destroyed by Yahweh, so Jerusalem and the temple will be destroyed as a result of the people's failure to hear and answer Yahweh's and Jeremiah's calls. As 7:13 and 27 state, the people's idolatrous practices are a direct result of the refusal to hear YHWH's and Jeremiah's word.

The thematic refrain of speaking/not hearing and calling/not answering reappears only one other time in Jer 35:17, also a deuteronomistic addition: "Therefore, thus says the Lord, the God of hosts, the God of Israel: Behold I am bringing on Judah and all the inhabitants of Jerusalem all the evil (*rāʿâ*) that I have pronounced against them; because (*yaʿan*) I have spoken (*dibbartî*) to them and they have not listened (*lōʾ šāmēʿû*), I have called (*wāʾeqrāʾ*) to them and they have not answered (*welōʾ ʿānû*)." The context of Jeremiah 35 pertains to the faithfulness of the Rechabites to the covenant commands and Jeremiah's speech is set in the confines of the temple (v 4). Jeremiah uses the faithfulness of the Rechabites as an object lesson for the inhabitants of the city. As in Jeremiah 7, the theme of speaking and not hearing is linked with the wayward cultic practices of serving other gods (v 15).

Jeremiah 35 provides another example of the thematic interplay explaining the destruction of Judah and Jerusalem in the context of the failure of the people to heed Yahweh's call through Jeremiah. Jeremiah

---

7:1–15 as reflecting a post-587 context: "[I]n the period after 586 B.C. when the Deuteronomistic history assumed its final form and when also, as we believe, the Jeremianic prose sermons were developed (at least substantially), the destruction of the Temple was a bitter reality which demanded explanation, an explanation which the Temple sermon in Jeremiah vii. 1–15 together with other discourses and narratives in Jeremianic prose tradition unquestionably provide."

[77] R. P. Carroll *Jeremiah*, 211. See W. Thiel, *Jeremia 1–25*, who attributes 7:13 to a deuteronomistic editor.

[78] *Jeremiah*, 218: "The unity [7:27–28] is shaped by v. 13 and demonstrates its truth by having the speaker [i.e., Jeremiah] ignored." See J. Gerald Janzen, *Studies in the Text of Jeremiah* (Cambridge: Harvard University Press, 1973) 38, where he argues that 7:27 is an "intrusion of a set expression" derived from 7:13.

35 represents the same circle of traditions which are found in Jer 7:1–34.[79] Because the compositional link is between variations on the theme of speaking/not hearing, calling/not answering and the destruction of Judah and Jerusalem unique to Jeremiah and the Jeremianic corpus of traditions, we are in a position to examine further how Prov 1:20–33 represents another such example of the similar theme. Gemser's earlier observation that there are similarities between Prov 1:24ff and Jer 7:24–28 can be developed further. Such similarities, we are arguing, offer evidence that Prov 1:20–33 is a derivative of the core message found in Jeremiah 7 and, as we shall see, Jeremiah 20:7ff.

PROV 1:20-33 AND THE REUTILIZED TRADITIONS FROM JEREMIAH 7 AND 20.

We can add to the contributions of contemporary scholars by listing other vocabulary and phraseology shared between Jer 7:1–34 and Prov 1:20–33.

1. *baḥûṣ*	"in the streets"	Prov 1:20
ûbĕḥuṣôt (yĕrûšālāim)	"in the streets (of Jerusalem)"	Jer 7:17
ûmĕḥuṣôt (yĕrûšālaim)	"in the streets (of Jerusalem)"	Jer 7:34
2. *tārōnnâ*	"(*ḥokmâ*) cries"	Prov 1:20
rinnâ	"a cry"	Jer 7:16
3. *qôlāh*	"her voice"	Prov 1:20
bĕqôl (YHWH)	"the voice of (the Lord)"	Jer 7:28
qôl	"voice"	Jer 7:34
4. *tiqrāʾ*	"(*ḥokmâ*) will call"	Prov 1:21
weqārāʾtā	"you (Jeremiah) will call"	Jer 7:2
wāʾeqrāʾ	"I (YHWH) called"	Jer 7:13
wĕqārāʾtā	"you (Jeremiah) will call"	Jer 7:27
5. *šĕʿārîm*	"gates"	Prov 1:21
bĕšaʿar, haššĕʿārîm	"in the gate"/"gates"	Jer 7:2
6. *baʿîr*	"in the city"	Prov 1:21
bĕʿārê (yĕhûdâ)	"in the cities (of Judah)"	Jer 7:17
mĕʿārê (yĕhûdâ)	"from the cities (of Judah)"	Jer 7:34
7. (*yiśnĕʾû*) *daʿat*	"(they hated) knowledge"	Prov 1:22, 29
(*ʾôdîʿâ (dĕbāray)*	"I will make known (my words)"	Prov 1:23

---

[79] See: W. Holladay, *Jeremiah*, 236, 238, 258, 666–667 where he notes the similarities in the traditions. Cf. also W. Thiel, *Die deuteronomistische Redaktion von Jeremia 1–25*, 113; *Die deuteronomistische Redaktion von Jeremia 26–45*, 47–48; L. Stulman, *The Prose Sermons of the Book of Jeremiah*, 107; and E. W. Nicholson, *Preaching to the Exiles, A Study of the Prose Tradition in the Book of Jeremiah* (Oxford: Basil Blackwell, 1970) 34, where 7:13, 27; 35:17 all appear in the deuteronomistic prose sections of Jeremiah.

	linked with *yir'at YHWH*, the fear of the Lord, cf. Prov 1:29	
(*lōʾ*) *yĕdaʿtem*	"(gods you did not) know"	Jer 7:9
8. *dĕbāray*	"my words"	Prov 1:23
haddābār/dĕbar	"the word/the word of (YHWH)"	Jer 7:2
dibrê (*haššeqer*)	"(deceptive) words"	Jer 7:4,8
wāʾădabbēr/wĕdabbēr	"I spoke"	Jer 7:13
9. *yaʿan qārāʾtî*	"because I called"	Prov 1:24
yaʿan + *wāʾeqrāʾ*	"because" + "I called"	Jer 7:13
10. *yiqrāʾunnî wĕlōʾ ʾeʿeneh*	"they will call me but I will not answer"	Prov 1:28
wāʾeqrāʾ ʾetkem wĕlōʾ ʿănîtem	"I will call call you and you will not answer me"	Jer 7:13
wĕqārāʾtā ʾălêhem wĕlōʾ yaʿănûkâ	"and you will call to them and they will not answer you"	Jer 7:27
11. *weyōʾkĕlû*	"and they will eat"	Prov 1:31
wĕʾiklû	"and eat"	Jer 7:21
12. *mipprî*	"fruit of"	Prov 1:31
pĕrî	"fruit of"	Jer 7:20
13. *darkām*	"their way"	Prov 1:31
darkêkem	"your ways"	Jer 7:3
14. *ûmimmōʿaṣōtêhem*	"their counsels"	Prov 1:31
bĕmōʿēṣôt	"in (their) counsels"	Jer 7:24
15. *tĕʾabbĕdēm*	"destroys them"	Prov 1:32
ʾābĕdâ	"is destroyed"	Jer 7:28
16. *wĕšōmēaʿ* (*lî*)	"the one listening" (to me)	Prov 1:33
šimʿû	"listen"	Jer 7:2
ʾênennî šōmēaʿ	"I do not listen"	Jer 7:16
šimʿû bĕqôlî	"obey my voice"	Jer 7:23
wĕlōʾ šāmĕʿû	"they did not listen"	Jer 7:24, 26, 28
wĕlōʾ yišmĕʿû	"they will not listen"	Jer 7:27
17. *yiškān*	"he will dwell"	Prov 1:33
waʾăšakkĕnâ	"I will (let you) dwell"	Jer 7:3
wĕšikkantî	"I will (let you) dwell"	Jer 7:7
18. *beṭaḥ*	"trust/secure"	Prov 1:33
(*ʾal*) *tibṭĕḥû*	"do not trust"	Jer 7:4
bōṭĕḥîm	"(you) are trusting"	Jer 7:8

In addition to this list of common vocabulary there are numerous thematic similarities. For example, as the refrain in Jer 7:13, 27 functions to call attention to the perceived reason for the destruction of Judah and Jerusalem, we are arguing that the announcement in Prov 1:28, *ʾaz yiqrāʾunnî wĕlōʾ ʾeʿěneh*, "then they will call me but I will not answer," and Prov 1:24, *yaʿan qārāʾtî wattĕmāʾēnû*, "Because I called and they refused to listen," are a direct play upon the same motif in Jer 7:13, 28. The fact that

Prov 1:28 couches its refrain in a future context and reverses the pronouns from "you" plural to "they" plural can be explained by recalling the proposed post-exilic context for Prov 1:20–33. By paraphrasing the refrain from Jeremiah and by setting it in a context of direct discourse, the refrain in effect looks back to the generation which refused to heed the words of the prophet. The alterations in tense and person thus do not diminish the intertextual play on traditions that are reflected in Proverbs 1. Instead, the alterations set the context of wisdom's speech and the perception of that speech in the historical situation which recall the words of Jeremiah to the pre-587 generation at Jerusalem.

Similarly, the shift to the third person plural in vv 28–31 effectively explains the reason for the fact that *that* people faced destruction. YHWH was not ineffective and hence not to be blamed for the fall of Judah and Jerusalem. Rather, the people brought doom upon themselves as stated in the result clause in Prov 1:29. Recontextualization of direct discourse lends itself not only to linking two disconnected· traditions together, but it also revivifies Jeremiah's discourse in a newly fabricated sapiential context.

We can see a similar example of recontextualization of direct discourse in Zechariah 7. While we will be taking a closer look at Zechariah 7 and its similarities with Prov 1:20–33 later on, we can tentatively cite Zech 7:13 as another example of a post-587 tradent reutilizing earlier traditions from Jeremiah concerning the fall of Judah and Jerusalem.

After Zechariah quotes the words of the "former prophets," *hannĕbî'îm hari'šōnîm*, in Zech 7:9–10, and reports the effect of their words in vv 11–12, Zech 7:13 reads: "As [I] called (*qārā'*) and they did listen (*welō' šāmē'û*) they will call (*yiqrĕ'û*) but I will not listen (*wĕlō' 'ešmā'*)."[80] 7:13 provides the reason for the fall of Jerusalem.[81] Framed as a quotation spoken by YHWH, 7:13 combines together a reference to the past, "As I

---

[80] There is a textual problem in 7:13. For "I called," the Hebrew reads, *qārā'* "he called." S has ܐܚܩ meaning *qārā'tî*, "I called." A third person singular verb is anomalous in the present context of Zech 7:13. We are following the RSV's translation which is supported by the S. See A. Petitjean, *Les Oracles du Proto-Zacharie, Un programme de restauration pour la commaué juive aprè l'exil* (Paris: J. Gabalda et Cie, 1969) 353–354, where he also argues for a reading of *qārā'tî* over *qārā'*. See H. G. Mitchell, *Zechariah* (ICC, Edinburgh, and T Clark, 1912) 202: where he translates 7:13 as: *It came to pass that, because, when he* (Yahweh) *called, they* (the fathers) *did not hear,*—There follows an apodosis in the Massoretic text, *so they call, and I will not hear, said Yahweh. . . ."*

[81] See A. Petitjean, *Les Oracles du Proto-Zacharie,* 353–354; H. G. Mitchell, *Zechariah,* 200.

called," as well as a reference to the future, "I will not listen," all in the same verse. The incongruous nature of the quote is alleviated by reading the words in the context of looking back on the destruction of Jerusalem and a view to the "future" explaining what YHWH is about to do, all of which is known to the post-587 readers of the text. A similar combination of past and future speech is contained in Prov 1:24–31.

Our argument for the reutilization of Jeremiah 7 within Prov 1:20–33 can be extended beyond the shared references to *qr⁾* in 1:24, 28 and by the refrain found in Prov 1:28. We have already noted how some scholars have sensed the tension between wisdom's invitation to hear in v 22–23 and the word of condemnation immediately following in vv 24–31. Our proposed reading for 1:24ff is based upon the perceived combination of differing layers of discourse introduced by a conditional phrase *tašûbû*, "if you turn." By reading vv 24–27 as a quotation and vv 28–31 as a further reflection upon vv 24–27, we see the tension disappears.

In a similar manner, scholars have concentrated upon the odd combination of conditional sentences admonishing the people to emend their ways along with a word of unconditional destruction in Jeremiah 7.[82] R. P. Carroll attributes the combination of admonition and condemnation to the editors who utilized past traditions by bringing them up to date with content addressed to the "prophet's" (i.e., the editor's) contemporaries. Carroll says:

> The history of not listening and not responding to the divine word comes to an end with the destruction of temple and city. . . . The history of non-hearing explains the fall of Jerusalem but does not account for the section recommending amendment of life (vv. 3–7). The two sections, admonition and destruction, do not belong together. They are about different matters. This is not the tension between Yahweh's absolute word of judgment and the conditional possibility of hope. . . , but two discrete elements brought together by the editors. . . . The word of denunciation explains why destruction has befallen Jerusalem; the call to amendment of life is addressed to those of the period after that fall. . . . Jerusalem fell, but those who survived that fall, and their descendants, needed to be taught the lessons of that fall.[83]

The editorial combination of older traditions for the purpose of teaching a lesson that Carroll detects in Jeremiah 7 is duplicated in Prov 1:20–33. The final two verses in Proverbs 1, introduced by a *kî* clause in v 32, functions as summary statement concerning the *pĕtāyim* and *kĕsîlîm*

---

[82] See: W. Holladay, *Jeremiah*, 236, 238; E. W. Nicholson, *Preaching to the Exiles*, 69–70; G. Fohrer, "Jeremias tempelwort," *ThZ*, 5 (1949) 401–417.
[83] *Jeremiah*, 211.

introduced in v 22. Moreover, as a summary their content is based upon the lesson from history represented by the discourse in vv 24–31.

Vv 32–33 allow the narrator to formulate a general rule based not upon his or her own experience, but upon Judah's history as exemplified in and through earlier traditions.[84] We should not be surprised to see that the narrator has culled from the traditions the overriding importance attached to *šmʿ*, "hearing" in v 33.

The thematic influence of Jeremiah 7 is also evident in the result of right hearing in Prov 1:33: one will "dwell secure," *yiškan beṭaḥ*, without "dread of evil," *mippaḥad rāʿâ*, if one "listens," *wĕšōmēaʿ*. Part of Jeremiah's message in Jeremiah 7 concerns dwelling (*škn*, vv 3, 7) in the land, based on heeding (*šmʿ*) YHWH's word. Security/trust (*bṭḥ* vv 4, 8) is part and parcel of such dwelling.

The underside of failing to heed, *šmʿ* in Prov 1:20–33, is the advent of *rāʿâ*, "evil," Prov 1:33—a word in Jeremiah which receives specific content in regards to the destruction of Judah and Jerusalem. For example, Holladay says the following for the occurrence of *rāʿâ* in Jer 18:20: "In this instance the 'evil' (רָעָה) is not that which the opponents inflict on Jrm but the 'disaster' that Yahweh has revealed to Jrm he will inflict upon the people. The word occurs repeatedly in Jer . . . ."[85] Elsewhere in the book of Jeremiah the expression *rāʿâ* is linked directly with the destruction of Judah and Jerusalem (see: 19:15; 26:3, 13; 36:31; 39:16; 42:17; 44:2, 11).

We are not arguing that the reference to *rāʿâ* in Prov 1:33 relates only to the now destroyed city of Jerusalem and its temple. Rather, *rāʿâ* manifests its importance *via* its lexical and thematic associations forged by the paraphrased Jeremian discourse in Prov 1:24–27, and the reflective verses in 28–31. We can further add to the above comparisons between Prov 1:20–33 and Jeremiah 7.

For one, the location of wisdom's speech as *šĕʿārîm bāʿîr*, "in the gates of the city," resembles the location of Jeremiah's words in 7:2. Jeremiah is commanded to stand *bĕšaʿar bêt YHWH*, "in the gate of the house of the

---

[84] Where v 22 mentions the *pĕtāyim, lēṣîm*, and *kĕsîlîm*, v 32 mentions only the *pĕtāyim* and *kĕsîlîm*. Trible ("Wisdom Builds a Poem," 517) explains the absense of the *lēṣîm* by saying: ". . . vs. 32 compresses the address of vs. 22 by omitting reference to scoffers." In the context of the passage it is not clear what is achieved by such compression. If anything, the ring structure is weakened by the omission of the *lēṣîm* in v 32. From the point of view of the passage itself, vv 32–33 do not exhibit close adherence to rhetorical features but rather highlight the thematic features of turning (*šûb*, vv 23, 32) and listening (*šmʿ*, vv 23, 33).

[85] *Jeremiah*, 531, 535.

Lord," and to address his words to *kol yĕhûdâ habbāʾîm baššĕʿarîm*, "all you men of Judah who enter these gates"(note plural). [86]

A reference to "cities" and "streets" is found in 7:17, 34. In this case, YHWH commands Jeremiah not to intercede for the people on account of what they are doing *bĕʿārê ûbĕḥuṣôt*, "in the cities and streets." [87] The activity of wisdom's public announcement of its message resembles the activity of Jeremiah's speaking in the gates and in the streets. [88] Both wisdom and Jeremiah articulate their *dĕbārîm*, "words," in such a way that their hearers have a choice of heeding their words or ignoring them and opting for others' "words." For example, all the verbs in 1:20 relate to wisdom's forthcoming speech. The answer to wisdom's accusing question in 1:22a, *ʿad mātay pĕtāyim tĕʾēhābû petî*, "How long, O simple ones, will you love simpleness?" lies in paying attention to her reproof, *lĕtokaḥtî*. Such reproof takes the form of wisdom making known her words: *ʾôdîʿâ dĕbaray ʾetkem*, "I will make known my words to you." As we have noted, the failure to listen results in destruction (vv. 32–33).

When Jeremiah stands before the people, he pits *dĕbar YHWH*, "the word of the Lord," against *dibrê haššeqer*, "deceptive words." Clearly, to trust, *bṭḥ*, deceptive words ultimately leads to being unable to "dwell in this place," *škn + māqôm*, v 7. Part of Jeremiah's monologue is framed in a question, vv 9–10, as *ḥokmâ* does in Prov 1:22. The safety of Judah and Jerusalem is linked to whose words the people obey, *šmʿ*. As Shiloh was destroyed, so Jerusalem and the temple face a similar fate: "because . . . I spoke to you persistently and you did not listen, and when I called, you did not answer," v 13.

---

[86] Concerning the ambiguous location of Jeremiah's speech in 7:2, R. P. Carroll (*Jeremiah*, 207) says: "The temple sermon is built around the ambiguous term 'place' (*maqom*), meaning 'temple' (v. 12) or 'land' (v. 7) or possibly 'city' . . . ." See W. Holladay (*Jeremiah*, 235) where he says the following for v 2b: ". . . the words are somewhat out of place, since the temple sermon was delivered not in the gate(s) but in the temple court (26:2). The words are similar to those found in 17:20; 22:2; and 26:2. . . ." In 11:6 YHWH commands Jeremiah saying: *qĕrāʾ ʾet kol haddĕbārîm hāʾēlleh bĕʿārê yĕhûdâ ûbĕḥuṣôt yerûšālaim*, "Proclaim all these words in the cities of Judah, in the streets of Jerusalem. . . ." See R. P. Carroll (*Jeremiah*, 490) where he places 11:1–13 in the same traditio-historical strand as 7:1–8:3. Also: W. Holladay, *Jeremiah*, 348–349; E. W. Nicholson, *Preaching to the Exiles*, 34.

[87] Cf. 5:1; 44:1, 6, 17 for similar references to places where Jeremiah spoke and where the people engaged in foreign cult practices.

[88] We recognize that other prophets delivered their messages in similar public arena. If the location of wisdom's speech were the only link that we had with the Jeremianic traditions then we would hardly have compelling evidence. However, in combination with other similarities with Jeremiah we can count the similar location in Jeremiah and Proverbs 1 as additional evidence for a resemblance of traditions by Proverbs.

Similarly, deviant cult practices are traced to the people "obeying a voice" other than YHWH's (v 23). As wisdom advises listening to her words as a preventive against $rā^câ$, "evil," 1:33, so too the people in Jeremiah's time fall prey to $rā^câ$, "hurt," Jer 7:6 and "wickedness," Jer 7:12, by not listening.

The rejection of wisdom's words which results in the rejection of YHWH is patterned upon Jeremiah's life, where rejection of his word amounts to rejection of YHWH's word (cf. Jer 7:27). We have already noted how Prov 1:20–33 adopts the unique phraseology from Jeremiah 7 concerning speaking/not hearing, calling/not answering. The combination of $śḥq$, "laugh," and l^cg, "mock," in Prov 1:26 appears in Jer 20:7. As Holladay states, the combination of $śḥq$ and l^cg appears no where else in prophetic literature. [89] The borrowing of the Jeremianic pair $śḥq$ and l^cg by Prov 1:26 becomes all the more probable when we take note of the similarities in context and point of view reflected both in Jeremiah and Proverbs.

Part of Jeremiah's lament enlists the expression pth, in Jer 20:7, 10. V 7a reads, $pittîtanî$ $YHWH$ $wā^eppāt$, "O Lord, thou hast deceived me, and I was deceived . . . ."(RSV) V 10c records the words of the "friends" of Jeremiah who look for his downfall: ^ûlay $yĕputeh$, "perhaps he will be deceived. . . ."(RSV) [90]

The accusing question in Prov 1:22 isolates the expression $pĕtāyim$, "simpletons," from the root pth. In the case of Jer 20:7, 10, Jeremiah is identified by means of pth, "someone easily persuaded." [91] Jer 20:7 emphasizes his dilemma. Jeremiah portrays himself as "persuaded/overcome," pth, by YHWH on account of the word that Jeremiah "speaks", ^adabber, "cries out," $^ez^cāq$, and "shouts," $^eqrā^c$. A similar association of pth, dbr, and $qr^$, appears in Prov 1:20–23 where wisdom addresses the $pĕtāyim$, "simple ones."

---

[89] W. Holladay, *Jeremiah*, 553.

[90] For a detailed discussion of the problems in translation and intepretation of Jer 20:7–8, see: D. J. A. Clines and D. M. Gunn, ""You Tried to Persuade Me" and "Violence! Outrage!" in Jeremiah XX 7–8," *VT* 28 (1978) 20–27. Cf. M. Fishbane, "'A Wretched Thing of Shame, A Mere Belly': An Interpretation of Jeremiah 20:7–12," in *The Biblical Mosaic, Changing Perspectives,* ed. by R. Polzin and E. Rothman (Philadelphia/Chico, California: Fortress Press/Scholars Press, 1982) 169–183; E. D. Lewin, "Arguing for Authority, A Rhetorical Study of Jeremiah 1.4–19 and 20.7–18," *JSOT* 32 (1985) 105–119.

[91] See Clines and Gunn, "Jeremiah XX 7–8," where they argue that "persuade" appears to be the best rendering of pth for Jer 20:7. Part of their argument is based on the observation that pth "describes an attempted act rather than a successful one."(p. 20)

Ironically, in the context of Jer 20:7 where Jeremiah perceives himself overpowered by the word of YHWH, Jeremiah's "friends" also see him as potentially "overpowered" in v 10. The context of such overpowering pertains directly to the word that Jeremiah speaks. The same "word" elicits derision from his hearers: "I have become a laughing stock (*śḥq*) all the day; everyone mocks (*lᶜg*) me."

According to E. D. Lewin, vv 7–13 are an example of a "Lament of the individual."[92] Set in the context of the community, Jeremiah's lament captures the anguish that Jeremiah experiences not only of the failure of the people to hear his word, but also of the ridicule that he faces because of that word.[93] The combination of such unique phraseology from Jeremiah 20 and Jeremiah 7 in Prov 1:20–33 is not at all surprisihg when we recall the futility that Jeremiah faced in getting YHWH's message to the pre-587 community at Jerusalem. As YHWH spoke through Jeremiah and was not heeded, called and not answered, so too, YHWH's word through Jeremiah met with laughter and mocking.

The turn-about context of Prov 1:20–33 where wisdom now accuses the people of being *pĕtāyim*, "simple ones," (v 22) and where *ḥokmâ* now "laughs," *śḥq*, and "mocks," *lᶜg*, (v 26) when calamity comes, can be explained by reading the text in a post-587 context. The Jeremianic traditions are recontextualized to serve the needs and purposes of a later community. From the narrator's viewpoint as well as from the viewpoint of the community to which the paraphrased discourse from Jeremiah is addressed, it is clear that the tables are turned. The *pĕtāyim* are identified with the earlier *pĕtāyim* in Jeremiah's time on the basis of their rejection of YHWH and Jeremiah and on the basis of their failure to hear/listen/answer. The fact that Prov 1:22 is the *only* example of a accusing question in all of Proverbs 1–9 pinpoints the perennial hardheartedness of wisdom's hearers to be different from their forebears: *ᶜad mātay pĕtāyim tĕᵓĕhăbû petî*, "How long, O simple ones, will you love being simple?"[94]

---

92 "Arguing for Authority," 111.

93 E. D. Lewin, "Arguing for Authority," 112: "It is specifically the prophetic word which causes Jeremiah's personal anguish and public shame (vv. 8–9). Jeremiah has made his enemies through preaching that word, and he cries out in protest and for deliverance to the God who overpowered him with the prophetic commission."

94 The only other places where questions appear in Proverbs 1–9 are 5:20 and 8:1. Prov 5:20 questions the involvement with foreign women and does not have the tone of an accusing question as in 1:22. The context in 8:1 is different from Prov 1:20ff. In 8:1 the narrator introduces *ḥokmâ* by gaining assent from the reader as to where *ḥokmâ* addresses them. Prov 1:22 in contrast accuses the *pĕtāyim* of being continually recalcitrant.

PROV 1:20–33, JEREMIAH, AND
RABBINIC COMMENTÁRY

In *Midrash Mishle* we can again see how other commentators have identified portions of wisdom's discourse in Prov 1:20–33 with traditions found in the book of Jeremiah. [95]

The first place where Jeremiah's name emerges in *MM* is at Prov 1:24—the same verse where we argue that *ḥokmâ* shifts to a quotation of Jeremianic speech. *MM* reads: *d"ʾ yˁn qrʾty. zh yrmyh shyh qwrʾ lhm lysrʾl byrwslym lʾswt tswbh wlʾ hyw mʾmynym lw*, "Another interpretation: "Because I have called and ye refused." (Prov. 1:24) This refers to Jeremiah. He called upon Israel in Jerusalem to repent." [96]

The rabbinic comments for Prov 1:24 confirm our argument that the referent "you" does not refer to those mentioned in Prov 1:22–23. In none of the examples drawn from scripture for Prov 1:24 in *MM* is there even a hint that the *pĕtāyim, lēṣîm*, or *kĕsîlîm* were in the minds of the rabbinic commentators when they read wisdom's word of judgment. Equally significant, *Yal Sh* reproduces Prov 1:23 but adds the particle *ʾim*, "if," making clearer the conditional case of the verse: *ʾm tswbw ltwkhty ʾbyˤh lkm rwḥi*, "If you turn to my reproof, then I will pour out my spirit." The addition of the particle *ʾim*, "if" is another confirmation of our earlier argument for a conditional form for 1:23.

MM also comments on *wĕtôkaḥtî lōʾ ʾăbîtem* in Prov 1:25 and attributes the words to Jeremiah: *wtwkhty lʾ ʾbytm. zh yrmyh sˤl kl twkhh wtwkhh shyh mwkyh ʾt ysrʾl hywh mbzyn ʾwtw wmlˤygyn ˤlyn, wʾmr lhm yrmyh hyykm sˤtyd ywm sybwʾ sksm sʾtm mlˤygyn ˤly wmshqym by bk ʾny ˤtyd ywm ʾhd lhlˤyg ˤlykm wlshq ˤlykm*, "'And would have none of my reproof.' [Prov 1:25] This refers to Jeremiah, for each and every reproof he gave to Israel they would spurn and mock him. Jeremiah said to them: By your lives! The day will come that just as you [now] mock me and make fun of me, one day in the Future I will mock (*śḥq*) and make fun (*lˤg*) of you." [97]

MM captures the essence of Prov 1:20–33 by its emphasis upon the people's failure to heed Jeremiah's word reflected in the Jeremianic traditions. Moreover, *MM*, detects a natural link between the theme of calling/not answering with the unique combination of *śḥq* and *lˤg*,

---

95 *MM* makes other cross-references besides Jeremiah. The plurality of references in *MM* does not detract from our analysis or from using *MM* as further evidence that other commentators have "heard" the voice of Jeremiah in Prov 1:20–33. Medieval Rabbinic commentators were not in the business of establishing the traditio-historical roots to portions Proverbs as we are doing. Their exegesis, however, is just as much sensitive to the inter-locking associations among the traditions as our work is.

96 B. Visotzky, *Midrash Mishle: A Critical Edition*, 1. 206.

97 B. Visotzky, *Midrash Mishle: A Critical Edition*, 1. 208.

"laughing" and "mocking" in Jer 20:7. The paraphrasing of Jeremiah's speech concerning laughing and mocking is even framed in such a way that a future context is evoked where the tables will be turned upon those who laugh and mock at Jeremiah. Just such a reversal, we are arguing, is preserved in Prov 1:20–33. As YHWH and Jeremiah called the people and they did not answer, so the time came (i.e., the destruction of Judah and Jerusalem) when they call but YHWH and Jeremiah do not answer. In the same way, as there was a time when the people laughed and mocked at Jeremiah, the time came (i.e., the destruction of Judah and Jerusalem) when Jeremiah laughs and mocks them. The rhetorical structure which we isolate for Prov 1:20–33 has concrete reality in the very history which the text represents. Structure reflects history.

CONTEMPORARY RESEARCH IN THE
REUTILIZATION OF JEREMIANIC TRADITIONS
IN ZECHARIAH AND THE PARALLELS WITH PROV 1:20–33.

MM uses Zech 7:11 as a prooftext for interpreting Prov 1:24 in conjunction with Jeremiah's warnings to the people of Jerusalem. Added to *MM*'s comments for Prov 1:24 is the following: *wlʾ hyw mʾmynym lw, snʾmr wymʿnw lhqsyb wytnw ktp swrrt (zkry z yʾ)*, "And was it not they who refused [to listen] to him? as it is said, 'But they refused to pay heed, they presented a balky back' (Zech 7:11)." [98]

The associations that the medieval commentators detect between Prov 1:24, Jeremiah's words to the people of Judah and Jerusalem, and Zech 7:11 have similarly been analyzed by contemporary scholars such as C. Kayatz, G. Boström, and H. Ringgren and W. Zimmerli. [99]

Equally instructive are the recent observations by W. A. M. Beuken. [100] At the close of his analysis for Zech 1:1–6; 7:7–14, Beuken detects a number of similarities in content and form found in Prov 1:23–28. Beuken presents the following outline for Prov 1:23–28:

Spr. 1,23: 1) Ein Anruf zur Umkehr (תשובו) ist in Nebenordnung, aber mit bedingender Bedeutung, Heilsverheissung gebunden - vgl. Sach 1,3.

---

[98] B. Visotzky, *Midrash Mishle: A Critical Edition*, 1. 206. With minor variations *Yal Sh* reads the same as *MM*. Cf. Nachmias' abbreviated interpretation: *wymʾnw lhqsyb wytnw ktp swrrh (zkryh z yʾ)*, "But they refused to hearken, and turned a stubborn shoulder" (Zech 7:11).

[99] *Studien zu Proverbien 1–9*, 119; *Proverbiastudien*, 29–31; *Sprüche/Prediger*, 17.

[100] W. A. M. Beuken, S.J., *Haggai-Sacharja 1–8*.

2) Die Ausgiessung des Geistes ist parallel zur Erkenntnis von Gottes דברים - vgl. Sach 7,12, wo der Dienst des Propheten parallel zur Vermittlung des Geistes ist.

V. 24:   1) "Weil ich rief und ihr nicht wolltet" - vgl. Sach 7,13a.

2) Dieselben Zeitworte קרא, מאן und הקשיב wie Sach. 7, 7(13). 11.

VV. 24–26 In einem Schema gleichen Verhaltens auf Gegenseitigkeit sind Ungehorsam gegenüber den Geboten (24–25) und Gottes Weigerung, in der Not zu helfen (26), auf einander bezogen-vgl. Sach. 7,13.

V. 28:   "Dann werden sie mich rufen, aber ich werde nicht antworten" - vgl. Sach. 7,13b. Das zweite Glied von V. 28 wiederholt dasselbe Schema in weisheitlichen Ausdrücken. [101]

The link between Zechariah 7 and Prov 1:23–28 lies primarily in their commonly shared expressions and form. Beuken arrives at his conclusion concerning the similarities between Zechariah and Proverbs through a detailed examination of the traditio-historical process (*die Endüberlieferung*) within Zechariah 7 which combines together *das deuteronomistische und das chronistische Geschichtswerk*. According to Beuken, a Levitical circle of tradents is responsible for the final form and content of the material. [102] A brief summary of Beuken's examination of Zechariah 7 deserves our attention, for his analysis highlights a number of important editorial devices which have complementary parallels in Prov 1:20–33.

At the conclusion of his analysis of Zech 7:14b Beuken sums up the tone and direction of Zechariah 7 as a whole:

V. 14b. "So machten sie das liebliche Land zur Wüste". Mit einer kurzen Schlussfolgerung, die auf die vorausgehende Strafansage zurückgrieft, schliesst dieser paränetische Rückblick auf Israels Geschichte. Der Entwurf der Endüberlieferung wird hier sichtbar: sie will nicht mit dem angeführten Jahwewort schliessen, sondern mit einer historiographischen Feststellung. Es ist die Geschichte, die sie interessiert; sie will aus dem, was über dieses Land kam, die Lehre ziehen. Diese ganze Erweiterung ist in erster Linie

---

[101] *Haggai-Sacharja 1–8*, 137–138.

[102] *Haggai-Sachariah 1–8*, 124. Because Beuken attributes the final form and content for Zech 1:1–6 and Zech 7:7–14 to the same circle of redactors, the following quote applies to both passages: "Dieser einleitende Bericht ist Werk jener levitischen Kreise, aus denen das deuteronomistische und das chronistische Geschichtswerk entstanden, wie auch eine besondere Jeremiaüberlieferung."

nicht Überlieferung prophetischen Nachlasses (ausgenommen VV. 9–10), sondern ein historischer Rückblick im Dienst der Paränese. [103]

The historical referent of Zechariah 7 is not altogether self-evident within its context for the modern reader. Only through a process of comparing the traditions within the passage with other prophetic traditions can Beuken make a case for the reutilization of a historical event in the present prophetic context. Furthermore, as *ein historischer Rückblick in Dienst der Paränese*, Beuken points out that what we have in Zechariah 7 is not so much original prophetic speech as a combination of specific prophetic traditions which have been woven together to form a hybrid of *Geschichtsparänese* and prophetic speech. [104]

Such things as the use of quotations of former prophets (vv 9–10), the combination of second and third person plural prophetic speech (vv 9–12), the theme of calling, *qrʾ*, and not hearing, *lʾ šmʿ*, (v 13), covenant formulary, storm imagery (v 14), as well as evidence of modified *Scheltwort und Drohwort* alert Beuken to the blending together of prophetic traditions within Zechariah 7. [105] Beuken locates the traditio-historical focus of Zechariah 7 within the complex of traditions concerning the 6th century destruction of Judah and Jerusalem as evidenced through the deuteronomic sections of the book of Jeremiah. As Beuken says:

> Schliesslich erhebt sich die Frage: auf welche prophetische Gerichtsankündigung, die in Negationen von Ausdrücken aus dem priesterlichen Heilsorakel abgefasst ist, spielt hier die paränetische Erweiterung an? Die Antwort ist nicht schwierig. In der deuteronomistischen Jeremiaüberlieferung trifft man auf ein gleichlautendes Unheilswort für Jerusalem und Juda. . . . [106]

---

[103] *Haggai-Sacharja 1–8*, 135.

[104] For example, Beuken says the following about the combination of *der Ich-Bericht* and history in Zechariah 7: "Man kann sagen: durch diese Überarbeitung kommt der Prophetenbericht in die Luft zu hängen, denn eine Antwort auf die Anfangsfrage bleibt aus. Der Ich-Bericht wird der Paränese wegen aufgeben. Es geht den Tradenten nicht so sehr um die einst von Sacharja gegebene Antwort, sondern um die unglückseligen Folgen, die die Abweisung ähnlicherprophetischer Aussprachen in der Vergangenheit hatten. Dieser Wechsel in der Gattung wird nur dadurch ein wenig verdeckt, dass diese Predigt aus des *Geschichte* eine Lehre zieht"(*Haggai-Sacharja 1–8*, 121).

[105] W. A. M. Beuken, *Haggai-Sacharja 1–8*, 130–132.

[106] *Haggai-Sacharja 1–8*, 132. Beuken further comments on the combination of covenant formulary and priestly oracles of salvation in Zech 7:10–14 which derive from the Jeremianic traditions concerning Jeremiah's words to the people of Judah

The appearance of traditions from Jeremiah concerning the destruction of Judah and Jerusalem is not at all surprising when we recall the opening verses of Zechariah 7. The references to fasting, the fifth month, the seventh month, and the seventy years are unmistakable plays upon the events surrounding the destruction of the Temple and Jerusalem in 587. [107] By framing his message with the backdrop of the Jeremianic tradition concerning the forthcoming destruction of Jerusalem and the temple because of the people's failure to listen, Zechariah lends further credibility to his own prophecy by playing upon earlier traditions which have come to pass. [108] Zechariah is a prophet like Jeremiah. But in Zechariah's case, he stands on the shoulders of the Jeremianic traditions. Thus, the emphasis falls not upon accurate historical quotation but upon paraphrastic use of earlier traditions in service to Zechariah's parenetic format.

A key to unravelling the traditio-historical background of Zechariah's message, as Beuken argues, lies in the paraphrased prophetic speech in Zech 7:9–10 which appears earlier in Jer 7:5–7. [109] Another key element in Beuken's analysis is the quoted words of Yahweh in 7:13: *wayĕhî ka'ăšer qārā' wĕlō' sāmē'û kēn yiqrĕ'û wĕlō' 'ešmā' 'āmar YHWH*

---

and Jerusalem (*Haggai- Sacharja 1–8*, 132): "Zusammenfassend dürfen wir sagen: die Sacharjaredaktion grieft in dieser Erinnerung an das Strafgericht auf eine Thematik zurück, die in der Jeremiaüberlieferung der levitischen Milieus ihre Gestalt erhielt und von dort her ihr bekannt war. In dieser Thematik waren Ausdrücke zweier alter Gattungen, des Bundesformulars und des priesterlichen Heilsorakels, in schöpferischer Weise zu einem neuen Inhalt zusammengefügt worden. Die Sacharjaüberlieferung selbst gab dieser Thematik die Form eines paränetischen Schemas, das sie öfter verwendet und das die praktische, erfahrbare Verhaltenweise der Bundespartner untereinander klar andeutet."

[107] See 2 Kgs 25:8–9, 25 where the Temple was burned in the fifth month and Gedaliah, the governor appointed by the Babylonians, was murdered in the seventh month. The seventy years refers to the period from 587 to 519. See: Jer 25:11; 29:10. H. G. Mitchell, *Zechariah*, 196, says: "The fast of the fifth month commemorated the destruction of Jerusalem and its temple by the Babylonians. . . . It had been observed ever since the Jews went into captivity (v. 5), a period of nearly seventy years." Cf. also: A. Petitjean, *Les Oracles du Proto-Zacharie*, 309–310; D. Petersen, *Haggai and Zechariah 1–8*, 284–285.

[108] See M. Fishbane's comments (*Biblical Interpretation*, 505) concerning the aggadic reutilization of the Jeremianic cycle of seventy years by Esther and Zechariah: "Given the learned nature of this citation [in Esther 8:16–17 and 9:30–31] from Zech. 8:19, it is not unlikely that the exegete responsible for it was aware, on the basis of Zech 7:1–5, which refers to these fasts in the same breath as a reference to the seventy-year oracle of Jeremiah, that the expectation of the end of the four fast-days commemorating the fall of Jerusalem signalled the fulfilment of the Jeremian prophecy."

[109] W. A. M. Beuken, *Haggai-Sacharja 1–8*, 123–124.

ṣĕbā'ôt, "As I called, and they would not hear, so they called, and I would not hear," says the Lord of hosts(RSV). [110]

Zech 7:13 provides the reason for the destruction of Judah. As Jeremiah's words went unheeded by the people of Judah and Jerusalem when there was still time for repentance, so YHWH ignored the pleas of the people when the Babylonians destroyed Judah and the temple. Thus, Beuken links the traditio-historical content of Zech 7:7–14 with the Jeremian traditions about the destruction of Judah and Jerusalem. Surprisingly, Beuken fails to address the possibility that Prov 1:20–33 may likewise reflect a similar reutilization of the Jeremian traditions concerning the destruction of Judah and Jerusalem. His failure to do so is perhaps explained by his favorable citation of C. Kayatz's earlier work on Proverbs, where she dates the traditions to the Solomonic period. [111] But in light of our above analysis which finds evidence of borrowing from Jeremiah 7 and 20, we can add to Beuken's initial observation about Prov 1:23–28. As Zechariah 7 represents *ein historischer Rückblick in Dienst der Paränese*, Prov 1:20–33 stands in the same editorial circle of tradents who play upon the perceived reason for the destruction of Judah and Jerusalem as preserved in the book of Jeremiah. [112]

---

[110] *Haggai-Sacharja 1–8*, 131–132. For Beuken, Zech 7:13 recalls Jer 11:11. The corresponding vocabulary is not exactly the same. The combination in Jer 11:11 is z⁽q + šmᶜ. Zech 7:13 has qr' + šmᶜ as in Jer 7:13, 27. Beuken's citation of Jer 11:11 is baffling when we recall that Beuken notes the traditio-historical similarites between Zechariah 7 and portions of Jer 7:5–6. In addition, both Zech 7:13 and Jer 7:13, 27 provide the "reason" for the destruction of Jerusalem. See W. Holladay, *Jeremiah*, 239, where he notes that Jer 7:13 functions as an added "reason" for the forthcoming destruction; and C. Westermann, *Basic Forms of Prophetic Speech*, 181, 221–222, where he discusses Jer 7:13 and its role in summarizing the reason for Jeremiah's word of judgment.

[111] See W. A. M. Beuken, *Haggai-Sacharja 1–8*, 138 where he notes C. Kayatz's work. Beuken also says: "Natürlich wollen wir damit nicht sagen, dass hier literarische Abhängigkeit vorläge. Wir wollen nur illustrieren, wie sehr die Gattung der Paränese an überlieferte Formen gebunden ist. Gewiss erhebt sich die Frage, in welcher Beziehung die levitische Predigt und die spätere Weisheit zueinander stehen, doch überschreitet diese Frage die Problemstellung unserer Untersuchung"(p. 138).

[112] Beuken is not the only modern scholar who has recognized both the similarities between Zechariah 7 and Prov 1:20–33 and how Zechariah 7 reutilizes past prophetic traditions in a historical *Rückblick* framework. For example, A. Petitjean (*Les Oracles du Proto-Zacharie* 354) comments on the similarities between Zech 7:13 and Prov 1:20–33: "Le couple qārā'/šāmaᶜ se retrouve en *Jer.*, XXIX, 12, et c'est peut-être par influence jérémienne qu'il s'est imposé en *Ez.*, VIII, 18b et en *Zach.*, VII, 13. L'idée exprimée dans ces deux derniers passages apparaît également en une péricope du livre des *Proverbes* (I, 22–33), marquee par le vocabulaire, le style et les idées prophétiques." Like Beuken, Petitjean isolates Zech 7:13 as the key verse which has corresponding

Over and above shared themes, the discourse of wisdom and Jeremiah utilize combinations of second and third person plural speech as a textual strategy. We have already analyzed how the refrain in Prov 1:28, as quoted direct discourse, recalls the earlier words drawn from Jeremiah. In Jeremiah 7:21–26 there is a remarkably similar combination of direct discourse addressed to the generation at the Exodus. V 21, by means of the phrase kōh ʾāmar YHWH ṣĕbāʾôt ʾelōhê yisrāʾēl, introduces YHWH's direct discourse which reads: ʿōlôtêkem sĕpû ʿal zibḥêkem wĕʾiklû bāśār. [113] The "you" plural in v 21 is speech directed to the Exodus generation. V 22 then shifts to "them," third person plural, again referring to the same generation, but this time from the perspective of Jeremiah's generation. V 23 shifts once again to the second person plural "you" only to return to the third person plural "they" in vv 24–26.

The ease by which the narrator combines second and third person discourse does not detract from the way the discourse works. The narrator, through the voices of the prophet and the deity, achieves a level of historical and theological continuity between the Exodus generation and Jeremiah's hearers by means of direct discourse. The links in the

---

parallel features with Jeremiah. Petitjean, however, limits his comments concerning other corresponding similarities in form and content between Proverbs and Zechariah. D. Petersen's comments (Haggai and Zechariah 1–8, 293) about Prov 1:20–33 are even briefer. Petersen considers "Dame Wisdom's" words in Prov 1:28 as a "similar expression" for Zech 7:13. Like Petitjean, Petersen says nothing more about their similarities. Both Petitjean and Petersen devote their analyses to traditio-historical details of Zechariah 7 and arrive at conclusions very similar to Beuken's earlier analysis concerning the combination of prophetic speech and historical reference to the destruction of Judah and Jerusalem. Petitjean and Petersen also agree with the historical character of Zechariah 7. For example, A. Petitjean calls the context in which Zechariah 7 appears a Geschichtspredigt: 7:7–14 is "comme une Geschichtspredigt destinée à mettre en lumière la signification de l'exil et de la destruction qui frappèrent la population et le pays de Juda. Le rappel des 'paroles des prophètes anciens' constitue la première partie de cette Geschichtspredigt qui évoque, en trois points, trois périodes de l'historie du peuple: la prédiction des prophètes, la désobéissance de la communauté et le châtiment"(p. 315). Framed in a post-exilic context, Zechariah appeals to past events by means of paraphrased prophetic speech. By appealing to earlier prophetic speech pertaining to the destruction of Jerusalem and the Temple in 587, Zechariah drives home his point concerning the outcome of the earlier generation's refusal to heed the prophet's warning. Along similar lines of Petitjean's Geschichtspredigt and Beuken's Rückblick auf die Geschichte, Petersen says: "What we have in Zech. 7:8–14 is an integrated historical essay exploring the demise of the Judahite state"(p. 296). Prophetic speech is integrated into the fabric of an historical account.
[113] W. Holladay, Jeremiah, 259, treats vv 21–23 as "parody of priestly torah" and treats vv 24–26 as an "accusation report."

temporal chain are the variations of the theme of speaking and not hearing. [114] Again, the strategy that the narrator assumes in Prov 1:24ff is not far removed from that of Jer 7:24–28.

<h2 style="text-align:center">SUMMARY</h2>

Our analysis of Prov 1:20–33 isolates a number of editorial devices for combining, in this case, prophetic speech in a sapiential context similar to our example in Prov 1:8–19. In Prov 1:8–19 we noted how the parent adds another dimension to his/her discourse by quoting the discourse of the "sinners." The vocabulary of the "sinners" in turn draws upon the broader inner-biblical associations between the "sinners'" discourse and the brothers' discourse in Genesis 37. Clusters of similar vocabulary link the texts together. A level of unity is also established within vv 8–19 by the very fact that the parent reappropriates the vocabulary of the "sinners" for his/her own purposes.

Prov 1:20–33 reflects a similar strategy. The narrator introduces wisdom in vv 20–21 by calling attention to her forthcoming speech in vv 22–23. Wisdom then adds another stratum of speech by introducing paraphrased prophetic speech from Jeremiah 7 and 20 in Prov 1:24–31. The parent stands back, as it were, in 1:19 and draws a general conclusion derived from his/her discourse. So also 1:32–33 offers a conclusion derived directly from the previous discourse. And in both cases, the conclusions are based upon refashioned scriptural traditions. While the length of both discourses is different, we detect a similarity in form. Traditions from the Torah and the Prophets are freely played upon in order to form new discourse units in a sapiential context.

The combination of second and third person speech found in Prov 1:24–31 is also a feature commonly found within the prophetic traditions. By appealing to different levels of reference, i.e., "you" and "they," which in effect refer to the same group of people but from different vantage points, the prophet Jeremiah, for example, can bridge the distance between generations. Such speech from the past is refashioned by the prophet in addressing a present community as in Jer 7:21–26. A similar technique is found in Zechariah 7 which Beuken rightly calls *ein historischer Rückblick in dienst der Paränese*. The presence of the same combination of speech in Prov 1:24–31 is further evidence that the editor of these verses was well versed in editorial techniques found elsewhere

---

[114] W. Holladay, *Jeremiah*, 263, comments on 7:25 by saying: "Not only did the generation at Sinai not listen, but neither has any generation since."

in scripture and makes use of such a technique in his/her discourse. Traditions from Judah's history are reutilized in a sapiential context.

We can also point to a number of factors which help to explain the juxtaposition of Prov 1:8–19 and 1:20–33. First of all, both units appeal to a form of *pth*, "entice," as a verb and "simpletons" as a noun in vv 10 and 22. Our early analysis of v 22 has important bearing here. As we showed, the book of Proverbs clearly differentiates between *pĕtāyim*, and *lēṣîm* and *kĕsîlîm*. Because Prov 1:10 and 22 both speak of *pth* in a positive manner in differentiation from *ḥaṭṭā'îm*, *kĕsîlîm*, and *lēṣîm* we can detect both a high degree of familiarity with the broader scope of the book of Proverbs as well as a design to maintain fidelity with the book. A degree of consistency is evident in the opening two lessons in Proverbs which match other references in the book. Even though we detect clear evidence of a reutilization of traditions from discourse events from Genesis and Jeremiah, we see a conspicuous absence of editorial reduplication of the traditions. Instead, the accounts from Genesis and Jeremiah are refashioned to fit into the framework of Proverbs. As a result, the traditions from the Torah and the Prophets are creatively woven into the larger pattern of the book of Proverbs.

Secondly, both the opening lessons in Proverbs pertain to Judah in some fashion. In Prov 1:8–19 the parent, especially in v 19, plays upon Judah's discourse from Genesis 37. In Prov 1:20–33 it is Judah as a nation which is alluded to in wisdom's discourse. Thus, not only do we recognize scriptural traditions from Israel's past in Prov 1:8–19 and 1:20–33, but we are given contexts which relate ostensibly to Judah.

4

Prov 6:1–19 and the Joseph Story.

A. Translation.
Prov 6:1–19

1) My son, if you have become surety
for your companion, and what's more, if
you have struck a bargain with a stranger,
2) if you are snared by the words
of your mouth, if you are caught by
the words of your mouth,
3) then do this, my son, and save yourself,
for you have come into your companion's
hand: go, hasten, and importune
your companion.
4) Give your eyes no sleep and
your eyelids no slumber;
5) save yourself like a gazelle
from the hand, like a bird from
the hand of the fowler.
6) Go to the ant, O sluggard;
consider its ways, and be wise.
7) Without having any chief, officer,

or ruler
8) it prepares its food in summer, and
gathers its sustenance in harvest.
9) How long will you lie there, O
sluggard? When will you arise from
your sleep?
10) A little sleep, a little slumber,
a little folding of the hands to rest,
11) and poverty will come upon you
as a traveler, and want as an
armed man.
12) A worthless man, a wicked man,
goes about with crooked speech,
13) winks with his eyes, speaks with
his feet, points with his finger,
14) with perverted heart he cultivates
evil, continually sowing discord;
15) therefore, calamity will come upon
him suddenly; in a moment he will be broken
beyond healing.
16) There are six things which the Lord
hates, seven which are an abomination to God:
17) haughty eyes, a lying tongue, and
hands that shed innocent blood,
18) a heart that cultivates wicked plans,
feet that make haste to run to evil,
19) a false witness who breathes out
lies, and a man who sows discord
among brothers.

Introduction

Scholars generally agree that Prov 6:1–19 is an interpolation which interrupts the otherwise smooth flow of the text between Proverbs 5 and 6:20ff. D. G. Wildeboer's assertion made in 1897 that "6, 20 schliesst sich ganz an 5, 23 an, so dass dies Stück 6, 1–19 einer Interpolation sehr gleicht," represents the opinion of many modern commentators.[1]

---

[1] *Die Sprüche*, 17. P. W. Skehan, "Proverbs 5:15–19 and 6:20–24," *CBQ* 8 (1946) 290–297, offers a detailed analysis where he argues for an earlier unit of tradition which links Proverbs 5 and 6:20–24. For Skehan, Prov 6:1–19, as a later addition to the text, interrupts the once natural connection between Proverbs 5 and 6:20ff. A revised form of the article appears in *Studies in Israelite Poetry and Wisdom* (CBQMS 1, Worcester,

It is not difficult to see why vv 1–19 are treated as an interpolation. Vv 1–19 interrupt the common theme of warning against involvement with the zārâ/nokriyyâ, "loose woman"/"adventuress" (5:20, RSV) and ʾēšet raʿ/nokriyyâ "evil woman"/"adventuress" (6:24 RSV). If vv 1–19 are removed, a common thematic thread between the end of Proverbs 5 and 6:20ff seems to re-emerge.

Besides the tension between 6:1–19 and its surrounding context there is the additional problem of an internal lack of cohesion in vv 1–19. The verses appear to be a *pastiche* of very different units of unrelated tradition. The four units can be easily divided:

1. vv 1–5: The parent adomonishes the son to gain release from a surety should the son be involved in one.
2. vv 6–11: These verses shift to an address warning the sluggard that slothfulness leads to agricultural privation and want. Reference is made to the ant and its food-gathering traits as an example which the sluggard should follow.

Massachusetts: The Heffernan Press, 1971) 1–8. See also: R. E. Murphy, *Wisdom Literature*, 59: "This [Prov 6:1–19] is a collection of disparate pieces which interrupt the sequence of lengthy instructions in chs. 1–9." B. Gemser, *Sprüche Salomos*, 37–38: "Diese vier Ermahnungen (1–5. 6–11. 12–15. 16–19) passen nicht recht in das Programm der ersten Sammlung (cf 2, 12–22), zerreissen den Zusammenhang zwischen dem vorigen (c. 5) und dem folgenden Abschnitt (6, 20–35), welche beide Ehebruch handeln ... sind also ... späterer Zusatz zum Kern der ersten Sammlung...." R. B. Y. Scott, *Proverbs*, 16: "In ... vi 1–5, 6–11, and 12–15 are found admonitions on the themes of ... rash pledges, sloth, and rascality. Together with the numerical proverb in vi 16–19 ... [they] disturb the order of Part I and may have been inserted later from other sources." C. H. Toy, *Proverbs*, 119: "The second half of the chapter (v. 20–35) is a discourse against adultery, similar to that of ch. 5.—The first half consists of four short sections wholly different in style from the rest of this Division (chs. 1–9); while the other discourses are general praises of wisdom, or warnings against robbery and debauchery, conceived in a broad and solemn way, these are homely warnings against petty vices, with one arithmetical enumeration of sins.... Since they interrupt the course of thought in chs. 1–9, it is not likely that they were here inserted by the author of this Division; they were more probably misplaced by an editor or scribe, and at an early period, since they occur here in all the Ancient Versions." H, Ringgren and W. Zimmerli, *Sprüche/Prediger*, 31: "Anscheinend ohne Zusammenhang mit dem Übrigen und ohne Verbindung zueinander stehen hier vier volkstümliche Ermahanungen aneinandergereiht, ein typisches Beispiel der praktischen Lebensweisheit der Spruchdichter. Warum sie hier eingefügt worden sind, bleibt unklar: sie brechen offenbar den Zusammenhang zwischen 5,23 und 6,20ff., wo wieder das Thema vom fremden Weib aufgegriffen wird." For similar comments questioning why 6:1–19 has been placed between 5:23 and 6:20ff see: O. Plöger, *Sprüche Salomos*, 61–62.

3. vv 12-15: A random list of the characteristics of a treacherous person whose ultimate demise is foretold. Various body parts represent the manifold aspects of the "worthless man."

4. vv 16-19: A similar list is found in vv 12-15. However, here the focus shifts to what God "hates" and what are "abominations" to YHWH. Again, body parts represent the evil characteristics of the "man." The form of vv 16-19 is that of a graduated numerical saying—the only example of such a form in Proverbs 1-9.

Equally significant is that while the parent directly addresses the son in vv 1-5 and the sluggard in vv 6-11, starting with v 12 the text shifts to third person discourse and concentrates on the characteristics of a "man." Such a hodgepodge of form and content in 6:1-19 stands in stark contrast to the otherwise clearly crafted direct discourse of the parent and wisdom in the remaining portions of Proverbs 1-9. As a result, R. Murphy's assessment accurately summarizes what other commentators have said about vv 1-19: "In themselves, these short units are instructional and designed to alert the student to the values concerned, but there is no connection among them."[2] Thus, Prov 6:1-19 exhibits independence from the surrounding context in two ways: 1) it is out of place in the larger context of Proverbs 5 and 6:20ff; 2) it lacks internal cohesiveness.

In the following pages, we will offer an analysis of Prov 6:1-19 which takes into consideration both the issues of the external context of vv 1-19 as well as the internal problem of the connection between the four units of vv 1-5, 6-11, 12-15, 16-19. Unlike many scholars who recognize the interruptive nature of 6:1-19 on the basis of how these verses are at odds with their surrounding context, we will start with a close analysis of the content and discourse-form of 6:1-19 and work outwards. By coming to terms with the internal compositional nature of 6:1-19 we will be able to offer another interpretation of these verses which in turn will provide us with another point of view for interpreting Proverbs 5 and 6:20ff. In our analysis of vv 1-19 we agree with other scholars who conclude that these verses represent a stage in the editorial process of the book of Proverbs. But our interpretation does not stop with an observation concerning the contextual awkwardness of vv 1-19. The question of the editorial composition of 6:1-19, we are arguing, is secondary to the primary question of what role the verses now play in their present canonical context not only for the book of Proverbs but also for the larger scope of the Hebrew Bible.

---

[2] *Wisdom Literature*, 59.

The following analysis of Prov 6:1–19 is broken down into two sections. The first section is an analysis of how vv 1–5, 6–11, 12–15, and 16–19 achieve a level of editorial cohesiveness by means of key words and phrases, common points of view, and alliteration. Such linking will take into consideration how Prov 6:1–19 represents similar, if not exact, traditions found in other portions of the book of Proverbs. In the second section we will argue that the rationale for the order of Prov 6:1–19 reflects a larger narrative context which echoes Judah's role in the Joseph story found in the book of Genesis. Special attention will be given to the discourse of the parent which implies earlier events from the Joseph story by means of abbreviated descriptive discourse. Again, the work of M. Bakhtin and M. Sternberg will play an important role in our analysis.

Earlier we saw how the words of Judah from Genesis 37 play a decisive role in our analysis of the levels of discourse in Prov 1:8–19. Similarly, Judah as a nation figures in the context of prophetic discourse reclaimed from Jeremiah in Prov 1:20–33. As for 6:1–19, we will argue for a similar inner-biblical play upon other events in Judah's life recorded in Genesis. But unlike Prov 1:8–19 and 1:20–33, where the narrator combines layers of identifiable first person discourse which achieves a mimetic representation of people and events from Israel's history, 6:1–19 reflects the strategy of a narrator who casts before his/her readers a series of juxtaposed units of tradition in 6:1–5, 6–11, 12–15, 16–19. And contrary to R. Murphy's assessment that "there is no connection between them," we will argue that the four discourse units in Prov 6:1–19 reflect a sophisticated level of composition which not only presents vv 1–19 as a meaningful unit of discourse but also links together portions of Genesis and Proverbs; i.e., Torah and Wisdom.

THE COMPOSITIONAL UNITY OF 6:1–19

For Prov 6:1–5 and vv 6–11, the first two didactic units in Prov 6:1–19, F. Delitzsch argues that these once independent units are interconnected on the basis of similar diction:

> These brief proverbial discourses, each of which forms a complete whole, have scarcely been *a priori* destined for this introduction to the Salomonic Book of Proverbs edited by the author; but he places them in it; and that he so arranges them that this section regarding sluggards follows that regarding sureties, may have been occasioned by accidental points of contact of the one with the other (cf. לְךָ, 6a, with 3b; שֵׁנוֹת ... תְּנוּמוֹת, ver.

10, with ver. 4), which may also further determine the course in which the proverbs follow each other. [3]

Delitzsch's comment about the joining together of units by means of common vocabulary is important for a number of reasons. The conjoining of proverbial discourses in 6:1–11 even on the basis of what Delitzsch calls "accidental points of contact" indicates an editorial level of redaction. Whatever the earlier context of the discourse units was, vv 1–11 now form a newly ordered unit with its own integrity. In addition, Delitzsch's initial observation which perceives textual associations on the basis of vocabulary invites a further investigation into how other diction in vv 1–19 aids in the broader formation of the text. We will argue later that a similar technique of linking other units together by means of vocabulary represents an editorial process which achieves a degree of cohesiveness for vv 1–19. [4]

The beginning and ending of vv 1–19 reflect a familial context. At the beginning, the mother/father addresses the son. The parent's initial advice to the son about extricating himself immediately from surety involving a *rēaᶜ*, "neighbor" in vv 1–5, conveys a common familial point of view with v 19. There a man who upsets the familial concord of *ʾaḥîm*,

---

[3] F. Delitzsch, *Proverbs*, 139.

[4] The combination of traditions to form cohesive literary units on the basis of vocabulary is a common phenomenon both in the literature of the ancient Near East and within the Hebrew Bible. For example, N. Sarna ("Psalm 89: A Study in Inner Biblical Exegesis," in *Biblical and Other Studies*, ed. by A. Altmann [Brandeis Texts and Studies; Cambridge: Harvard University Press, 1963] 29–46) says: "The combination of originally unrelated elements into an integrated unit is a literary phenomenon familiar to us from the ancient world. The classic example is the Gilgamesh epic of Babylon, many of its component parts having been formerly independent episodes borrowed from Sumerian compositions, while the twelfth tablet has been appended to the epic without any attempt at integration . . . . The identical tendency is not lacking in Biblical literature. This is true of Psalm 19, in which an old nature hymn (verses 1–7) has been combined with a Torah hymn (verses 8–15). Psalm 70 has been incorporated into Psalm 40 (verses 14–18) and Psalm 108 is a composition of parts of Psalm 57 (verses 8–12) and 60 (verses 7–14). In these particular instances it is not always easy to distinguish the principle by which integration has been effected. However, there is an ever growing recognition of the fact that many Biblical passages have been placed in juxtaposition solely on the basis of association of ideas, words, or phrases" (pp 29–30) Sarna utilizes the principle of integration in his analysis of the three divisions of Psalm 89 as we are doing in our analysis of the four divisions in Prov 6:1–19. See p. 30, n. 7 of Sarna's article for references to other works which draw attention to the practice of integration by means of vocabulary. We can also recall W. Holladay's use of common vocabulary to mount his case for the compositional unity Jeremiah 7:1–34 in *The Architecture of Jeremiah 1–20*.

"brothers" by sending "discord," *mĕdānîm*, among them is condemned as an "abomination." By returning in v 19 to a similar familial context initiated in v 1, the text offers further hints as to the import of vv 1–19 as a whole. We are not reading a hodgepodge of unconnected discourse units as much as we are given a series of integrated traditions.

In the following pages we will build upon Delitzsch's observation which places emphasis upon vocabulary as a means of combining the units in Prov 6:1–19. In the process we will take note of some of the predominant editorial devices which achieve a level of cohesiveness for vv 1–19. We will also locate sections elsewhere in Proverbs which are remarkably similar to portions of Prov 6:1–19.

Separate Units and Perceived Unity: The Composition of Prov 6:1–19.

Of all the references to providing surety, *ʿrb*, in the Hebrew Bible, Proverbs is the only book which consistently warns against engaging in it. [5] But even though Prov 6:1–5 represents another example which addresses the issue of going surety/taking a pledge, Prov 6:1–5 does not so much contain a warning against surety/taking a pledge as the verses offer the parent's advice as to why it is necessary to extricate oneself from a surety/pledge. Lurking in the shadows is a "man" into whose hands the son is liable to fall. The reference to the "hand"/"hand of the fowler" in 6:5 denotes both an undesirable situation and an undesirable man. The "man" is further alluded to in vv 12–19.

It is also clear that the parent in vv 1–5 is speaking either from experience or experience based on tradition. Being involved in a surety places a person in someone else's hand. Prov 6:1–5, moreover, is the only example where the theme of going surety/taking a pledge is set in a conditional context: "My son, if you become surety for your companion," "if you have given your pledge for a stranger," thus setting the text of the passage in a future context. As unusual as the conditional context is for introducing the topic of a surety/pledge, we encountered a similar use of the conditional form in Prov 1:8–19 and 1:20–33. In both cases we

---

5 See: Prov 11:15; 14:10; 17:18; 20:16; 20:19; 22:26; 24:21; 27:13. Gen 43:9; 44:32 are the only examples in the Hebrew Bible where someone stands as surety for someone else. The following examples, even though they employ the root *ʿrb*, reflect a variety of meanings ranging from commercial dealings to religious contexts: Gen 38:17, 18, 20; Isa 36:8; 38:14; Jer 30:21; Neh 5:3; Ez 27:9, 13, 17, 19, 25, 27, 34; Pss 106:35; 119:122; Job 17:3; Ezra 9:2; 2 Kgs 18:23. The expression to *tqʿ* + *kp*, literally, "to strike the hands," in v 1b is found only in the book of Proverbs (cf. 11:15; 17:18; 22:26). The combination of *ʿrb* and *tqʿ* + *kp* is unique to Prov 6:1.

argue for the preproductive nature of speech which draws upon past traditions in order to address an issue in the parent's time frame. While we are not in the position at this point to reach a conclusion about another example of conditional discourse, we can at least be aware that the parent's discourse in 6:1–19 continues a similar mode of address found earlier in Proverbs 1–9.

The emphasis laid upon extricating oneself immediately from a surety is linked further by the parent with the dangers inherent in speech in vv 1–5, thus making Prov 6:1–5 the only example which connects providing surety/taking a pledge with being caught by what one says: *nôqaštā bĕ'imrê pîkā nilkadtā bĕ'imrê pîkā*, "if you are snared by the words of your mouth, if you are caught by the words of your mouth," v 2. [6]

The stress on speech and words in 1:2 which is conveyed by the expression *bĕ'imrê pîkā*, "by the words of your mouth," reflects a common topic in vv 1–19. For example, later on in v 12 the *'ādām bĕliyyaʿal* "worthless man," goes about literally with "a crooked mouth," i. e. "crooked speech," *ʿiqqĕšût peh*—an expression found also in 4:24 and 19:1. V 13 also records that the same man *mōlēl bĕraglāw*, "speaks with his feet," a derogatory reference to the man's actions which metaphorically speak. [7] In the same vein, one of the things which is an abomination and hated by YHWH is *lĕšôn šāqer*, "lying tongue," v 17. The expression *yāpîāḥ kĕzābîm ʿēd šāqer*, "a false witness who breathes out lies," in v 19 relates directly to speech.

While there is no exact lexical parallel among all the above references to speech, one recognizes a similarity in the importance attached to

---

[6] See Prov 12:13; 18:7; 20:25; for similar expressions about being "ensnared," *yāqōš*, by what one says.

[7] The expression *mōlēl bĕraglāw* in v 13 which is translated by the RSV as "scrapes with his feet," literally means "speaks with his feet." BDB, 576, lists *mōlēl* as a verbal derivation of *mĕlîlâ*, "ear of wheat," meaning "rub," "scrape." But Prov 6:13 is the only example where *mll* as a verb appears in the Hebrew Bible. Given the emphasis on speech in vv 1–19, the expression *mōlēl bĕraglāw* is best understood as a metaphor meaning that the worthless man's actions *vis á vis* his feet bespeak his character. Along with the expressions *qōrēṣ bĕʿēnāw*,"winks with his eyes," and *mōreh bĕʾeṣbĕʿōtāyw*, "points with his fingers," *mōlēl bĕraglāw* "speaks with his feet," is understood in the sense of sending non-verbal signals which amount to unspoken language. See W. O. E. Oesterley, *Proverbs*, 42: "*speaketh*. This is the lit. meaning of the Hebr. word, and is better than the R.V. marg. 'shuffleth' . . . . The expression denotes insincerity, the movement or 'language' of the feet indicating something different from that uttered by the tongue." Cf. D. G. Wildeboer, *Die Sprüche*, 19: "מֹלֵל deutet. wörtl. redet, Part. Kal bei Pi. מְלֵל, wie auch דֹבֵר neben דִּבֶּר. . . . 'Mit den Füssen reden ist ein Ausdruck der Zeichensprache, um die Falscheit anzudeuten." W. O. E. Oesterley, *Proverbs*, 42: "*maketh signs* . . . Here again there is reference to the language of signs."

speech and actions which speak. The "son's" fate is determined directly by what he says. Moreover, the charactêr of the "man" is manifested by speech or actions which speak.

The topic of speech is not the only link between vv 1–5 and the remaining verses in 6:6–19. In v 4 the parent further admonishes the son by saying *ʾal tittēn šēnâ lĕˤêneykā ûtenûmâ lĕˤapˤappeykā*, "give your eyes no sleep or slumber to your eyelids." Because involvement in a surety is so potentially damaging, the son must put aside even sleep until he has extricated himself from the surety. The demand of the moment is to act. The necessity to act quickly is conveyed by the imperative *ʾal tittēn*. [8]

Sleep vocabulary reappears in v 10, the section addressed to the sluggard. Similar to the message addressed to the son, the parent admonishes the *ˤāṣēl*, "sluggard," to avoid sleeping. Where the parent says to the son in v 4: *ʾal tittēn šēnâ lĕˤêneykā ûtenûmâ lĕˤapˤapeykā*, "give your eyes no sleep or slumber to your eyelids," in vv 9–10 the parent questions how long the sluggard will continue sleeping: *ˤad mātay ˤāṣēl tiškāb mātay tāqûm miššĕnātekā mĕˤaṭ šēnôt mĕˤaṭ tĕnûmôt mĕˤaṭ ḥibbuq yādayim liškāb*, "How long will you lie there, O sluggard? When will arise from your sleep? A little sleep, a little slumber, a little folding of the hands to rest." [9] The sleep motif adds to the lexical and thematic links between vv 1–5 and vv 6–11.

Other connections can be noted. The parent commands both the son and the sluggard, *lēk*, "go," in v 3c and v 6a. The imagery of the hand, *yād*, plays a role in both vv 1–5 and vv 6–11 in conjunction with a metaphorical appeal to wildlife and an insect. The son is commanded to save himself "like a gazelle from the hand," *miyyād*, "and like a bird from the hand of the fowler," *miyyād yāqûš*, v 5. [10] The reference to the

---

[8] Cf. F. Delitzsch, *Proverbs*, 138: "The immediateness lying in לְךָ . . . is now expressed as a duty, ver. 4f. One must not sleep and slumber . . , not give himself quietness and rest, till the other has released him from his bail by the performance of that for which he is a surety."

[9] See C. Rabin, " מעט חבק ידים לשכב (Proverbs vi, 10; xxiv, 33)," *JJS*, 1 (1949) 198, where he offers this translation: "A little sleep, a little slumber, a little to lie down with hands folded." F. Delitzsch (*Proverbs*, 141) attributes the words in v 10 to the sluggard: "The words, ver. 10, are not an ironical call (sleep only a little while, but in truth a long while), but *per mimesin* the reply of the sluggard with which he turns away the unwelcome disturber. The plurals with מעט sound like self-delusion: yet a little, but a sufficient!" Cf. C. H. Toy, *Proverbs*, 124, where he also suggests that v 10 contains the quoted reply of the sluggard. There is no indication, however, that one should read v 10 as a quotation. Delitzsch's argument would be more credible if there were a *verbum dicendi* or some other nominal indicating speech.

[10] Prov 6:5 reads: *hinnāṣēl kiṣĕbî miyyād ûkĕsippôr miyyād yāqûš*, "save yourself like a gazelle from the hand, like a bird from the hand of the fowler" (my translation). The

gazelle/bird is immediately followed by a reference to the ant. In vv 6–11 the parent appeals to the feature of the *nĕmāla*, "ant," which, like a gazelle/bird in v 5, provides the analogical model for the sluggard's well being. The parent warns the sluggard that to choose *mĕ⁽aṭ ḥibbuq yādayim*, "a little folding of the hands," v 10, leads ultimately to *rē⁾šekā* "your poverty" and *ûmaḥsōrĕkā* "and your want" in v 11. To avoid the "hand," v 5, a synecdoche for a "man," the son must avoid sleep until he is released from the surety. Folding of the "hands" which signifies sleep in v 11 has the potential of leading the sluggard into upcoming privation and want which arrives as a "traveller" and an "armed man", v 11. There is not so much an evolving sense of contrast between the son caught in a surety and the slothfulness of the sluggard as there is an emerging similarity in outcome for both. Both involvement in a surety and slothfulness potentially entraps the son or sluggard with someone else who has power over them.

Furthermore, attention to work and agricultural planning for lean times in vv 6–11 saves one from want and privation which comes as a "traveller"/"armed man." As such, the theme of sleep supplies more than just a neat link between vv 1–5, the lesson on surety, and vv 6–11, the lesson about obtaining stores of food. The lexical and thematic integration of an account concerning surety/taking a pledge with the warning to the sluggard concerning possible agricultural privation suggests a mutual connection between the opening two units in Proverbs

---

expression *miyyād* in v 5a is a problem. Scholars generally emend the reference *yād*, "hand," to specify "hunter" or "trap." For example: O. Plöger, *Sprüche Salomos*, 61: "Lies: מִצַּיָּד statt des einfachen מִיָּד ("aus der Hand")." W. McKane, *Proverbs*, 323: "In v. 5, the emendation of *yād* to *ṣayyād*, 'hunter', is a smaller alteration than *māṣod*, 'net' (cf. LXX ἐκ βρόχων 'from meshes [of the net]')." C. H. Toy, *Proverbs*, 129–130: "מיד, here impossible . . here we must either supply a word, as צַיָּד . . . or פֹּ . . . ." W. O. E. Oesterley, *Proverbs*, 40: "*from the hand.* A textual error . . . ; read 'out of a snare' (מִפַּח)." B. Gemser, *Sprüche Salomos*, 38: "aus dem Netz." R. B. Y. Scott, *Proverbs*, 56: "[Until you] escape like a gazelle from a hunter's hand . . . ." H. Ringgren and W. Zimmerli, *Sprüche/Prediger*, 31: "Entweder hat *jad*, "Hand", hier eine sonst nicht belegte Spezialbedeutung "Falle", "Netz" . . . Oder ist *sajjad*, "Jäger", zu lesen?" H. Wiesmann, "Das Buch der Sprüche. Kap 6, 1–19," 243: "Das alleinstehende מיד ist gewiss unrichtig; die alten Übersetzungen ausser Vulg. (= de manu) geben den Begriff פֹּה oder מצוֹר . . . wieder." D. G. Wildeboer, *Die Sprüche*, 18, who reads as מִצַּיָּד. But any emendation for *miyyād* in v 5a is a retrojection from the LXX to a non-extant Hebrew *Vorlage*. We will argue later that the combination of "surety" and "hand" is a deliberate play upon Gen 43:9 where Judah says: *⁾ānōkî ⁾e⁽erbennû miyyādî tĕbaqšennû*, "I will be surety for him; from my hand you shall require him." Thus, while we recognize the unusual expression *miyyād* in Prov 6:5, we retain the MT without emendation. To emend the text has the disadvantage of covering over one of the unique expressions in Prov 6:1–5 which achieves a potential inner-biblical link.

6. The failure to extricate himself immediately from a surety potentially traps the son in an unwanted social tangle with someone else—i.e. the metaphorical "hand"/"hand of the fowler," v 5. Likewise, the sluggard who fails to model himself upon the industrious ant will meet poverty and want which comes personified as a "traveller"/"armed man." A clear warning about undesirable social entanglements characterizes both discourse units in vv 1–5 and vv 6–11.

The third discourse unit, vv 12–15, also links up with the surrounding sections by means of shared vocabulary and point of view. Where both vv 1–5 and vv 6–11 end with reference to an anonymous "man" whom the son and sluggard are warned about, v 12, the first verse in the third discourse unit, begins with reference to characteristics of a thoroughly undesirable "man:" *ʾādām bĕliyyaʿal ʾîs ʾāwen hôlēk ʿiqqĕšût peh*, "a worthless man, a wicked man, goes about with crooked speech." The expression *ʾîš ʾāwen*, "wicked man" who *hôlēk* (*hlk*) "goes about" in v 12 echoes the *mehallēk* (*hlk*) "traveller" and *ʾîš māgēn*, "armed man," in v 11, thus providing another lexical and topical link between the second and third sections. [11]

The reference to *peh*, "mouth," in v 12 recalls a similar reference in v 1ab. *yād*, "hand," appears again in v 17 (cf. v 5, 10). As part of the sevenfold graduated numerical saying, *yād*, in v 17b, forms part of the third thing that YHWH hates: *wĕyādayim šōpĕkôt dām nāqî*, "and hands shedding innocent blood," an expression very similar to Prov 1:16. The reference to avoiding the "hand" in v 5 now receives further specification because from the "hands" of a man comes potential shedding of innocent blood, *yādayim šōpĕkôt dām nāqî*.

---

[11] Prov 6:11: *ûbāʾ kimhallēk rēʾšekā ûmaḥsorĕkā kĕʾîš māgēn*, "and poverty will come upon you as a traveller, and want as an armed man." The RSV's translation of *mĕhallēk* as "vagabond," is possible but not necessarily the best translation of an otherwise common expression *mĕhallēk* in the Hebrew Bible. The root of *mĕhallēk* is *hlk*, meaning "to go," "to travel" without the added connotation carried by "vagabond." See: *BDB*, 235. The expression *ʾîš māgēn*, "armed man," (RSV) adds to the difficulty of translating v 11. McKane, *Proverbs*, 324–325, asserts: "The simile in v. 11 is transparent, despite the uncertainty which attaches to the meaning *māgēn*." McKane translates *māgēn* as *mōgēn* or *maggān* based on the Ugaritic *mgn* meaning "beggar." Even though McKane recognizes the difficulty in the expression *ʾîš māgēn*, he interprets the otherwise common expression *mĕhallēk* in an uncommon fashion as "vagrant" based on a Ugaritic parallel. As McKane, *Proverbs*, 324–325, says: *mĕhallēk* has the pejorative nuance of 'vagrant'. . . , or of the word 'tinker', which on the lips of a farmer in Scotland is often associated with a possible threat to property." The general meaning of the text seems to be that "poverty" and "want" will come upon the slothful as an outsider, i.e., as a "traveller"/"armed man" would take away the provisions of a person.

The expression *qōrēṣ běʿênāw*, "winks with his eyes," is one of the characteristics of the "worthless" and "wicked man" in vv 12–13. Earlier reference was made to *lěʿêneykā*, "your eyes," v 4, where the son is admonished not to go to sleep. Again in v 17a the expression *ʿênayim rāmôt*, "haughty eyes," appears as one of the seven things hated by YHWH.

ḥōrēš rāʿ in v 14a translated as "cultivating evil," continues the agricultural theme found in vv 6–11 and complements the parallel agricultural expression *midānîm yěšallēaḥ*, "sowing discord" in v 14b. [12] In v 19 the combination of *šlḥ* + *mědānîm* again appears. A contrast is struck between vv 6–11 and vv 12–15. [13] Where the parent admonishes the son to use the ant as a model for cultivating/harvesting food, the "worthless man" cultivates evil and sows discords.

Besides lexical and thematic connections between vv 1–11 and vv 12–19, starting with v 12 the text shifts to the third person and concentrates solely on the identifying characteristics of "a man." The narrowing of focus in content for vv 12–19 leads Delitzsch to argue that vv 12–15 and vv 16–19 are not really two discourse units but one. [14] We can build on Delitzsch's analysis by arguing that there is a common focus that emerges in vv 1–19 as a whole. The shift to the third person descriptive speech in vv 12ff adds to the strategy of the parent who now calls attention to a particular "man." The previous warnings in vv 1–5 and vv 6–11 against involvement with someone else gains clarity and precision by the identification of a worthless man. Moreover, one detects in vv 16–19 a tightening of the structure which culminates in v 19. In vv 12–15 the random references to body parts such as *peh*, "mouth," *ʿênayim*, "eyes," *raglayim*, "feet," *ʾeṣbaʿ*, "finger," *lēb*, "heart," are combined with *ʾîš*/*ʾādām*, "a man," in order to characterize the "man." Body parts are inseparable from the "man."

---

[12] See W. McKane, *Proverbs*, 326, who favors translating *ḥrš* as "cultivate:" "The metaphor is then based on farming and not craftsmanship." Cf. F. Delitzsch, *Proverbs*, 145, who recognizes the agricultural reference underlying *ḥrš*.

[13] There is a textual problem in v 14 *midānîm* and v 19 *mědānîm*, both translated as "strife." While both forms derive from the root *dîn*, *midānîm* in v 14 is anomalous. The *qere* offers *midyānîm*. The same form as the *qere* appears once again in 18:18 and as a construct in 19:13. As for the form *mědānîm*, it appears once in Prov 10:12 translated as "strife" and again in Gen 37:36 as the gentilic "Midianites."

[14] *Proverbs*, 146: "What now follows is not a separate section . . . , but corroborative continuation of that which precedes. The last word (מדנים, strife) before the threatening punishment, 14b, is also here the last. The thought that no vice is a greater abomination to God than the (in fact satanical) striving to set men at variance who love one another, clothes itself in the form of the numerical proverb . . . ."

By contrast, in vv 16–19 the random body parts receive isolated attention apart from reference to the "man." Cast in the form of a graduated numerical saying, vv 16–19 list a surprising number of corresponding features with vv 12–15. While in some cases the expressions are not exactly the same, we can offer a close approximation in our lexical comparison of vv 16–19 and vv 12–15 on the basis of the five body parts listed in each unit.

v 17	*ʿênayim rāmôt* "haughty eyes"	v 13	*qōrēṣ bĕʿênāw* "winks with his eyes"
v 17	*lĕšôn šāqer* "lying tongue"	v 12	*ʿiqqĕšût peh* "crooked speech"
v 17	*wĕyādayim šōpĕkôt dām nāqî* "and hands that shed innocent blood"	v 13	*mōreh bĕʾeṣbĕʿōtāyw* "he points with his finger"
v 18	*lēb ḥōrēš maḥšĕbôt ʾāwen* "a heart that cultivates wicked plans"	v 14	*tahpukôt bĕlibbo ḥōrēš rāʿ* "with perverted heart he cultivates evil"
v 18	*raglayim mĕmāharôt lārûṣ lārāʿâ* "feet that make haste to run to evil"	v 13	*mōlēl bĕraglāw* "he speaks with his feet"

The emphasis solely on parts of the body in vv 16–18 adds to the intensifying effect of the graduated numerical saying. By literally moving from top to bottom, i.e., from the eyes to the feet in vv 17–18, the narrator ends up with a whole man in v 19: *ûmĕšallēaḥ mĕdānîm bên ʾaḥîm*, "and a man who sows discord among brothers"—the ultimate abomination.[15] The expression *ûmĕšallēaḥ mĕdānîm* in v 19 appears also in v 14, *midānîm yĕšallēaḥ*. Only now in v 19 the text specifies exactly the familial context of *ʾaḥîm*, "brothers"—something not done in vv 12–15 but alluded to earlier in 6:1–5. The five references to body parts in vv 12–14 has a corresponding list to five body parts in vv 17–18. But now the parent in vv 16–19 enlists the potential evil that attaches to parts of the body listed in vv 12–14 in order to give crystal clarity to the truly abominable man in v 19.

Besides the editorial interconnections between vv 1–5 and vv 6–11, scholars note how vv 6–11 present vocabulary, topics, and whole sections which are unique only to the book of Proverbs. For example, the

---

15 W. Roth, *Numerical Sayings*, 86, says the following about the structure of vv 16–19: "The list enumerates seven sins, the first five being connected with one organ of the body respectively (eye, tongue, hand, heart, feet) and all reflecting a prophetic concept of 'abomination'. . . . The abominations listed here are selected in order to mark out the ethically evil man."

only other place where the "ant," *nĕmālâ*, is mentioned in the Hebrew Bible is in Prov 30:24–28, a graduated numerical saying. Like Prov 6:6–11, 30:24–25 associates *ḥkm*, "wisdom," with the *nĕmālâ*, "ant," on the basis of its ability to provide food in lean times: *ʾarbāʿâ hēm qĕṭannê ʾāreṣ wĕhēmmâ ḥăkāmîm mĕḥukāmîm hannĕmālîm ʿām lōʾ ʿāz wayyākînû baqqayiṣ laḥmām*, "Four things on earth are small, but they are exceedingly wise: the ants are a people not strong, yet they provide their food in the summer," i.e., in a period of potential want before the harvest. Prov 6:6–7, however, refers to the ant in the singular unlike 30:25. Also, Prov 6:7 adds *ʾăšer ʾên lāh qāṣîn šōṭēr ûmōšēl*, "without having any chief, officer, or ruler," emphasizing the ant's ability to provide food for itself without overseers. Nothing is said of the *ʿāṣēl*, "sluggard," in 30:24–28. If there is any common ground between the "ant" and the "sluggard" in the traditions within the book of Proverbs, it is the agricultural context as found in 6:6–11. The common ground can be seen when we look at references to the *ʿāṣēl* elsewhere in the book of Proverbs.

Like the reference to the "ant," the reference to the *ʿāṣēl*, "sluggard," is also unique to the book of Proverbs. [16] In a number of cases the reference to the sluggard is teamed up with agricultural imagery and sleep as in 6:6–11. For example:

19:15 *ʿaṣlâ tappîl tardēmâ wĕnepeš rĕmiyyâ tirʿāb*
"Slothfulness casts into a deep sleep, and an idle person will suffer hunger."

20:4 *mēhōrep ʿāṣēl lōʾ yaḥărōš yĕšāʾal baqqāṣîr wāʾāyin*
"The sluggard does not plow in the autumn; he will seek at harvest and have nothing."

24:30–34 (30) *ʿal śĕdēh ʾîš ʿāṣēl ʿăbartî wĕʿal kerem ʾādām ḥăsar lēb*

(31) *wĕhinnēh ʿālâ kullô qimmĕśōnîm kāssû pānāyw ḥărullîm wĕgeder ʾăbānāyw neḥĕrāsâ*

(32) *wăʾehĕzeh ʾānōkî ʾāšît libbî rāʾîtî lāqaḥtî mûsār*

(33) *mĕʿaṭ šēnôt mĕʿaṭ tĕnûmôt mĕʿaṭ ḥibbuq yādayim liškāb*

(34) *ûbāʾ mithallēk rēšekā ûmaḥsōreykā kĕʾîš māgēn*

(30) "I passed by the field of a sluggard, by the vineyard of a man without sense;

(31) and lo, it was all overgrown with thorns; the ground was covered with nettles, and its stone wall was broken down.

(32) Then I saw it and considered it; I looked and received instruction.

---

[16] Prov 6:6, 9; 10:26; 13:4; 15:19; 19:15, 24; 20:4; 21:25; 22:13; 24:30; 26:13, 14, 16; 31:27. Cf. C. H. Toy, *Proverbs*, 123: "The term *sluggard* appears to belong to the parenetic vocabulary of the OT.; it occurs only in the book of Proverbs."

(33) A little sleep, a little slumber, a little folding of the hands to rest,

(34) and your poverty will come upon you like a robber, and your want like an armed man."

26:14 *haddelet tissôb ʿal ṣîrāh wĕʾaṣēl ʿal miṭṭātô*

"As a door turns on its hinges, so does a sluggard on his bed."

Commentators recognize the striking similarities, if not exact duplication, between portions of 6:6–11, on the one hand, and 30:24–25, (the "ant") and 24:33–34 (the "sluggard"), on the other hand. [17] The problem of deciding whether there is a case of borrowing between these texts is difficult to solve. As Toy indicates, the similarities between 6:6–11; 30:24–25; 24:33–34 may well be explained by positing a now lost documentary source which was tapped by all three examples. [18] Whatever the case, a decision now concerning the history of 6:6–11 is not crucial for our analysis. It is clear that because Prov 6:6–11 reflects themes found only in the book of Proverbs we can turn to other texts to help in our interpretation of 6:6–11 and its relationship with 6:1–5. Specifically, the juxtaposition of the ant and the sluggard on the basis of an agricultural motif found only in 6:6–11 is further clarified by the other references to the ant and sluggard in the book of Proverbs.

Our intent in the above paragraphs is to isolate the various compositional features which unify vv 1–19. We agree with those scholars who argue that vv 1–19 appear to be a combination of four unrelated units. However, the text *as it now stands* presents a number of clues which suggest that editors combined independent units of tradition

---

[17] See: F. Delitzsch, *Proverbs*, 142; W. O. E. Oesterley, *Proverbs*, 41; R. B. Y. Scott, *Proverbs*, 58–59; O. Plöger, *Sprüche Salomos*, 64; W. Nowack, *Die Sprüche Salomo's*, 41; H. Ringgren and W. Zimmerli, *Sprüche/Prediger*, 32; B. Gemser, *Sprüche Salomos*, 39; A. Barucq, *Le Livre des Proverbes*, 79.

[18] C. H. Toy, *Proverbs*, 122: "The example of the ant is adduced, and the sluggard warned that poverty will overtake him. The tone is perhaps satirical; the passage is a specimen of the popular teaching of the sages.—The parallel passage, 24:30–34, does not adduce the ant, but describes the neglected condition of the sluggard's field, and has the same conclusion as our section: 24:33. 34 = lit. 6:10. 11. The two paragraphs are variations on the same theme; both have taken the ending from the same source (some familiar expression, or some earlier collection of aphorisms, now lost), or one has borrowed from the other. In either case our passage has a clearer unity than that of ch. 24, in which our v. 9 must be introduced before v. 33 in order to connect the conclusion with what precedes. . . . Obviously our section does not belong in its present place, though when and how it was misplaced we cannot say; the change was made early, since the Versions here accord with the Hebrew."

to form an integrated discourse. The isolation of common diction and topics represents an editorial strategy found elsewhere in the Hebrew Bible. Contrary to Murphy's assessment that there is no connection between the four units at hand, we detect many lexical and thematic features which indicate an emerging logic to the compositional content for Prov 6:1–19. Similarly, Delitzsch's comment that we can account for the union of the units on the basis of "accidental points of contact" fails to recognize that once united accidental points of contact give way to a verbal and thematic web of lexical associations which generate "meaning." The text reads now not as a disjointed hodgepodge but as a potentially meaningful didactic unit.

PROV 6:1–19: MIMETIC REPRESENTATION
BY MEANS OF ACTIONAL AND DESCRIPTIVE SPEECH.

Introduction

In the previous section we offered an analysis of Prov 6:1–19 which concentrates on the composition of these verses in terms of various editorial devices. Whatever the earlier context was for the four discourse units, we can speak of a degree of cohesiveness within the text as it now stands.

Along with the issue of internal editorial composition we can add the strategy of the editor who couches his/her discourse in the framework of direct speech. Stratified levels of speech is another example of how direct discourse implies the broader inner-biblical associations of traditions and speech *via* dialogic relationships. By concentrating on the parent's discourse we will carry our argument beyond the internal traces of composition to argue for a larger inner-biblical reading on the basis of the discourse found in 6:1–19. In our earlier examples of Prov 1:8–19 and 1:20–33 we saw the importance attached to the combination of different levels of direct discourse which are set off either by a *verbum dicendi* or by nominals used to introduce speech. The isolation of speech within speech allows us to posit examples of inner-biblical interpretation based on otherwise unrelated discourse examples found elsewhere in the Hebrew Bible.

For our example from Prov 6:1–19, however, there is no single example of a similar use of a *verbum dicendi* or nominal which serves to introduce another discourse level. Instead, Prov 6:1–19 preserves a number of descriptive references concerning the act of speech along with a number of other descriptive references to action which are framed in the direct discourse of the parent. For example, and by way of contrast, the parent in Prov 1:10 introduces his/her discourse with a conditional particle, "My son, if sinners entice you. . . ." which serves to introduce further the sinners' speech, "if they say. . . ," in v 11f. M. Bakhtin's assertion that "conditional discourse [set in a larger context of speech-events] is always double-voiced discourse,"[19] is born out well by the conditional format of Prov 1:8–19. Speech from Genesis 37 appears in a refracted form in the parent's discourse and the "sinners'" quoted words.

In Prov 6:1–2 the parent again addresses the son in conditional discourse, "My son, if you have become surety for your companion. . . if you are snared by the words of your mouth. . . ." As much as the conditional particle and the expression referring to "the words of your mouth" invites a potential quotation of the son's words, a tactic assumed by the parent in 5:12–14, the parent instead continues admonishing the son as to how he should act in vv 3–5. The parent's words are packed with imperatives related to expressive action: *ʿăśēh zōʾt*, "do this," *hinnāṣēl*, "save yourself," *lēk*, "go," *hitrappēs*, "hasten," *rĕhab* "importune," *ʾal tittēn*, "do not give," and, a second time, *hinnāṣēl*, "save yourself."

Emphasis upon expressive action dominates the content of Prov 6:1–19 to such an extent that any possibility of double-voiced discourse seems to give way to the monologue of the parent. As the son is admonished to act in vv 3–5 so is the sluggard in vv 6–11. Moreover, the rationale for holding together the four discourse units seems to be strained by the odd combination of the direct discourse of the parent addressed to the son and sluggard in vv 1–11 which abruptly shifts to describe a "man" by means of a random listing of expressive action in vv 12–15 and by a graduated numerical saying in vv 16–19. We will argue, however, that the combination of parental discourse and descriptive third person speech is not as odd as it appears once we recognize that the rationale for the whole of Prov 6:1–19 lies in its mimetic representation of events drawn from portions of the Joseph story. By alluding to earlier events from the Joseph story, the parent's didactic lesson represents another example of how content unique to the book of Proverbs is conjoined to other traditions within the Hebrew Bible by means of discourse. One hears, as a result, not only the words of the parent but also one hears in the background the words of the ancestors from Israel's past.

In order to perceive how the combination of different modes of speech achieves mimetic representation of earlier events from Israel's history we will return to Sternberg to see how different forms of discourse imply the speech and identity of another person. How these

---

[19] *Problems of Dostoevsky's Poetics*, 190.

verses construe "meaning" by imaging earlier events involving Judah and his brothers depends upon the order and content of the parent's discourse. The combination of actional and descriptive discourse in Prov 6:1–19 further illustrates inner-biblical interpretation.

Action and Description: Quoting the Unspoken

In an article entitled "Ordering the Unordered: Time, Space, and Descriptive Coherence," [20] Sternberg addresses the problem of whether or not we can speak of a "principle of coherence" in any random listing of descriptive features pertaining to places, objects, and people. Because Prov 6:1–19 combines together separate discourse units which likewise utilize a random listing of expressive body parts to describe an anonymous "man," Sternberg's article has direct bearing on our interpretation of these verses.

In contrast to actional discourse which establishes a principle of coherence "according to the logic of progression inherent in the line or chain of events itself; from earlier to later and from cause to effect," [21] the presence of random ordering in descriptive discourse lacks a requisite beginning, middle, and end. [22] As one example of descriptive writing that focuses on "static entities," Sternberg cites the opening passage from Charles Dickens' *A Tale of Two Cities*:

> It was the best of time, it was the worst of time, it was the age of wisdom, it
> was the age of foolishness, it was the epoch of belief, it was the epoch of

---

[20] *Yale French Studies*, 61 (1981) 60–88.

[21] "Ordering the Unordered," 61.

[22] "Ordering the Unordered," 60: "In pictorial discourse, where both the represented object and the representational medium distinctively extend in space, the sequential problems of beginning, middle and end relate less to the structure of the finished product than to the accidentals of its genesis. Objective temporality (say, the 'pregnant moment') is here neither mandatory nor dominant but subdued, and the aspirations to the condition of narrative, exceptional and indeed rare; whereas actional discourse, whether literary or historical or cinematic, presupposes temporal extension in both object (the series of events unfolded) and medium (the series of signs unfolding them). The temporality common to the action and its rendering and reading does invest all questions of sequence with prime significance, structural as well as genetic, and does invite no end of ordering manipulations. But, again, it also provides a natural principle of coherence, one that enables the narrator to construct his presentational sequence (and the reader to re-construct that sequence, however chronologically deformed) according to the logic of progression inherent in the line or chain of events itself; from earlier to later and from cause to effect."

incredulity, it was the season of Light, it was the season of Darkness, it was the spring of hope, it was the winter of despair. [23]

Sternberg argues that the descriptive elements in Dickens' passage hang together only "by virtue of their coexistence within a common frame of reference . . . that serves to integrate them," i.e., they appear within a larger narrative context. [24] Unlike a chain of reported events which move from cause to effect, there is nothing inherent in the "static entities" themselves which could hinder the production of another order of the same elements along lines either of coexistence or contiguousness. Because a sense not only of time but also of an inherent reason for its particular order is missing in Dickens' passage and in other similar passages cited by Sternberg, juxtaposed items in themselves leave Sternberg to question why one item should precede another and why a list starts and ends where it does. Moreover, Sternberg raises the question of whether or not a seemingly random list of static objects can reflect a larger narrative pattern.

Sternberg goes so far as to argue that even such things as analogous features, similarities, and correspondences in a descriptive list of a spatial object do not offer an explanation for a particular ordering. If anything, similarity and contiguity such as in Dickens' passage serve only to limit the descriptive range of possibilities. [25] Any explanation that posits an inherent quality to a random spatial series fails to recognize that such a series floats without any sense of progression or meaning. According to Sternberg, one way that we can account for a "natural line of progression" for the description of a spatial object is to "postulate some extrinsic *point(s) of reference*" of which could be an established narrative sequence or the narrated description of a character's action and speech.[26]

The remainder of Sternberg's article is devoted to examples of what he terms "the various ordering mechanisms imposed on spatial existence."[27] Chiefly significant for us, however, is how Sternberg perceives the complementary function of "action" discourse and "description" discourse. "Action" discourse and "description" discourse

---

[23] "Ordering the Unordered," 62.
[24] "Ordering the Unordered," 62.
[25] As Sternberg says: "By themselves, in short, the principles of similarity and contiguity serve throughout the reading-process less to prepare and account for the emergence of descriptive items in a certain order than to narrow down the range of ordering possibilities into a determinate, more or less closed set"("Ordering the Unordered," 69).
[26] "Ordering the Unordered," 69.
[27] "Ordering the Unordered," 70.

are not mutually exclusive ways of communicating in a narrative context. Instead, they are facets of the same communicative process whereby a text projects its own point of view. Whether one is reading discourse dominated by either "action" or "description," each communicative strategy presupposes the other as being an element of discourse.[28]

In short, a person or event can be alluded to not only by playing upon a character's speech but also by ordering a series of actions which reflect a similar chain of events from the past. An element of complementarity is discernible between active and descriptive discourse to the degree that each form of discourse can represent various identifying features of the same state of affairs, event, or person.[29] The choice of portraying a person, for example, along lines of actional discourse or discourse geared to description lies with the strategy of the narrator. Whatever a narrator's motive for utilizing actional or

---

[28] "Ordering the Unordered," 72–73: "Actional mimesis presupposes a descriptive element, however implicit or even camouflaged. For each component event is located in space as well as in time; and each speech-event, from authorial statement to figural dialogue, also abounds in references to features and entities that coexist within the speaker's world: to persons and things, properties and relations, topographical details and psychological conditions, local or temporary states of affairs and canons of probability governing reality as a whole. So the represented action that synthesizes these events not only take place but make place, not only changes and moves existents but portrays existence. Its very development through time unfolds and populates and realizes for us the work's spatial arena with its assorted static dimensions and configurations. Indeed, the point of the action itself may largely consist in spatial representation, its dynamics so manipulated as to enable the author to specify or encompass as much as possible of his world's fixtures."

[29] "As already indicated, the temporal development of a process at times subserves, and always entails and directs, spatial development. But the opposite also holds true in principle: the mere listing of static items may operate as a cover or shorthand for the propulsion of actional dynamics. Thus, the tripartite descriptive-looking series listed by Humbert Humbert 'A shipwreck. An atoll. Alone with a drowned passenger's shivering child' coheres as the highlights not of a melancholy seascape but of an imaginary sexcapade. Just as the equally unconcatenated series of references to sound that follows Alice's attempt to drive the White Rabbit away from the window—"she heard a little shriek and a fall, and a crash of broken glass" (*Works of Carroll*, p. 46)—makes up not a disorderly simultaneous cacophony but a minature plot, progressing by causal-chronological sequence from the intruder's panic to his landing on a cucumber-frame. In each instance, the chronological-causal mechanism offers a better integration and explanation of the facts than the merely configurative. It enables the reader to tighten the linkage of the referents beyond the limits of even the strongest nonlinear contiguity and to account for the ordering as well as the selection of information by projecting the formal statics . . . of space into the irreversible dynamics of time"("Ordering the Unordered," 73–74).

descriptive writing, far more important is the potential effect upon a reader who comes across varieties of discourse as we do in Prov 6:1–19. In these verses the parent combines together both his/her discourse about surety and slothfulness with a running description of a man who is, among other things, "worthless." However, his "worthlessness" is conveyed to us as readers not by quoting his words but by describing his actions *via* a creative play upon his body parts which in effect "speak." Moreover, as we have shown, there is clear evidence that these verses exhibit a high degree of cohesiveness whereby the parent's word about surety and slothfulness meld with the description of the "worthless" man. While Prov 6:1–19 at first glance fails to project a sense of being a coherent whole which moves from cause to effect, action to reaction, these verses still function mimetically by means of their abbreviated descriptive elements. Because "actional mimesis presupposes a descriptive element,"[30] a catena of seemingly unrelated descriptive elements thus functions as abbreviations for action which develop over a span of time. Since actional and descriptive discourse are equally mimetic, the reader is required to exercise a reading competence that allows the text to project its own lines of intra-textual and inter-textual orientation through either chronological or spatial means.

The reference to the mimetic nature of actional and descriptive discourse recalls Sternberg's analysis of quotation that we addressed in our examples from Prov 1:8–19 and 1:20–33. The mimetic nature of active and descriptive discourse also offers a complementary sequel to his argument concerning representational speech. Because the domain of mimetic representation *via* quotation ranges beyond merely a play upon someone else's speech to include expressive behavior, inner-biblical links can be established by means of a concentration upon descriptive speech.

Sternberg further argues that because quotation is representational (i.e., mimetic) "its object [i.e., the person or persons being represented] is itself a subject or manifestation of subjective experience: speech, thought, and otherwise *expressive behavior* . . . ."[31](emphasis added) Alongside the example of mimetic speech of the parent in Prov 6:1–19, we also have examples of both "thought" and "expressive behavior." That the parent can perceive the internal workings of the perverted heart that cultivates evil (see vv 14, 18) indicates more than the attributed omniscience of the parent; it serves to reveal a literary strategy which gives concrete reality to a "man" *via* a rich lexical montage. Such a lexical montage signals internal and external characteristics outside the realm of direct speech. According to Sternberg, to represent someone else one need not rely

---

[30] "Ordering the Unordered," 72.
[31] "Proteus in Quotation Land," 107.

solely on verbal quotation. Actions likewise speak and such speech is quotable. Thus Sternberg offers a corrective to the view held by some scholars that an "original message must be a 'verbal communication.'"[32] For Sternberg, the world of expression is not limited to speech, written or spoken; rather, reported discourse can tap what he calls the "three objects of quotation," that of speech, thought, and mute reality, i.e., expressive behavior.[33] In other words, "verbal messages" and "nonverbal things" each can function as mimetic representatives of character and events.

The amount of translation of action into descriptive speech is tied directly to the strategy of the reporter. Mimetic representation comes into play by how much and in what way a narrator interprets action. Whether the reporter interprets the action correctly or incorrectly is besides the point. And it is inconsequential if the originator of the expressive act meant to convey a message. The combination of a nonverbal message *and* the interpreter's translation of that message into direct speech achieves a mimetic representation of character. The two go together. Thus the recasting of someone else's discourse reminds us of both Bakhtin's and Sternberg's arguments that to quote someone else is to interfere with the other person's original message. And such interference is knowingly done for the benefit of the communicative structure of the reporter.

The difference that exists between quoting someone else's words and quoting someone's action Sternberg terms an intersemiotic transfer.[34] Nonverbal objects of representation cannot be verbally reproduced; they can only be translated into the medium of direct discourse. Sternberg says:

> The point is, in other words, that original signals constitute nonverbal objects of representation, just like any external event or internal process. . . . And as such . . , they cannot by definition be verbally reproduced. They can only be verbally represented ("imitated") as action and/or converted ("translated") into speech. In either case, moreover, owing to the discrepancy in medium there is no natural way of verbalizing these signals, neither as regards reporting form nor extent nor lexical choice, etc. The

---

[32] "Point of View," 90.

[33] "Proteus in Quotation Land," 134.

[34] M. Sternberg, "Proteus in Quotation Land," 91: ". . . The reporter here variously combines his perspective with that of reportee so as to recast . . . some signal into a direct-speech paraphrase. The difference consists in the nature of the original signal—all these being instances of intersemiotic rather than intralingual transfer. The reportees can be referred to as speakers, accordingly, only in a figurative though indeed well-established sense, by virtue of conventional metonymic shifts."

resultant quotation is, accordingly, inevitably combined with the perspective of the reporting interpreter, and the question is only one of degree.[35]

The payoff for a narrative strategy which recasts nonverbal signals into direct discourse is the way in which a narrator can telescope what would otherwise be lengthy story sequences into a few words. A well-chosen word or phrase being representational of action can allude to a whole series of events for an attentive reader.[36] The conciseness that is achieved through the translation of acts into representative speech allows the narrator to achieve a level of "perspective interplay" that would otherwise be difficult to carry out in other forms of quotation.[37] The usefulness of Sternberg's analysis of descriptive discourse which literally quotes action becomes evident when we look once again at the content of Prov 6:1–19. In the two earlier examples in Prov 1:8–19 and 1:20–33, the inner-biblical links were established mainly on how earlier discourse from Genesis 37, Jeremiah 7 and 20 was recontextualized. For Prov 6:1–19, however, the bridge between vv 1–19 and portions of Genesis is formed on the basis of earlier action echoed by means of combined allusive imagery.[38] Because Prov 6:1–19 represents portions of

---

[35] "Point of View," 92.

[36] See W. Iser, *The Act of Reading, A Theory of Aesthetic Response*, (Baltimore/London: The John Hopkins University Press, 1980) 53–85, esp. pp 79–81, for his discussion of the importance of a repertoire of a literary work and the function of "literary allusion" which situates a text and a reader in familiar territory. For Iser, various elements quoted from familiar literary traditions offer a reader orientation points which add to meaning. See p. 79 where Iser speaks briefly of quotation. Unlike Sternberg, however, Iser does not provide a detailed discussion of the function of quotation or the various ways a narrator can quote.

[37] "Point of View," 92–93.

[38] See M. Bakhtin, *Problems of Dostoevsky's Poetics*, 195 where he speaks of double-voiced discourse which does not play upon the words of someone else but where the implied speech is imaged in the allusive discourse of a reporter: "In both stylization and parody, that is, in both of the preceding varieties of the third type, the author makes use precisely of other people's words for the expression of his own particular intentions. In the third variety, the other person's discourse remains outside the limits of the author's speech, but the author's speech takes it into account and refers to it. Another's discourse in this case is not reproduced with a new intention, but it acts upon, influences, and in one way or another determines the author's discourse, while itself remaining outside it. Such is the nature of discourse in the hidden polemic, and in most cases in the rejoinder of a dialogue as well. . . . The other's discourse is not itself reproduced, it is merely implied, but the entire structure of speech would be completely different if there were not this reaction to another person's implied words." See also V. N. Volosinov, "Reported Speech," in *Readings in Russian Poetics: Formalist and Structuralist Views*, ed. by L. Matejka and K. Pomorska

the Joseph story *via* descriptive speech which alludes to earlier traditions, we will appeal both to shared vocabulary and descriptive speech to establish inner-biblical points of contact as we did for Prov 1:1–19 and 1:20–33. These verses, we are arguing, imply events (i.e., the action) in the Joseph story concerning Judah's role both in the selling of Joseph and in the surety for Benjamin.

Prov 6:1–19 and Judah's Role in the Joseph Story.

Scholars have long recognized the central role that Judah plays in the fate of Joseph and his brothers. J. Ackerman notes that Judah plays "*the* key role in catalyzing the reconciliation between brothers."[39] Judah is also the "spokesman and leader" of the brothers.[40] G. Savran states that Judah is the "ringleader in the plot against Joseph in 37:26."[41] According to Savran, Judah's speech in Gen 44:18–34 is the second longest narration by a biblical character indicating the central role that Judah plays in the Joseph story.[42] R. Alter concludes that "since he [Judah] was the one who proposed selling Joseph into slavery instead of killing him (Gen. 37:26–27), he can be thought of as the leader of the brothers in the deception practiced on their father."[43] Lastly, E. Good also recognizes the role of "central actor" that Judah plays elsewhere in the Joseph story: "There are two earlier incidents in which Judah is a central actor: the selling of

---

(Ann Arbor, Michigan: Michigan Slavic Studies, 1978) 167 where he discusses the aspect of how an image of a character is formed by means of his/her thinking, speaking, and by mannerisms which imply speech.

[39] "Joseph, Judah, and Jacob," 99.

[40] "Joseph, Judah, and Jacob," 103.

[41] "The Character as Narrator in Biblical Narrative," 8.

[42] "The Character as Narrator," 3. The longest speech in the Hebrew Bible is by Abraham's servant in Gen 24:34–49. As Savran says: "From among all the instances of characters retelling the past, two texts stand out as exceptional pieces of rhetorical art, and as the two most lengthy examples of narration by a character in biblical narrative. In Gen. 24:34–49 Abraham's anonymous servant recounts to Laban his master's charge to bring back a wife for Isaac, and the ensuing events at the well when the servant meets Rebecca. In Gen. 44:18–34, Judah reminds Joseph of the hostile encounter between the brothers and Joseph, the command to bring Benjamin down to Egypt, and Jacob's reaction to that ultimatum. . . . Where the average length of instances of narration by a character is between 2–4 verses, Abraham's servant speaks continuously for 16 verses (239 words), and Judah for 17 verses (218 words)."

[43] *The Art of Biblical Narrative*, (New York: Basic Books, Inc., 1981) 10.

Joseph into captivity (37:18–35) and the sordid affair with Tamar (ch. 38)"[44]

Only a few scholars have noted another aspect of Judah's role in the Joseph story. Judah stands out in the Hebrew Bible as the only one who provides surety for someone else.[45] In this case, Judah gives himself as surety for Benjamin in Genesis 43. An awareness of his unique role in providing surety for Benjamin helps us to take a fresh look at how a particularly knotty problem in Prov 6:1 can best be explained by positing an inner-biblical link between Genesis and Proverbs. Specifically, the fact that *lĕrēʿekā*, "for your neighbor" stands in parallel with *lazzār*, "for a stranger," in v 1 adds another dimension to our interpretation which takes into consideration the larger issue of "providing surety" for someone. The parent warns about the potential outcome of entering into a surety for a *rēaʿ*, "neighbor," in vv 3–5 but says nothing about the *zār*, "stranger." The tension between v 1a and v 1b needs further analysis for it has direct bearing upon how we understand Prov 6:1–19 in its larger inner-biblical context.

The Parallel Expressions lĕrēʿekā, *"for your neighbor," (RSV)*
and lazzār, *"for a stranger" in Prov 6:1–5.*

The difficulty in understanding the parent's words in 6:1 is reflected in the LXX. The LXX rendering of v 1 reflects a perceived difference between the *rēaʿ* and *zār*: *uie, ean egguēsę son philon paradōseis sen cheira echthrǭ*, "Son, if you become a surety for your friend, you will deliver your hand to an enemy." The LXX differentiates between *philon* and *echthrō*. Accordingly, to become a surety in the LXX sense one in effect

---

[44] "The 'Blessing' On Judah, Gen 49:8–12," *JBL* 82 (1963) 429.
[45] For instance, L. A. Snijders, "The Meaning of *zār*," 81, n. 40: "Evidence concerning sureties in the O.T. is scarce and its conditions are completely missing in the O.T. legislation. Yet this transaction must have been known, as appears from the application of it as an image in several prayers to God (Is. xxxviii 14, Ps. cxix 122). In the Pentateuch only the story of Judah, who stands surety for his brother Benjamin (Gen. xliii 1–14) speaks of sureties. But this is an exceptional case." C. H. Toy, *Proverbs*, 121: "Of the details of the old Heb. law of suretyship or endorsement we have no information. Besides the procedure of Judah in pledging himself for Benjamin (Gen. 43:9), and a couple of allusions to the practice (Job 17:3 [Ps] 119:122), we find in the OT., outside of Pr., only one description of a business-transaction involving personal security (Neh. 5:1–11), and this is rather of the nature of a mortgage given by a man on his children regarded as his property." W. O. E. Oesterley, *Proverbs*, 39: "The law says nothing about suretyship. A reference to it occurs in Gen xliii. 9, where Judah tells Jacob that he will be surety for Benjamin's safe return. Otherwise it is mentioned only in post-exilic literature . . . ."

hands oneself over to *kakon*, "evil men" (v 3), who are associated with *echthrǭ*, "the enemy" (v 1).[46]

The structure of the MT, which presents vv 1–2 as the protasis to the apodosis beginning in v 3, is abridged in the LXX. Such an abridgement produces a different reading for the LXX. The LXX presents the protasis in v 1a and the apodosis in v 1b. By syntactically linking *ʿārabtā lěrēʿekā*, "becoming surety for your neighbor" *tāqaʿtā lazzār kappeykā*, "striking a bargain with a stranger," in 1:1, with *bě*ʾimrê *pîkā*, "with the words of your mouth," in 1:2ab, the MT emphasizes the oral aspect of giving surety and a bargain. In the LXX, v 2 reads as a result clause with emphasis not on speech but upon *egguēsē* (= *ʿrb*), "surety."[47] The LXX reading perhaps represents an attempt to overcome a number of other difficulties in translating v 1.

For one, the combination *ʿrb* + *l* appears nowhere else in Hebrew scripture.[48] Another difficulty in the MT for 6:1, as we have noted, is the

---

[46] Cf. A. Baumgartner, *Du Livre des Proverbes*, 65: "La LXX n'pas compris que la portee du s'etendait egalement au 2d m.: elle met donc le verbe תקעת au futur et dit: (1a) ἐὰν ἐγγυήσῃ. (1b) παραδώσεις . . . . 'Si tu cautionnes ton prochain . . . .[il arrivera que] tu te seras livre a un etranger'. Mais tel n'est pas le sens du passage, qui n'etablit pas d'opposition entre רעך et זר; ces deus mots sont presque synonymous ici, et indiquent une personne quelconque, en dehors de celle qui cautionne (comp. XXVII, 2)."

[47] Cf. C. H. Toy, *Proverbs*, 129.

[48] F. Delitzsch, *Proverbs*, 135: "The phrase ל ערב is not elsewhere met with, and is thus questionable." See: G. Boström, *Proverbiastudien*, 101: ". . . 1.) wird für Jemanden bürgen im Alten Testament mit *ʿārāb* und Akkusativ (siehe Spr. 11:15; 20:16; 27:13), und nicht mit *lᵉ* ausgedrückt." W. McKane, *Proverbs*, 321: "Since *ʿrb* in the sense of 'going surety for' someone usually takes the accusative, the construction with *lᵉ* is an initial difficulty in v. 1 . . ." L. A. Snijders, "The Meaning of *zār* in the Old Testament, An Exegetical Study," *OTS*, 10 (1954) 81: "The construction *ʿrb le* is unusual. He, for whom surety is stood is referred to in the accusative (Gen xliii 9, Is. xxxviii 14, Ps. cxix 122, Prov. xx 16, xxvii 13). *ʿrb lfny* (Prov. xvii 18) indicates the one in whose presence the action of going surety happens, very probably the creditor. Further evidence is lacking to be able to determine with certainty the value of the preposition *lᵉ* with regard to the procedure." Snijders, however, goes on to say that since the general meaning of *ʿrb* conveys the negative sense of meddling in the affairs of others, we can read *ʿrb lě* as a verb plus accusative combination: "The one who gives himself up as a guarantee, has meddled with the man for whom he is a surety. As a result of these considerations it is the natural thing to put the meaning of *ʿrb lᵉ* on a par with *ʿrb* plus accusative"(p. 82). For further discussion on the unusual combination of *ʿrb lě* in Prov 6:1, see: D. G. Wildeboer, *Die Sprüche*, 17; H. Wiesmann, "Das Buch der Sprüche. Kap. 6, 1–19," 242. O. Plöger, *Sprüche Salomos*, 61, 63; H. Ringgren and W. Zimmerli, *Sprüche/Prediger*, 32.

unusual pairing of *lĕrē'ekā*, "for your neighbor" and *lazzār*, "with a stranger" which are set in a context of providing "surety."[49] Commentators have offered a number of interpretations for the combination of *lĕrē'ekā* + *lazzār*. Boström argues that *rēa'* and *zār* are two different people who interact in a common commercial context of creditor and debtor. Specifically, *rēa'*, the "neighbor," is the creditor and *zār*, the "stranger," is the debtor.[50] Boström translates the phrase *'im 'ārabtā lĕrē'ekā* as: *wenn du bei deinem Nächsten gebürgt hast*, "if you have given surety to (*bei*) your neighbor" (i.e., neighbor as creditor) in contrast, for example, to the RSV's, "if you have become surety for your neighbor" (i.e., neighbor as debtor, presuming Boström's commercial context). For v 1b, *tāqa'tā lazzār kappeykā* Boström translates as: *deine Hand für einen Fremdling gegeben hast*, "have given your pledge for (*für*) a stranger[51]

---

[49] See: W. McKane, *Proverbs*, 321: "[T]he question [is] whether *zār* is intended as an exact parallel of *rēa'*. That some difficulty was felt in respect of this second point by LXX is suggested by the reading 'enemy' in v. 1b, for a neighbour can be an enemy, but hardly a stranger." W. Nowack, *Die Sprüche Salomo's*, 39: "Schwerlich ist auch hier auf זר neben רע Gewicht zu legen . . . ." G. Gerleman, *The Studies in the Septuagint*, 18, attributes the LXX reading to a proclivity among the Greeks to substitute antitheses for synonymous parallelism.

[50] G. Boström, *Proverbiastudien*, 100–101.

[51] G. Boström's translation was made earlier by D. G. Wildeboer, *Die Sprüche*, 17: "*Für deinen Nächsten* übersetze lieber: *bei deinem Nächsten*: der Nächste ist hier nicht der Schuldner, für den man gut spricht, sondern der Gläubiger selbst." Boström translates the first *lamed* in v 1a as a dative "to your neighbor," and the second *lamed* in v 1b is also translated as a dative but with the meaning "in place of," i.e., in place of the stranger. McKane, *Proverbs*, 321-322, agrees with Boström's argument. The neighbor, *rēa'*, is also the creditor. McKane, however, recognizes the difficulties Boström's argument presents by his interpretation of the same particle *lĕ* in two different ways in the same verse. As McKane says: "Boström's translation assumes a different force of *l^e* in v. 1a (where it is used with a dative) as compared with v. 1b (where it means 'in place of'). This is not a decisive objection, although it is unexpected [!] in relation to the parallelism"(p. 322). O. Plöger, *Sprüche Salomos*, 60, also translates the first *lamed* as *bei* and the second *lamed* as *für*. In contrast, see: B. Gemser, *Sprüche Salomos*, 36, where he translates both *lemādoth* as *für*. L. A. Snijders, "The Meaning of *zār*," 84, n. 45, also says: "He [Boström] bases this contrast [between *rēa'* and *zār*] of the sentence-parts on G who renders *rēa'* and *zār* with φίλος and ἔχθρος, resp. Ἔχθρος is indeed very unusual as an equivalent of *zār* (ἔχθρος need not, however, be a foreigner!). It must be assumed that G reads צר instead of זר. (cf. G. Ps xliii 6, 11, lxxiii, 10, lxxvii 61, 66 Job vi 23, xix 11, Si. xii 16 etc.) This alteration is connected with the fact that the Greek translator of Proverbs did not understand the expression *tq' l^e*, (cf. xi 15, xvii 18, xxii 26) and judges giving credit differently from Proverbs."

L. A. Snijders offers another interpretation. He translates *lĕrēʿekā* as *lazzār* as synonymous expressions referring to the *same* person. Snijders translates 6:1 as "My son, if you stand surety for your fellow, (you) strike hands for the sake of the *zār*."[52] As a *zār*, the person is not a stranger or foreigner, but a disenfranchised figure within the community.[53] But then Snijders envisages a third party creditor alongside the *rēaʿ* and *zār*.

McKane offers another interpretation and translates vv 1–2 as: "My son, if you have given surety to your neighbour, and struck hands for a stranger, you are snared by your own words, trapped by your own utterances."[54] He reasons that one goes to the "neighbor" because the "neighbor" is the creditor. For McKane the *zār* is the third party debtor.[55]

But for all the differences in interpretation and translation between Boström, Snijders, and McKane, they all agree that a commercial context forms the backdrop for understanding the nature of going surety for someone.[56] Oddly enough, nothing resembling commercial interests is reflected in vv 1–5. Instead, the one going surety is alerted to the "power" (*kap*, v 3,; cf. v 1) the "neighbor" now has. Thus it is questionable whether we can read into the text a commercial context where we can identify clearly both the creditor and the debtor as some scholars have done. Equally questionable is the argument which posits a

---

52 "The Meaning of *zār*," 83. Snijders also says: "In verse 3 *rēaʿ* also means the same person, viz. the one for whose sake the guarantee is given. Here the *zār* is the fellow-citizen who, however, is outside the daily way of life of the guarantor"(p. 84). Snijders does not explain the social significance of someone who "is outside the daily life of the guarantor" or how he arrived at his conclusion.

53 "The Meaning of *zār*," 84. In his article on זוּר/זָר in *The Theological Dictionary of the Old Testament*, trans. by D. E. Green (Grand Rapids: Eerdmans, 1980) 57, Snijders says: "The 'stranger' is clearly someone who does not belong to the family (members of a family regulate their affairs privately, without official transactions). The *zār* can, through insolvency, bring the creditor into the house of the guarantor, and thus represents a threat to his well-being." Again, Snijders does not explain how he has arrived at his conclusion. Snijder's interpretation of the *zār* as a person who jeopardizes the house of the creditor is a projection by Snijders which lacks any support from within the Hebrew Bible.

54 W. McKane, *Proverbs*, 322: "The assumption that the neighbor is the creditor agrees with v. 3b, 'for you have come into the presence of your neighbor'. . . ." Ironically, Delitzsch, *Proverbs*, 135, referring to the same reference, *rēʿekā*, "your neighbor," in v 3, says: "If we look to ver. 3, the רֵעַ (רֵעֶהָ) mentioned there cannot possibly be the creditor with whom one has become surety, for so impetuous and urgent an application to him would be both purposeless and unbecoming."

55 *Proverbs*, 219.

56 Such as: W. McKane, *Proverbs*, 322; G. Boström, *Proverbiastudien*, 101–102; H. Ringgren and H. Zimmerli, *Sprüche/Prediger*, 32; W. O. E. Oesterley, *Proverbs*, 39.

synonymous relationship between *rēa^c* and *zār* when there are no other examples in the Hebrew Bible to support such a reading.

A Proposed Translation and Interpretation of lěrē^{c}kā and lazzār.

Prov 6:1 reads, *běnî 'im ^{c}ārabtā lěrē^{c}ekā tāqa^{c}tā lazzār kappeykā* "My son, if you have become surety for your neighbor, have given your pledge for a stranger"(RSV). Because the MT elsewhere registers other examples for the expression *rēa^c* which approximate relationships closer than a "neighbor," we are arguing that a more inclusive translation of *lěrē^{c}ekā* would be "friend," "companion," "fellow," as rendered by BDB.[57] For example, there are cases where *rēa^c* stands parallel to *'aḥ*, "brother," thus indicating a relationship far closer than a "neighbor."[58] While "neighbor" is possible, we are arguing that in the context of Prov 6:1ff a specific term such as "companion" is more appropriate. The parental warning about a surety arrangement involving a "companion" is further specified by a parallel reference to a *zār*, "stranger." Even though a contrast is struck by combining "companion" and "stranger," we can explain their appearance by turning to J. Kugel's recent work on biblical parallelism. He offers us a number of fresh insights into the various ways parallelism functions within scripture.[59]

Kugel argues that parallel expressions in A + B clauses need not have the same or approximate meaning. Instead, Kugel describes a variety of ways expressions in parallel clauses can converge or diverge in meaning.[60] For Kugel, all parallelism is synthetic parallelism and best rendered by the conjunctive expression, "A, and what's more, B."[61]

---

[57] *BDB* 945–946.

[58] Cf. Jer 9:3; Ps 35:14. See also Jer 3:20 where *mērē^{c}āh* refers to "her husband." Another use of *r^{c}h* is understood as "lover" in Jer 3:1, and Hos 3:1.

[59] J. Kugel, *The Idea of Biblical Poetry: Parallelism and Its History* (New Haven/London: Yale University Press, 1981), esp. pp. 1–58.

[60] For instance, Kugel says the following about a number of examples which combine pairs of expression found in scripture: "The use of pairs does not mean the *clauses* are equivalent, and what is interesting in these lines [i.e., the examples cited by Kugel] are the subtle variations—including, of course, *who* is being summoned and in what order: Heaven and Earth, kings and noblemen, nations and people. These are what tell the story. This point is important, for in the enthusiasm following the discovery of the pairs, the differences between A and B have sometimes been overlooked" (*The Idea of Biblical Poetry*, 31). Kugel later offers his definition of "biblical parallelism: "What then is the essence [of biblical parallelism]? In asserting the primacy of our form————/————// we are asserting, basically, a sequence: first part—pause—next part—bigger pause. . . . But even this sequence is a bit of a shorthand for the real point, for what those pauses actually embody is the *subjoined, hence emphatic*, character of B. The briefness of the brief pause is an expression of B's connectedness to A; the length of the long pause is an expression of

Kugel's analysis of biblical parallelism helps in interpreting Prov 6:1. Thus, our translation of 6:1: "My son, if you have become surety for your companion, and what's more, if you have struck a bargain with a stranger." Instead of treating the parallel expressions *rēaᶜ*, "companion," and *zār*, "stranger," synonymously, as some commentators are prone to do, we are employing Kugel's recent analysis of biblical parallelism to indicate the *difference* between the paired expressions in 6:1.

Kugel's analysis of parallelism helps us in other ways. While other commentators have wrestled with the unique combination of *ᶜrb* + *l* and the identity of the *rēaᶜ* and *zār*, we believe that there are a number of other unusual features in vv 1–5 which require further attention. For instance, the expression *tāqaᶜtā lazzār kappeykā* is difficult to translate. The RSV renders the text as, "[you] have given your pledge for a stranger." The combination *tqᶜ kp* literally means, "to strike hands," presumably as a sign of agreement between two people.[62] In what sense the son would strike a bargain "for a stranger" is not addressed in the text. Even though *tqᶜ* appears elsewhere in Prov 11:15; 17:18; and 22:26, it is combined with *kp* + *l* only in Prov 6:1 and Job 17:3b. However, Job 17:3b reads: *mî hûʾ lĕyādî yittāqēᶜa* which the RSV translates as "who is there that will give surety for me." Where Prov 6:1 employs the Qal form of *tqᶜ*, Job 17:3 uses the Niphal *yittāqēᶜa*. The different verb forms in combination with *l* result in markedly different translations. R. Gordis argues that the Qal results in the understanding of "giving" a pledge, while the Niphal means "accepting" a pledge and he translates Job 17:3 *śîmâ naʾ ᶜārĕbēnî ᶜimmāk mî hûʾ lĕyādî yittāqēᶜa*, as, "God, pray take my pledge with You; Who else would accept a surety from my hands?"[63] In other words, the combination of Niphal *tqᶜ* + *l* designates Job as the one whose "hand" no one but God could dare strike in a bargain.

---

the relative disjunction between B and the next line. What this means is simply: B, by being connected to A—carrying it further, echoing it, defining it, restating it, contrasting with it, *it does not matter which*-has an emphatic 'seconding' character, and it is this, more than any aesthetic of symmetry or paralleling, which is at the heart of biblical parallelism. To state the matter somewhat simplistically, biblical lines are parallelistic not because B is meant to be a parallel of A, but because B typically *supports* A, carries it further, backs it up, completes it, goes beyond it" (pp. 51–52).

[61] J. Kugel, *The Idea of Biblical Poetry*, 57–58.

[62] See: L. A. Snijdars, "The Meaning of *zār*," 82–83; F. Delitzsch, *Proverbs*, 136; C. H. Toy, *Proverbs*, 120.

[63] R. Gordis, *The Book of Job: Commentary, New Translation, and Special Studies* (New York: The Jewish Theological Seminary of America, 1978) 172, 181. Earlier, F. Delitzsch (*Job*, trans. by F. Bolton [Grand Rapids Michigan: Eerdmans, 1976] 295–296) arrived at a similar translation as Gordis'.

The sense of Prov 6:1 also seems to convey the idea that just as the son may get involved in a surety with a *rēa*ᶜ, "companion," he may also find himself getting involved with a *zār*. Hence, the meaning of the *l* in Prov 6:1 is ambiguous: it could mean "to," "for," or even "with."[64] Given the lack of other examples of *tq*ᶜ + *kp* + *l*, we are interpreting the combination in Prov 6:1 on the basis of the context in Proverbs 5 and 6 where the parent warns against involvement with *zārâ/zārîm*. Our translation of *lazzār* as "with a stranger" is designed to capture the idea of warning against involvement with a stranger.[65]

To compound the problem of how to interpret Prov 6:1, there is no other example in Hebrew scripture where *zār*, "stranger," and *rēa*ᶜ, "neighbor," ever appear together in a context of going surety or taking a pledge. Prov 6:1 is the only example.[66] While scholars have puzzled over how to interpret the combination of *rēa*ᶜ and *zār*, no one raises the question of why these two words appear together only in 6:1 or what their relationship is with Proverbs 5. The five cases of going surety and taking a pledge in the book of Proverbs further indicate the unusual combination in Prov 6:1:

Prov 11:15   *ra*ᶜ *yēroā*ᶜ *kî* ᶜ*ārab zār wĕśōnē*ʾ *tôqĕ*ᶜ*îm bôṭēaḥ*
He who gives a surety for a stranger will smart for it, but he who hates suretyship is secure.

Prov 17:18   ʾ*ādām ḥăsar lēb tôqēa*ᶜ *kāp* ᶜ*ōrēb* ᶜ*arubbâ lipnê rē*ᶜ*ēhû*
A man without sense gives a pledge, and becomes surety in the presence of his neighbor.

Prov 20:16   *lĕqaḥ bigdô kî* ᶜ*ārab zār ûbĕ*ᶜ*ad nokriyyām hablēhû*
27:13   Take a man's garment when he has given surety for a stranger, and hold him in pledge when he gives surety for foreigners.

Prov 22:26   ʾ*al tĕhî betōqĕ*ᶜ*ê kāp ba*ᶜ*ōrĕbîm maśśā*ʾ*ôt*
Be not one of those who gives pledges, who become surety for debts.

---

[64] See R. Williams, *Hebrew Syntax*, 48–49, for examples of how *l* can be translated as "with" expressing involvement. Cf. GKC. par. 119u.

[65] R. B. Y. Scott, *Proverbs*, 56, also translates Prov 6:1b as we are doing: "Or have struck a bargain with a stranger."

[66] The combination of expressions which do not appear elsewhere in scripture is a feature noted by Kugel. As J. Kugel says: "The 'principle of parallelism,' however loosely defined, will not generate most of the actual lines found in biblical poetry, and on the other hand it *will* generate all sorts of lines that *never* appear in the Bible. . . The generating principle of this style is that of the added-on, subjoined clause, the 'part B' that always follows A and restates it or carries it further, intensifies its meaning, refines it, follows it in sequence, and so forth" ("A Feeling of Déjà Lu," *JR* [1987] 75).

None of these examples link *rēaᶜ* and *zār*. Also, the above examples do not connect going surety/taking a pledge with speech as Prov 6:1–5 does. Prov 6:1–5 is framed in a conditional context indicating a future case of taking surety unlike the simple declarative sentences for the other examples in Proverbs.[67] Even though Prov 17:18 is the only other example besides 6:1–5 where *rēaᶜ* is mentioned in a context of surety, 17:18, however, reads, *lipnê rēᶜēhû*, "before his neighbor," while 6:1 reads, *lĕrēᶜekâ*, "for/to your companion."[68]

Each example in Proverbs where *zār* appears in a discussion of surety always conjoins *ᶜārab + zār*. Prov 6:1 is the only example where *ᶜārab* and *zār* are separated. In view of our analysis of the unusual combination of *ᶜrb + lĕrēᶜekā* in 6:1a, the mention of the *zār* in 6:1b, the sustained interest in the *rēaᶜ* in 6:3–5, and the unique linkage between surety and speech, we are arguing that these features can best be explained by positing a larger inner-biblical context to which these verses allude. Hence, the unusual combination that we note for *ᵓārabtā + lĕ + rēᶜekā* is just one factor among others in the composite picture of Prov 6:1–5.

PROV 6:1–19, THE JOSEPH STORY, AND MIMETIC REPRESENTATION *via* ACTIONAL DISCOURSE.

In our summary of Sternberg's analysis of mimetic representation we described how a narrator can play upon earlier events by ordering elements of actional discourse. Alongside original messages, which are sometimes verbal events, we also are presented narration which gives a predominant place to action. Our analysis and translation of Prov 6:1 attempts to be faithful to the unusual aspects of this verse: we detect the close social relationship with the *rēaᶜ* as one who is a "companion" while

---

[67] There are no other examples in the Hebrew Bible which warn against going surety for someone. Cf. Gen 43:9; 44:32; Neh 5:3; Ez 27:9, 27; Ps 105:35; 119:122; Isa 36:8; 38:14; Ezra 9:2; 2 Kgs 18:23 for other references of the use of the verb *ᶜrb*.

[68] See: L. A. Snijders, "The Meaning of *zār*," 81: "'*rb lfny* (Prov. xvii 18) indicates the one in whose presence the action of going surety happens, very probably the creditor." For a similar reading, see: C. H. Toy, *Proverbs*, 347. But W. McKane, *Proverbs*, 503, offers an equivocating analysis: "The neighbor is in all likelihood the one on whose behalf financial liability is incurred, and the phrase indicates that he would be present at the proceedings of going surety. There is another possibility, more remote but not excluded entirely. If the translation 'in the presence of his neighbour' is pressed, the neighbour may be the one to whom the guarantor will be liable, should a third party for whom he has assumed financial responsibility be in default of his obligations." See: F. Delitzsch, *Proverbs*, 366; and B. Gemser, *Sprüche Salomos*, 72–73.

at the same time recognizing the added dimension of the parallel expression, *zār*, "stranger." The difference between them should not be lost in a hypothetical commercial context of creditor and debtor. More important, however, is the question of why *rēaʿ* and *zār* are joined only here and nowhere else in Hebrew scripture. Only by positing an inner-biblical context can we perceive how Judah's role in giving surety for Benjamin in Genesis 43 is reflected in Prov 6:1–19.

ʿăśēh zōʾt ʾēpôʾ Prov 6:3/*ʾēpôʾ zōʾt ʿaśû* Gen 43:11.

The inner-biblical context of Prov 6:1–19 can be seen in a number of unique features. For example, Prov 6:3 records an expression strikingly similar to one found in Gen 43:11, the section dealing with Judah's request that he be allowed to go surety for Benjamin. After Judah has convinced Jacob to allow him to stand surety for Benjamin, Jacob says: *ʾim kēn ʾēpôʾ zōʾt ʿăśû*, "if so, then do this. . . ." Following this expression Jacob advises Judah to take a "present" in the form of "a little balm and a little honey, gum, myrrh, pistachio nuts, and almonds," in Gen 43:11 in order to placate the Egyptian overlord (i.e., Joseph).[69] By placating the Egyptian overlord Judah has a better chance to return with both the food and Benjamin. The ultimate fate of Benjamin lies with the Egyptian overlord. If Judah fails then Benjamin will join Simeon as another prisoner of the Egyptian. In Prov 6:3 the parent says: *ʿăśēh zōʾt ʾēpôʾ*, "then do this. . . ," the same phrase as found in Gen 43:11 but in reverse order. *BDB* notes that the example from Prov 6:3 appears in a command context while Gen 43:11 appears in a conditional context.[70] Prov 6:3, however, is likewise introduced by *ʾim* in v 1.

Both examples exhibit a clear conditional context. As *ʾēpôʾ zōʾt ʿăśû* in Gen 43:11 introduces an apodosis, the same holds for Prov 6:3.[71] The combination of words *ʾēpôʾ zōʾt ʿăśû* / *ʿăśēh zōʾt ʾēpôʾ* appear only in Gen 43:11 and Prov 6:3. And for both surety examples, Genesis 43 and Proverbs 6, a third party literally decides the outcome of the surety.

---

[69] See J. Ackerman, "Joseph, Judah, and Jacob," 92: "Jacob, after a long struggle, has finally been convinced that the family will not survive if Benjamin is not sent to Egypt. The wily father hopes for the best and does what he can by sending gifts to the Egyptian lord (43:11). Thus Benjamin departs for Egypt; and with him go balm, honey, gum, myrrh, pistachio nuts, and almonds—the very goods that accompanied Joseph twenty years before (37:25)."

[70] *BDB*, 66.

[71] As Wildeboer (*Die Sprüche*, 17) earlier noted, v 3 represents the beginning of the apodosis for vv 1–2. G. R. Driver's suggestion ("Abbreviations in the Massoretic Text," *Textus*, 1 [1960] 128) that "the meaningless אֵפוֹא in אֵפוֹא זֹאת עֲשֵׂה 6:3a, is an abbreviation for אֲשֶׁר פָּקַדְתִּי אֵלֶיךָ is ingenious but unconvincing. Driver's reading derives from a retrojection of the Greek *poiei uie ha ego soi entellomai*, in 6:3.

The "Reversed" Framework of Prov 6:1–19 and
Judah's Role in the Joseph Story.

The probability that the parent's words in Prov 6:1–19 echo events from the Joseph story becomes all the more real when we recall the first and last speech-events of Judah. The first time Judah speaks is when he suggests to his brothers that they sell Joseph to the Ishmaelites/Midianites in Gen 37:26–27. In his last speech-event Judah informs the Egyptian overlord (i.e., his brother Joseph) that he has gone surety for Benjamin his brother in Gen 44:32–34. Each speech represents a turning point in the story.[72] Before the selling of Joseph in Gen 37:26 and after the surety explanation in Gen 44:32–34 Judah never speaks. The two speeches of Judah literally frame the context in which Judah reveals his own character by means of both what he says and what he does.[73]

Prov 6:1–19 has the same thematic framing, albeit reversed. The *first* lesson in Prov 6:1–5 concerns the parent's discourse on why the son should extricate himself from a surety should he be involved in one. Judah's explanation of his surety is the *last* thing he says in Gen 44:32. The very *last* words in Prov 6:19 pinpoint the abominable man as: *mĕšallēaḥ mĕdānîm bên ʾaḥîm,* "one who sends strife between brothers." The *first* words of Judah pertain to selling Joseph to the Ishmaelites/Midianites in Gen 37:26–28. The word *mĕdānîm* translated by the RSV as "strife" in Prov 6:19 is the exact same word as in Gen 37:36 and translated as "Midianites;" that is, the caravaneers who carried Joseph to Egypt thus separating the brothers.

The first and last didactic lessons in Prov 6:1–19 concern familial relationships, as does the Joseph story. Judah plays a role both by

---

[72] J. Ackerman in "Joseph, Judah, and Jacob," 103, also notes the important role assumed by Judah in Genesis 37 and 43: "Judah has become the spokesman and leader. The main turning point is reached, however, when Judah offers to assume personal responsibility for Benjamin's life in verses 8–10 [of Genesis 43]. Just as chapter 37 forced us to contrast the two brothers' attempts to deliver Joseph from death, the analogy between the offers of Reuben and Judah to be responsible for Benjamin forces us to contrast their words in order to see why Reuben's offer hardened Jacob's resolve not to send Benjamin, whereas Judah's words won him over. Unlike Reuben, Judah is successful because he sets Jacob's decision in a larger context."

[73] In *Midrash Rabbah, Genesis,* trans. by H. Freedman, third ed. (London/New York: Soncino Press, 1983) LXXXIV:17 the darshan notes that Judah spoke on three occasions on behalf of his brothers: "On three occasions Judah spoke before his breathren, and they made him king over them . . . ;" i.e., the time when he suggested they sell Joseph to the caravaneers in Gen 37:26–27, and the two occasions when Judah spoke to Joseph in Gen 44:14, 18. The last occasion records Judah's words concerning his surety for Benjamin. Hereafter, *Gen. Rab.* = *Genesis Rabbah,* Soncino.

dividing the family when he sells Joseph to the Midianites (the last thing mentioned in Prov 6:19) and by bringing the family together again when he goes surety for Benjamin (the first lesson in Prov 6:1–5). By reversing the order of acts associated with Judah, the parent in Prov 6:1–19 effects a reading of the text which ends with Judah's abominable act of selling his brother Joseph.

The parent's words in Prov 6:1–5, as we mentioned earlier, explain why it is necessary to avoid being involved in a surety. Undesirable social entanglements can result. In the Joseph story, Judah himself, by going surety for Benjamin, gets entangled not only with Jacob his father, but with the Egyptian lord—the ostensible "stranger." Judah's going surety for Benjamin unwittingly entangles Benjamin in a web of relationships that leave him dependent both on Judah and on the Egyptian lord. Is it any wonder then that the parent in Prov 6:1–5 admonishes the son as he/she does! The sweeping admonition of the parent in Prov 6:1–5 lends itself to the nature of suretyship itself. The "hand" in Prov 6:5 lays hold of not only the creditor and debtor in a surety but anyone else who plays a role in the fate of even one of the characters. In addition, the reference to *yād*, "hand," in Prov 6:5 recalls Judah's words to Jacob in Gen 43:9, *ʾānōkî ʾeʿerbennû miyyādî tĕbaqšennû*, "I will be surety for him, from my *hand* you will require him."

There is a good deal of irony attached to Judah's words about going surety for Benjamin his brother in Gen 43:9 when we recall his earlier words to his brothers concerning Joseph in Gen 37:26–27: "What profit is it if we slay our brother (*ʾaḥ*) and conceal his blood? Come, let us sell him to the Ishmaelites and let not our hand (*yād*) be upon him, for he is our brother (*ʾaḥ*), our own flesh." While Judah's "hand" was not directly upon Joseph, surely Joseph's fate was directly tied to Judah's devious action. Now Benjamin's fate is in the "hand" of the same deceiver as was Joseph's fate. While Judah thinks he was ridding himself of Joseph forever in Genesis 37, Judah's treachery backfires upon him. Now Judah's fate as well as Benjamin's is caught in the very hand of the Egyptian overlord who is actually their brother.[74] Judah's lengthy

---

74 G. Savran, "The Character as Narrator in Biblical Narrative," 7–8, is sensitive to the interlocking social relationships that are generated by Judah's acts and how Judah tries to get his way by indirectly blaming the Egyptian overlord for Jacob's premature death: "Concomitant with this display of familial devotion is Judah's corollary, that Joseph must show a corresponding degree of sensitivity to Jacob's situation. . . . By pointing out the effect of Benjamin's departure upon Jacob, twice through quotations (44:22, 27–29) and twice more in his own words (44:31, 34) Judah reveals to Joseph the true implication of his selfish demands. The true beauty of Judah's remarks lies in his ability to affirm explicitly his own responsibility, while effectively 'blaming' Joseph for his father's anticipated death. As Judah has become

monologue in Gen 44:18–44 captures the complexity of the interlocking associations within the Joseph story. Moreover, the linking of going surety with being "snared" and "caught" by one's words recalls Judah's self-imposed dilemma.

J. Goldin argues that Judah plays a role in the Joseph story only at the point where Judah can now assume the part played by the "favored" son. With Simeon, Levi, and Reuben having fallen into disfavor in their father's eyes, Judah is next in line as heir apparent only if he can be rid of Joseph. As Goldin says:

> Is it surprising that the one who speaks up now [in Gen 37:26–27] is Judah? "Let us get rid of that boy, sell him. There's nothing to be gained from killing him—that leaves a stain on the soul: we are not Cains." The objective is attained by selling him or letting those passing Ishmaelites-Midianites sell him. Joseph is finally removed, and there are no traces. Henceforth Judah is never out of sight. In anticipation we have already met him successfully prevailing on his father to send Benjamin along with them to Egypt. And when the cup is found in Benjamin's sack, who comes back before Joseph? Judah and his brothers, the verse says, not just "they." And who pleads, "What can we say and how can we prove our innocence?" Still Judah. And who makes the irresistible appeal (one of the highest achievements of biblical eloquence), which finally breaks Joseph down? Judah. And whom does *Jacob* send ahead to inform Joseph of their coming? Judah (Gen 46:28). (The very man responsible for the sale of Joseph.) In short, from the moment Judah speaks up in chap. 37, with the advice of how to get rid of Joseph (and simultaneously contriving [?] to make impossible Reuben's rehabilitation), it is Judah who is the chief spokesman, and hopefully the successor.[75]

Goldin concludes: "The smoothest tongue in Genesis is Judah's."[76]

Judah's words not only propel the action of the Joseph story in a new direction starting in Gen 37:26–27, but also they literally trap Judah, his brothers, and Jacob in a web of unforeseen circumstances. The parent's words in Prov 6:1–5 play upon the same theme of surety and speech. As we noted earlier, no other text in Proverbs or elsewhere links surety and speech as Prov 6:1–5 does. But if we read the issue of speech and surety in connection Judah's role in the Joseph story, then we can understand the import of the parent's words in Prov 6:1–5.

---

personally liable for Benjamin, so the obligation to prevent Jacob's death rests on Joseph's shoulders alone."

75 "The Youngest Son or Where Does Genesis 38 Belong," *JBL*, 96 (1977) 42.

76 "The Youngest Son," 41.

The Pairing of Surety and Agricultural Readiness in Prov 6:1-11
and Events from the Joseph Story.

Significantly, the context in which Judah has to go surety for Benjamin relates directly to the lack of food in a time of famine. According to Gen 43:2 Jacob commands his sons, *ʾabîhem šubû šibrû lānû mĕʿaṭ ʾōkel*, "Go again, buy us a little food." Judah and his brothers refuse to depart without Benjamin. Only at the point where Jacob relents and agrees to send Benjamin on the basis of Judah's surety do the brothers go. Again, Judah's convincing speech propels the action. Moreover, Judah and his brothers have already bound themselves to the Egyptian overlord by the fact that they left Simeon in Egypt when they took grain. By going surety for Benjamin Judah is going through a formality which has already been presaged by Joseph's request for the younger son to come and by Jacob's refusal to relinquish Benjamin.

As for Prov 6:6-11, the second discourse unit, the content of the unit revolves around food, harvest, potential privation and the necessity to be agriculturally industrious. Judah's surety for Benjamin is set in a context of agricultural want in Genesis. The parent's lesson on surety in Prov 6:1-5 is linked to his/her discourse concerning agricultural planning for lean times. If we recall the earlier dream episode in Genesis 41 concerning the upcoming famine, we can note a number of parallel features between Prov 6:6-11 and Genesis. Joseph interprets Pharaoh's dream sequence. The seven years of plenty are followed by seven years of famine. Joseph's interpretation of the dreams as well as his advice to appoint an *ʾîš nābôn wĕḥakām*, "a man discreet and wise," wins the top administrative post in Pharaoh's court. In addition, the famine extends not only over Egypt but over the whole earth: *wĕkol hāʾāreṣ bāʾû miṣrayĕmâ lišbōr ʾel yôsēp kîḥāzaq hārāʿāb bekol hāʾāreṣ*, "and all the earth came to Egypt to Joseph to buy grain, because the famine was severe over all the earth" (Gen 41:57).

Joseph's *ḥākām*, "wisdom," and his preparation for the upcoming famine allows the Egyptians to manage in a time of food scarcity. As such, Joseph excels over others by his ability to prepare the land for a period of famine. And like Joseph, the ant is the paradigm of one who foresees want and prepares for it. That the lesson on surety in Prov 6:1-5 is followed immediately by a lesson concerning food, harvest, and privation achieves a level of mimetic representation with the events when Judah goes surety for Benjamin.

As Joseph demonstrates his wisdom, *ḥākām*, in storing food for the period of the famine, the sluggard is admonished to "Go to the ant . . . , consider its ways, and be wise" (Prov 6:6). The wisdom of the ant lies not only in its ability to have a constant supply of food even in the lean times of summer, it also does so *ʾên lāh qāṣîn sōṭēr ûmōšēl*, "without having any chief, officer or ruler." The ant's industriousness is related directly to its own initiative. As for Joseph, the Pharaoh made him the overseer of the whole land of Egypt in Gen 41:40–41 thus indicating Joseph's unquestionably independent role in preparing for the famine. In contrast, the brothers in Gen 42:1 are portrayed as aimlessly looking at each other when the famine strikes. Only at Jacob's command do the brothers do anything.

The parallel features that we note between the Joseph story and Prov 6:6–11 have been noted in part by D. Daube. In an article devoted to an analysis of the graduated numerical saying in Prov 30:24–28, Daube argues that there is a "link-up" between figures in Israel's history and the imagery associated with the "Quartet of Beasties" in Prov 30:24–28.[77] In his analysis of the *nĕmālîm*, "ants," in Prov 30:24, Daube turns to the parallel references to the *nĕmālâ*, "ant," in Prov 6:6–11. Daube sees a connection between the attributes of the ant and Joseph. Even though Joseph is not named in Proverbs 6 or 30, he functions, according to Daube, as the "archetype" for the portrait of the ant.[78] Joseph's ability to organize, his wisdom, in addition to the theme of storing food lead Daube to conclude that one of the "sources of inspiration" for Prov 30:24–28 is the Joseph story.[79] Daube's argument can be further developed for Prov 6:1–19. The combination of themes in Prov 6:1–19 is designed to imply the larger network of literary and thematic associations found in the Joseph story. Vv 6–11 are one section which adds to an inner-biblical reading.

The allusion to Joseph by means of the figure of the ant is not unusual when we recall the many passages where non-human animate figures are used to represent characters in Israel's history. We have only to remember Jacob's blessing on his sons in Genesis 49 where Judah is a "lion's whelp," Isaachar a "strong ass," and Dan "a serpent."

The function of the ant in Prov 6:6–11 is to allude to other circumstances in the story. As the first lesson concerning surety in Prov 6:1–5 warns against possible involvement with another person, the second lesson in vv 6–11 ends on a similar note. The failure to store food for the future will eventuate in possible involvement with another. Poverty comes as a "traveller" and want as an "armed man." Hence, the first two discourse units in Prov 6:1–11 establish a case of mimetic representation where events in the Joseph story are implied. As readers we are not given recontextualized speech of Judah and his brothers. We

---

77 "A Quartet of Beasties in the Book of Proverbs," *JTS*, 36 (1985) 380–386.
78 "A Quartet of Beasties," 381.
79 "A Quartet of Beasties," 380.

are presented instead with discourse units which when combined call to mind episodes relating to Judah's relationship with his brothers and Jacob. From a lesson concerning the intricacies of unforeseen social relationships in a surety, the text moves to the need to be agriculturally industrious. Again, the parent's discourse is not merely a warning to the son and sluggard. The parent's words specify why it is necessary to extricate oneself from a surety as well as to avoid slothfulness. Each act leads to unforeseen results.

Third Person Discourse, "a Worthless Man," (inter alia),
and Judah's Role in the Joseph Story.

The shift to third person discourse which describes at length the characteristics of an *ʾādām bĕliyyaʿal*, "a worthless man," in v 12 adds further clarity and authority to the parent's lesson. By concentrating on the "man" the parent effectively identifies the man not by his speech but by his actions, which relate to bodily movement.

The listing of the body parts with their corresponding bodily movements in 6:12–19 at first appears to be a random combination without a clue to the significance of its order. Reference has already been made to Delitzsch's observation that Prov 6:12–19 is actually one unit.[80] The basis for Delitzsch's linking vv 12–15 and vv 16–19 together is the element of redundancy in vocabulary and themes. Besides the common expression *midānîm/mĕdānîm* present in vv 14,19, we have already noted the number of other commonly shared words such as *ʿênayim*, "eyes," *raglayim*, "feet," and *lēb*, "heart." But while there is a level of redundancy between vv 12–15 and vv 16–19, such redundancy adds to the intensifying effect of vv 12–19. A hierarchical order emerges in the arrangement of references to body parts and the "man" in vv 12–15 and vv 16–19. In the latter the parent enlists not only what YHWH hates and what proves to be abominable to YHWH, but also frames the discourse in a graduated numerical saying form. Similar body parts and their movements receive a different perspectival ordering. And by combining together third person discourse describing a man *via* his action in vv 12–15, the graduated numerical saying in vv 16–19, and YHWH's reaction to

---

[80] F. Delitzsch, *Proverbs*, 149: "Vers. 16–19. What follows is not a separate section. . . , but the corroborative continuation of that which precedes. The last word (מדנים , strife) before the threatening of punishment, 14b, is also here the last. The thought that no vice is a greater abomination to God than the (in fact satanical) striving to set men at variance who love one another, clothes itself in the form of the numerical proverb . . . ."

certain kinds of action, the parent orders both the point of view of the text and the point of view of the reader.[81]

Sternberg, for example, argues that cases of "hierarchical ordering," as we have in Prov 6:12–19, are not necessarily accidents of composition but reflect a larger narrative context. As Sternberg says: "Hierarchical ordering must thus carry perspectival implications, so that when we invest a series with scalar significance we *ipso facto* relate it to some refracting medium, responsible for its deliverance from the randomness of brute fact."[82] The presence of the graduated numerical saying in vv 16–19 functions as just such an example of "hierarchical ordering." The overlapping of vocabulary and themes with vv 12–15 works to adjust the reader's perspective of otherwise "brute fact(s)" into a concise order with an outside reference point. Sequential ordering of descriptive characteristics actually reflects a larger narrative context. As Sternberg asserts:

> As a reflection of a world picture—converting rank into sequence and scalar into serial position—hierarchical (dis)ordering structure of priorities, the reader accounts for the temporal order imposed on the intrinsically unordered aggregate by inferring a reference-point in the form of a more or less definite view-point; and for the clashes and discrepancies in the ordering of the same aggregate, by constructing a system of perspectival oppositions between different observers. It is not just that we invoke hierarchical sequence where a certain perspective has been established. We often establish (discover, fill out, judge) a perspective by the treatment and signals of hierarchy.[83]

Another way of saying this is that the ordering of descriptive characteristics as we have in the graduated numerical saying in Prov 6:16–19 is done by the parent on the basis of events and people outside the scope of these verses. The reader establishes the fuller chronological sequencing of events and characters. In addition, the discovered ordering of the description reveals the perspective of the one who does the

---

[81] See: M. L. Pratt, *Toward a Speech Act Theory of Literary Discourse* (Bloomington/London: Indiana University Press, 1977) 46–48, where she discusses "*Evaluative commentary,*" i.e., narrative strategies which reveal a narrator's attempt to draw attention to the point he/she is making. Even though Pratt does not discuss the function of graduated numerical sayings, we can posit a parallel between her discussion "evaluation devices" and the strategy of the parent who combines the graduated numerical saying with reference to YHWH. Cf. pp. 63–66.

[82] "Ordering the Unordered," 82.

[83] "Ordering the Unordered," 81.

ordering and does not represent an altogether objective representation of the facts. Sternberg says:

> Order of discovery, of perception, of emergence and disappearance, of association by contiguity and similartiy: these forms of perspectival sequencing are all grounded in the conditions and constraints that govern a subject's reading of reality. What distinguishes perspectival logic is thus its making sense of the world through the mediation of a reflector from within that world: a dramatized teller, a dialogist or monologist, a focus of narration, a vessel of consciousness, an imaginary spectator.[84]

As for Prov 6:16–19, the parent's "reading of reality," as it were, enlists the support of YHWH in a graduated numerical saying to bolster his/her own words in vv 12–15. Those features which overlap between the parent's words in vv 12–15 and YHWH's words in vv 16–19 are then elevated to the point that the parent's words are equated with YHWH's. Moreover, because hierarchical order is utilized in vv 16–19 *we* and the son see what the parent wants us to see: the man who sends strife between brothers is an abomination and is to be avoided.

We have already indicated that the play on words in 6:19b alludes to Judah and his role in selling Joseph to the Midianites. Prov 6:19b as a brief *description* thus condenses earlier *action*. Because v 19b forms the seventh and most despicable descriptive trait in the series, v 19b literally sets the stage for re-reading the previous six descriptions. We can fill in the actional spaces left open by the remaining descriptive expressions. Since 6:19b locates us as readers back in Genesis 37, we can see other actional contexts for the remaining six descriptive things hated by YHWH.[85]

Prov 6:17c records one of the six things hated by YHWH: *wĕyādamim šōpĕkôt dām nāqî*, "and hands shedding innocent blood." In Gen 37:22

---

[84] "Ordering the Unordered," 84.

[85] See W. Iser's analysis (*The Act of Reading*, 107–134) of the "wandering viewpoint" of a reader which literally travels *"inside"* the forward and backward movement of a text: "Thus, in the time-flow of the reading process, past and future continually converge in the present moment, and the synthesizing operations of the wandering viewpoint enable the text to pass through the reader's mind as an ever-expanding network of connections. This also adds the dimension of space and that of time, for the accumulation of views and combinations gives us the illusion of depth and breadth, so that we have the impression that we are actually present in a real world."(p. 116) As Sternberg earlier notes the interplay between space and time configurations involved in mimetic representation, Iser also speaks here of space and time correlates of a literary "real world." See also R. Fowler, "Who is 'The Reader' in Reader Response Criticism?" *Semeia* 31 (1985) 5–23; esp. pp. 18–21 where he talks about *"Reading as a Temporal Experience."*

Reuben attempts to save Joseph by saying to his brothers: *ʾal tišpĕkû dām hašlîkû ʾōtô ʾel habbôr hazzeh ʾăšer bammidbār wĕyād ʾal tišlĕḥû bô lĕmaʿan haṣṣîl ʾōtô miyyādām lahăšîbô ʾel ʾābîw,* "'Shed no blood. Throw him [Joseph] in this pit which is in the wilderness and lay no hand upon him,' in order that he might rescue him from their hand to return him to his father." The text associates "shedding blood" with the two references to the "hands" of the brothers. Judah's words also link the brothers' "hands" with Joseph's "blood" in Gen 37:26–27. Reuben's unsuccessful ruse leads to Judah's suggestion that they sell Joseph to the Midianites as alluded to in Prov 6:19b, *ûmĕšallēaḥ mĕdānîm bên ʾaḥîm,* "and a man who sends strife/Midianites between brothers."

Alongside the brothers' strategy of ridding themselves of Joseph by selling him is their planned deception of their father Jacob. Even though none of the remaining terms in Prov 6:17–19 have corresponding lexical examples in Genesis 37, we can match the references to deception in Prov 6:17–19 with the brothers' acts of deception in Genesis 37. As we saw in Sternberg's examples of how other authors quote action and how action and description are variables of representational discourse, other corresponding features are found between Genesis 37 and Prov 6:16–19.

No word of judgment is used by the narrator in Gen 37:29–36 to describe the brothers' deceptive action in despatching Joseph's blood-stained cloak to Jacob. Their action bespeaks identity. Alter addresses the element of deception which characterizes the activity of the brothers with their father Jacob.[86] The remaining features in Prov 6:17–19 translate the brothers' action as *lĕšôn šāqer,* "a lying tongue," *lēb ḥōrēš maḥšĕbôt ʾāwen,* "a heart that devises evil," and *yāpîaḥ kĕzābîm ʿēd šāqer,* "a false witness who breathes out lies." The brothers' attestation that *zōʾt māṣāʾnû,* "this we found," i.e., Joseph's coat, in Gen 37:32 is a lie. Their posturing before Jacob when they ask if he recognizes his son's coat is deception and a case of "devising wicked plans" in Prov 6:18b. Lastly, by allowing Jacob to conclude that a *ḥayyâ rāʿâ,* "evil beast," has devoured Joseph when the brothers know the truth exemplifies "a false witness," in Prov 6:19.

---

[86] *The Art of Biblical Narrative,* 10. The same theme of deception which plays upon the root *nkr,* "to recognize," occurs earlier in the episode of Jacob and his sons and reoccurs when Tamar deceives the arch deceiver, Judah: "The first use of the formula [i.e., a play on *nkr*] was for an act of deception [in deceiving Jacob into thinking that Joseph was killed by a wild animal]; the second use is for an act of unmasking. Judah with Tamar after Judah with his brothers is an examplary narrative instance of the deceiver deceived . . . . Now he [Judah] becomes their surrogate in being subject to a bizarre but peculiarly fitting principle of retaliation. Taken in by a piece of attire, as his father was, learning through his obstreperous flesh that the divinely appointed process of election cannot be thwarted by human will or social convention."

The expresion *raglayim mĕmahărôt lārûṣ lārāᶜâ*, "feet that make haste to run to evil," is very similar to Prov 1:16, *kî raglêhem lāraᶜ yārûṣû wîmahărû lišpak dām*, "for their feet run to evil, and they make haste to shed blood." Prov 1:16 appears to be a gloss from Isa 59:7. In concert with other vocabulary and themes in Prov 1:8–19, we saw how 1:16 adds to the thematic play upon Gen 37:26–27. As for Prov 6:18b, this verse, in conjunction with v 17b, *wĕyādayim sōpĕkôt dām nāqî*, "and hands shedding innocent blood," recalls Prov 1:8–19 and the context of Genesis 37. Similarly, *ᶜênayim rāmôt*, "haughty eyes," are interpreted in context with the remaining six features in Prov 6:16–19 as part and parcel of the deceptive features.

But where the brothers act in concert by following Judah's lead in Genesis 37, the parent in Prov 6:16–19 piles negative attribute upon negative attribute in such a way that they are all tied to the "man who sows discord/Midianites between brothers." The narrowing of focus upon a man identified typologically with Judah complements further our interpretation of the parent's didactic lesson as a whole. By drawing upon a familiar tradition within Israel's historical traditions the parent's lesson establishes itself firmly within the developing identity of the people.

PROV 6:1–19, THE JOSEPH STORY, AND RABBINIC COMMENTARY.

We saw from analyses of Prov 1:8–19 and 1:20–33 that the rabbis in *MM* made connections between Proverbs and portions of the Torah and the Prophets. *Gen. Rab.* similarly connects Judah's lengthy speech in Genesis 45:18–34, where he mentions his surety for Benjamin, with the parent's discourse on going surety in Prov 6:1–5.[87] For the two places in Gen 43:9 and 44:32–34 where Judah's surety is mentioned, *Gen. Rab.* links the narrative events with Prov 6:1–5.

> THEN JUDAH CAME NEAR UNTO HIM, AND SAID: OH LORD, etc. (XLIV, 18). It is written, *My son if thou art become surety for thy neighbour, if thou hast struck thy hands for a stranger—thou art snared by the words of thy mouth, thou art caught by the words of thy mouth—Do this now, my son, and deliver thyself*, etc. (Prov. VI, 1ff.). . . . Another interpretation: 'My son, if thou art become surety to thy neighbour' applies to Judah, who said: *I will be surety for him* (Gen. XLIII, 9). 'If thou hast struck thy hands for a stranger'—*Of my hand shalt thou require him* (ib.). 'Thou art snared by the words of thy mouth'—*If I bring him not unto thee, and set him before thee* (ib.) 'Do this now, my son'—cast thyself

---

[87] *Gen. Rab.*, XCIII:1.

in the dust at his feet and proclaim him king over thee; hence it is written, THEN JUDAH CAME NEAR UNTO HIM, AND SAID: OH MY LORD.[88]

Gen. Rab. also recognizes a wordplay on *midānîm*/*mĕdānîm* in its comments of Gen 37:28: "AND THERE PASSED BY MIDIANITES, MERCHANT MEN (XXXVII, 28). Their contentions [hatred] passed."[89] The following note by the editor explains the internal wordplay on *mĕdānîm* and "contentions:" "This is a play on *midyānîm* (Midianites), which is connected with *mĕdānîm*, 'discord,' 'strife': No sooner had they sold him than they regretted it, their hatred having evaporated."[90] The combination of words in Prov 6:19, we are arguing, suggests a broader inner-biblical context *via* a wordplay on *mĕdānîm*. It was Judah's initiative which literally sent the *mĕdānîm*, i.e., the Midianites, between brothers in Gen 37:28, 36. The reutilization of the form *mĕdānîm* which appears in Gen 37:36 and Prov 6:19, and the reference to "brothers" which appears nowhere else in Proverbs 1-9, indicates an intention in the text to remind the reader of the broader inner-biblical outcome of a man who sends *mĕdānîm*, "Midianites"/"strife" among brothers. More is at stake than familial discord; such a "man" is an abomination before God. And a backward glance at Judah's sordid role in the sale of Joseph illustrates well the parent's lesson.

---

[88] *Gen. Rab.*, XCIII:1. Note how *Gen. Rab.* weaves together portions of the discourse from Judah's speech in Genesis 43 and 44 with Proverbs 6:1–5. *Yal. Sh. Misle Shlomo* likewise associates Prov 6:1–15 and Gen 44:18 at the point where Judah comes before Joseph to plead on behalf of his brothers and their father Jacob. *Yal. Sh.* reads: *bny ᵓm ᶜrbt lrᶜk: zh yhwdh snᵓmr ᵓnky ˣrbnw nwqst bᵓmry pyk wybᵓ yhwhdh wᵓhyw byth ywsp ᶜsh zᵓt ᵓyph bny wrhb rᶜki wygs ᶜlyw yhwdh lpyysw*, "'My son, if you have become surety to your companion' [Prov 6:1]. This is Judah who said, 'I will be surety for him' [Gen 43:9]. 'If you are snared by the words of your mouth;' [Prov 6:2] 'and Judah and his brothers came to Joseph's house;' [Gen 44:14] 'do this then my son and importune your companion;' [Prov 6:3] 'and Joseph drew near to him'" [Gen 44:18] (my translation). *Yal. Sh.* associates not only the parent's discourse with Judah's surety for Benjamin but also with Judah's speech-event when he pleads with Joseph in Gen 44:18–34. In addition, the reference to being snared by one's speech in Prov 6:1–2 is linked by the darshan with the social entanglement with Joseph as the Egyptian overlord in Gen 44:18–34.

[89] *Gen. Rab.*, LXXXIV:18.

[90] *Gen. Rab.*, 783.

SUMMARY

Our reading of the text offers an alternative to the view that Prov 6:1–19 is no more than a random combination of traditions between Prov 5:1–23 and 6:20ff. The combination of traditions that are both unique to the book of Proverbs, such as the ant and the sluggard theme, and those that receive special attention such as the theme of going surety and are found elsewhere in the Hebrew Bible, locates us as readers both within the book of Proverbs as well as in the larger context of the canon. Prov 6:1–19 thus does not stand in isolation either from the Writings or from the Torah.

From the point of view of the parent's lesson, which is firmly fixed within portions of the Joseph story, we can again identify a historical shift between Torah and Proverbs. There emerges a sense that we are not reading examples of interpretations which slavishly copy traditions from the Torah; rather we are in the presence of an ongoing creative combination of traditions, points of view, and dialogue. Because our text reflects an attempt to locate the reader in the larger context of Israel's traditions, i.e., both Torah and Proverbs, a constructive understanding of the parent's discourse depends on the reader's ability to perceive textual transformations. Such transformations affirm a degree of continuity between past and present. Moreover, by alluding to events from Israel's past, the parent underscores the paradigmatic nature of the Joseph story and how certain kinds of action lead to particular results.

Our awareness of such transformations within the traditions as represented in our example from Prov 6:1–19 helps us to account for the parent's allusive reference to portions of the narrative sequence from Genesis. The events in the Joseph story function as the given background for the parent's lesson. Vv 1–19 move in such a way as to cast a backward glance to Judah and his relationship with his brothers in order to lay claim to a broader (re-)interpretation as represented in the parent's discourse. Even though the parent does not cite overtly the earlier episodes from the Joseph story, there are clear examples of covert citations *via* the rich combination of themes about surety, famine, and the familial relationship of brothers. Thus, the focus of the parent's discourse is not the Joseph story but rather how well events from Genesis assist the parent in making his/her case to the son in the context of the book of Proverbs.

Interestingly, Prov 6:1–19 is the third example where Judah plays a role in the tradition. We saw how Judah's discourse in the selling of Joseph is reutilized in Prov 1:8–19. In Prov 1:20–33 wisdom plays upon the theme of Judah's failure as a nation to heed Jeremiah's words. In Prov 6:1–19 Judah's earlier acts and speech again provide the impetus for the parent's lesson. Judah is not far removed from text and context especially when he is alluded to in the graduated numerical saying in 6:16–19. As we argued earlier, the order of Judah's decisive speech-events in Genesis 37 and 43 are reflected in Prov 6:1–19 but in reverse order. The text and the context of scripture for Prov 6:1–19 situates us as readers in a world populated by recognizable figures from the traditions which in turn lend credibility to the parent's discourse. The parent's words take on a refreshingly broader theological and historical dimension when we hear the expansive nature of Israel's biblical traditions. By recalling the events surrounding Judah, his brothers, and Jacob, we are further instructed in the "meaning" of the parent's lesson as well as cautioned concerning types of action.

5

THE IMPLICATIONS OF OUR
ANALYSIS FOR PROVERB 1–9.

INTRODUCTION

Having established correspondences between portions of Proverbs 1–9 and traditions from Genesis and Jeremiah, we can raise the question concerning what role each of these units of discourse plays in the overall content of Proverbs 1–9. In contrast to a scholar like S. R. Driver who avers that there is "no definite arrangement in the subjects treated"[1] in Proverbs 1–9, we are prepared to offer an assessment of the emerging rationale for the parent's discourse in Proverbs 1–9 which takes into account Prov 1:8–19, 1:20–33, and 6:1–19. In the following section we will first describe other features in Proverbs 1–9 which pick up themes and allusions initiated by the opening chapter of Proverbs. Afterwards we will concentrate on the role of Prov 6:1–19.

THE OPENING AND CLOSING OF PROVERBS 1–9.

One of the goals of C. Camp's analysis of the "feminine" in the book of Proverbs is to account for the diversity of content not only for

---

[1] S. R. Driver, *An Introduction to the Literature of the Old Testament*, 395.

Proverbs 1–9 but also for the book of Proverbs as a whole. According to Camp, the imagery of the "feminine" functions as the conceptual framework for binding the book together.[2] While we are in basic agreement with her attempts to discover some order within Proverbs, we cannot agree with a number of her conclusions.

Her analysis of the bracketing effect of the opening and closing chapters in Proverbs works only if portions of the text are ignored. Most notably, Camp leaves out of consideration all of Prov 1:8–19 in her analysis of the role of "feminine" imagery.[3] According to Camp, "feminine" imagery functions as the content of the inclusio in the opening and closing chapters of the book of Proverbs.[4] In the chapter titled, "Proverbs 1–9 and 31: The Literary Re-contextualization of the Proverb Collection," Camp argues for an intentional "canonical shaping" of the book of Proverbs. As evidence for "canonical shaping" Camp points to the similarity in content between the opening and closing chapters in Proverbs. Camp says:

> [T]he bracketing of the proverb collection by the poems on personified wisdom [i.e., Prov 1:20–33; 8] and the woman of worth [i.e., Proverbs 31] makes a contribution in literary craft sufficient to re-orient the proverb

---

[2] In the conclusion to her book, Camp states: "[T]he female imagery works as a golden cord that binds the book of Proverbs together, tying beginning to end and weaving a web with the many other images scattered throughout the book, providing a woof to their warp. Although the formal contrast between the introductory poems [i.e., Proverbs 1–9] and the collection of proverbs [i.e., Proverbs 10–30] remains clear, a striking degree of integration has been brought to the book by means of the external framework of poems about women, and by the internal web of images tied to the dominant female image. This integration is emphasized, moreover, by the use of the stylistic device of personification, which brings a sense of unity to the multiplicity of the proverb collection, without sacrificing nuance and concreteness"(*Wisdom and the Feminine*, 289).

[3] Earlier, E. Pfeiffer (*Introduction to the Old Testament*, 647) also argued for a similar "shaping" of Proverbs 1–9 on the basis of the opening and closing wisdom discourses. Like Camp, Pfeiffer ignores Prov 1:8–19. He also rearranges Proverbs 9 so vv 7–12 come after 9:18.

[4] The only place that she mentions Prov 1:8–19 is on p. 200. In her comparison between the content of Prov 23:22–24:4 and Prov 1:10–19 and 6:24–35, she says: "Prov 1–9 does not include any warning against strong drink, but is concerned throughout with the two other major themes of 23.22–24.4. In particular, those admonitions placed in the mouth of the mother as well as the father voice clearly the dangers of violent men and harlotrous women both of whom 'lie in wait' (ʾarah) [sic, ʾarab] for their victims, (1.10–19; 6.24–35)." Contrary to Camp, the verb ʾarab does not appear anywhere in 6:24–35.

collection from its original function as a schoolboy lesson-book to its later
function as part of a canon of religious literature.5

Camp's analysis, however, lacks support from Proverbs. Far too
much of the content of the first nine chapters is passed over by Camp.
Moreover, the opening lesson is Prov 1:8–19, and it concerns the parent's
discourse about the "sinners" who are identified as men and *not* the
feminine figure of wisdom as Camp leads the reader to believe.6

A level of editing which achieves a degree of shaping for Proverbs 1–
9 can still be described. We have already seen the commonly shared
features shared by Prov 1:8–19 and 1:20–33 which indicate that they are
to be read as complementary opening lessons. The issues addressed in
the opening two discourse units (i.e., Proverbs 1) are returned to in
Proverbs 9, thus forming a closure to the first major section in Proverbs.
For example, in both Prov 1:10 and 1:22 the *petî/pĕtāyim*, "simple ones"
are addressed. In Prov 9:4a, the closing discourse in Proverbs 1–9,
wisdom's maids call out to the *petî* saying: *mî petî yāsur hēnnâ,* "whoever

---

5 *Wisdom and the Feminine,* 182. See pp. 187–188; 191; 201; 252; 255 for similar
statements about the bracketing effect that is achieved by beginning and ending the
book of Proverbs with feminine imagery.

6 Even if 1:20–33 were the opening discourse in the book, as Camp says, it is difficult
to make an argument for "female imagery" when there is nothing in 1:20–33 which
alludes to wisdom being feminine. Camp assumes that the masculine and feminine
noun endings in Hebrew are gender specific, i.e., a feminine ending is synonymous
with specific sexual identity. But we know from other cases in the Hebrew Bible that
masculine and feminine noun endings do not necessarily specify gender. A noun
ending can be used to represent both masculine and feminine objects just as either
can mean "it." See *GKC* 122q. Recently, D. Michel (*Grundlegung einer hebräischen
Syntax: Teil 1—Sprachwissenschaftliche Methodik, Genus und Numerus des Nomens*
[Neukirchen-Vluyn: Neukirchener-V., 1977] argues that the so-called feminine plural
ending, as we have in *ḥokmôt* in Prov 1:20, can be translated as a plural form *nomen
unitatis,* i.e., an "individual plural"(pp. 34–63) without regard to gender. Even if one
could make the argument that the reference to wisdom in 1:20 represents an
overriding interest in the nature of the feminine, as Camp does, then one is faced
with the conspicuous absence of any other reference to wisdom as a female figure in
vv 21–33. The absence of any expressed interest in wisdom in 1:20–33 as a feminine
figure is all the more striking when we recall that in other places in Proverbs we can
clearly identify the attributes of the "feminine," such as in Proverbs 31. The dominant
interest in Prov 1:20–33 concerns the failure of others to respond to *words* which are
associated with wisdom with no indication whatsoever that wisdom's gender plays
any role in her discourse. Camp does not address the problem of the plural ending of
wisdom, *ḥokmôt,* in 1:20. Moreover, in Prov 8:1, the other text important for Camp's
analysis of the "feminine," instead of *ḥokmôt,* the text combines *ḥokmâ,* "wisdom,"
with *bînâ,* "understanding," without any further reference to gender, either feminine
or masculine.

is simple, turn in here." In 9:6 wisdom says to the *petî*: *ᶜizbû pĕtāyim wiḥyû wĕʾišrû bĕderek bînâ*, "leave simpleness and live, and rejoice in the way of understanding." In contrast, the *ʾēšet kĕsîlût*, "foolish woman," in 9:13 competes with the maids' call to the *petî* in 9:4 by framing her invitation in exactly the same words as the their invitation in 9:4. Prov 7:7 and 8:5 are the only other places outside of Proverbs 1 and 9 where the *petî* are mentioned. Of the eleven uses of the form *pth* in Proverbs 1–9, Proverbs 1 and 9, the opening and closing chapters of the first major division of Proverbs, record eight instances of *pth*.

Furthermore, Prov 9:7–12 contains a section very much reminiscent of Prov 1:22. In our analysis of Prov 1:20–33 we indicated how 1:22 contains references to the *pĕtāyim*, "simple ones," *lēṣîm*, "scoffers," *kĕsîlîm*, "fools," and how the book of Proverbs consistently portrays the *lēṣîm* and *kĕsîlîm* as unreprovable in contrast to the *pĕtāyim*. Wisdom's discourse in 1:20–33 is framed in such a way that her words are addressed only to the *pĕtāyim*. In Prov 1:22–33 wisdom implies that the *lēṣ* are among those who refuse to heed her earlier word.

As for 9:7–12, wisdom and her maids pause in their direct address to the *petî* in vv 1–6 to describe the ways of a *lēṣ*, "scoffer," in the third person. Many commentators treat 9:7–12 as an interpolation which has been mistakenly inserted into Proverbs 9.[7] But in the context of the larger scope of Proverbs 1–9 and especially in comparison with Prov 1:8–19 and 1:20–33, these verses offer a concluding comment which links the beginning and ending of Proverbs 1–9.

A striking similarity is evident in the characterization of the *lēṣ* in Prov 1:22ff and 9:7ff that we do not meet in a developed manner elsewhere in Proverbs 1–9.[8] Prov 9:7–8 indicates the uselessness of "reproving" *yākaḥ*, a *lēṣ*. Prov 1:22–33 discloses the same point of view.

---

7 C. H. Toy (*Proverbs*, 183) says: "Standing between these two descriptions [of wisdom in 9:1–6 and folly in vv 13–18], and interrupting their connection, is the paragraph v. 7–12, composed of separate aphorisms; it belongs by its contents in the succeeding scribal error." W. O. E. Oesterley (*Proverbs*, 69) refers to 9:7–12 as "*Some stray Proverbs*." R. B. Y. Scott (*Proverbs*, 74–75) rearranges Proverbs 9 as follows: 9:1–6, 10–12, 7–9, 13–18. He treats vv 7–9 as an "expanded proverb" brought in by an editor because of the content of v 12. W. McKane (*Proverbs*, 359) also notes that 9:7–12 "disturb both the balance and the continuity of the chapter." B. Lang (*Wisdom and the Book of Proverbs*, 87–89) treats Prov 9:7–10 as an intrusion. These verses, according to Lang, represent the original ending of Proverbs 1–9 but have been rearranged as a result of an editorial reworking of the text under the influence of the LXX. Cf. also, W. Frankenberg, *Die Sprüche*, 63. K. Delitzsch (*Proverbs*, 201) recognizes the consistency in wisdom's discourse in differentiating between the *pĕtāyim* "simple" and the *lēṣ*, "scoffer" that we find elsewhere in the book of Proverbs.

8 Only in Prov 3:34 is the *lēṣ* mentioned again.

Wisdom calls the *pĕtāyim*, "simple ones," to heed her "reproof" which by implication the *lēṣîm* have ignored. In 1:25, 30 the issue of "reproof" appears. Those who reject wisdom's "reproof" face ruin, according to Prov 1:32–33. Prov 9:7–12 indicates that the *lēṣ*, by rejecting "reproof" contributes to his own destruction. Where wisdom's speech in 1:20–33 indicates the scoffers' "hate" for knowledge (cf. 1:22, 29a), wisdom warns against "reproving" a scoffer for all one will receive is his "hate," 9:8.

As much as commentators note the intrusive nature of the discussion of the *lēṣ* in 9:7–12, vv 7–12 contribute to the editorial attempt to offer a closure to the opening chapter in Proverbs. Such a closure registers the importance the opening chapter has for establishing that the parent's discourse is not fabricated out of thin air. Rather, the veiled references to events from the Torah and Prophets lend a high degree of credibility to the value of the parent's discourse as it is couched in a new sapiential context.

Other factors indicate a level of editing which ties the opening and closing chapters of Proverbs 1–9 together. In Prov 1:7, the text offers the motto for the book of Proverbs: *yirʾat YHWH rēʾšît dāʿat ḥokmâ ûmûsār ʾewîlîm bāzû* "The fear of the Lord is the beginning of knowledge; fools despise wisdom and knowledge." Moreover, those who have not heeded wisdom's earlier call "hated knowledge and did not choose the fear of the Lord," *śānĕʾû dāʾat wĕyirʾat YHWH lōʾ bāḥārû*, 1:29. Prov 9:10 returns to the same theme in the context of the description of the "scoffer" and the "wise man:" *tĕḥillat ḥokmâ yirʾat YHWH wĕdaʿat qĕdōšîm bînâ*, "The fear of the Lord is the beginning of wisdom, and the knowledge of the Holy One is insight." As we have just seen, the "scoffer," hates "reproof." In the context of 9:7–12 the text implies that the "scoffer" is not identified with those who fear YHWH. In contrast, the "wise man" gains a long life on the basis of his fear of the Lord and his ability to accept reproof.

A thematic play on the idea of *derek*, the "way" resonates between Proverbs 1 and 9. In Prov 1:15 the son is warned not to go in the sinners' "*way*," and "hold back your foot from their paths." Also, in 1:31 those who refuse to heed wisdom's call will be consumed by *darkām*, "their way," much like the person who will bear the consequences of being wise onto himself in 9:12. In 9:6 wisdom and her maids invite the *petî* (cf. 1:10) "in the way of insight." In contrast, the *ʾēšet kĕsîlût*, "foolish woman," tries to allure the *petî* from his "way," in 9:15, *liqrōʾ lĕʿōbĕrê dārek hamĕyaššĕrîm ʾōrĕḥôṭām*, "calling to those who pass by, who are going straight in their *way*." Her way leads to death, v 18, while the way of wisdom is life, v 6.

Furthermore, in the opening lesson in Prov 1:8–19 the parent quotes the words of the "sinners" where they try to entice (*pth*) the son to lie in wait for the innocent in order symbolically to consume him *kišě'ôl*, "like Sheol," 1:12. The ironic twist, according to the parent's discourse in 1:17–19, is that if anyone is to be consumed by Sheol it will be the "sinners." In 9:18, the concluding verse to Proverbs 1–9, the discourse returns full circle to the topic of Sheol and strikes a reminiscent chord with the parent's opening discourse in Proverbs 1:8–19. In place of the first person discourse of the sinful *men*, which represents the first example of reported discourse, now the "foolish *woman*" is given center stage when she speaks in first person discourse in 9:16–17. The opening and closing discourse units start and end with speech from the very people the son is warned to avoid! In 9:16–17 she entices (*pth*) the "simple one" who passes by just as the "sinners" in 1:11–14 entice the son. Where the "sinners" promise financial gain by lying in wait for the innocent in 1:10–14, the "foolish woman" promises pleasantries for those who consort with her. Yet in Prov 9:18 those who populate Sheol are those who associate with the likes of a *'ēšet kěsîlût*, "foolish woman."

A complementary point of view is thus maintained between the opening and closing discourse units in Proverbs 1–9. Contrary to appearances, those who associate with either the "sinners" or the likes of a "foolish woman," for reasons of personal gain or for illicit sexual involvement, will end up contributing to their own destruction. Thus we witness a common focus in the opening and closing didactic lessons of Proverbs 1–9. In the first lesson the "sinners" portrayed as men entice the potentially "enticeable" to participate in the shedding of innocent blood. In the last lesson, the "foolish woman" entices the potentially "enticeable" to engage in illicit sex. But Sheol awaits them all.

PARENTAL WARNINGS ABOUT "SINFUL MEN" AND "STRANGE/ FOREIGN WOMEN:" THE ROLE OF PROV 1:8–19 AND 1:20–33 AS INTRODUCTION.

Because the opening and closing words in Proverbs 1–9 address similar issues we can look for further clues as to the focus of the parent's discourse. In fact, the allusions to the "way" either as a way to life or a way to ruin, play a key role in further identifying the kinds of men and women whom the son is to avoid. The references to the way in the opening and closing sections of Proverbs 1 and 9 are not the only times that these expressions occur. Indeed, the variety of references to the way as *derek*, "way," *'ōrḥôt*, "paths," *minnětîbâ* "path," and *ma'gāl* "course"/"path" throughout Proverbs 1–9 helps to provide a degree of unity to the various discourses of the parent.

Commentators have long recognized that the parent narrows his/her focus upon two types of people in Proverbs 1–9 whom the son is to avoid: sinful/wicked men and strange/foreign women.[9] Even though Prov 2:12–22 is the first time that we are introduced to the combination of men and women whom the son is to avoid, the groundwork has already been laid in Proverbs 1 for the parent's reasons to avoid them.

After the opening discourse units in Prov 1:8–19 and 1:20–33, where the parent and wisdom combine different levels of discourse, the focus of the text shifts to what the parent has to say without direct reference to anyone else's speech. Commentators note that all of Proverbs 2 can be read as one long sentence of the parent.[10] Interestingly, R. B. Y. Scott argues that Proverbs 2 probably stood as the opening discourse of the book of Proverbs.[11] But as the text now stands, the parent's discourse is prefaced by lessons drawn form earlier biblical traditions.

The placement of Prov 1:8–19 and 1:20–33, with their content from the Torah and the Prophets, assumes a significant role in how the following discourse of the parent is read. We know from Psalm studies, for example, that the opening two psalms orient the reader to the Psalter by establishing a point of view based upon the Torah and the Prophets.[12]

---

[9] As A. Robert ("Les attaches littéraires bibliques de Prov. I-IX," 51) says: "Les recommandations pratiques de Prov. I-IX veulent mettre le jeune homme en garde contre deux séductions trés dangereuses: celle du gain facile et illicite réalisé principalement par les malfaiteurs de grand chemin, et celle de la luxure, envisagée uniquement sous l'aspect de l'adultére." Cf. R. B. Y. Scott *Proverbs,* 42; C. Camp, *Wisdom and the Feminine,* 256.

[10] See : C. H. Toy, *Proverbs,* 31; R. B. Y. Scott, *Proverbs,* 42; and O. Eissfeldt, *Introduction to the Old Testament,* 473. E. Pfeiffer (*Introduction to the Old Testament,* 647) treats Proverbs 2–7 as "the main part of the speech" of Proverbs.

[11] Scott (*Proverbs*) points out that Proverbs 2 was probably the opening chapter in the book of Proverbs. He bases his analysis on how the content of Proverbs 2 establishes "a kind of prospectus" (p. 42) for the remaining chapters: "Evidently the purpose of this chapter is programmatic, since its several parts are later resumed as the subjects of several discourses"(p. 43). Cf. p. 16.

[12] See: J. L. Mays, "The Place of the Torah-Psalms in the Psalter." Mays concentrates mainly on Psalms 1; 2; 19; and 119. His article adds to the current interest in how Psalms 1 and 2 direct the reader's attention to the intentional editing of the Psalter. Mays notes the interconnections made between the the canonical collection of the Psalms, and the Torah and Prophets. Connections are made ostensibly *via* the reference to the Torah in Psalm 1 and the Prophets in Psalm 2. Mays also notes how Psalms 1 and 2 delineate two different groups of people: the inner circle of those who identify with Torah teaching and the reprobates outside the circle of pious believers. A degree of specificity is established by alluding to persons from Israel's past. By

As in the case of Psalms 1 and 2 (with their orientation to the Torah and the Prophets), which serve to introduce the Psalms of David starting with Psalm 3, the parent's first lengthy discourse in Proverbs, starts only after introducing discourse from the Torah and Prophets in Prov 1:8–19 and 1:20–33.

Prov 1:8–19 with its allusive play on Genesis (i.e., Torah) and Prov 1:20–33 with its allusive play on Jeremiah (i.e., Prophets) constitute a point of view which is reiterated in a variety of ways throughout Proverbs 1–9. As Psalms 1 and 2 initiate a reading of the Psalter by referring the reader to the Torah and the Prophets, Prov 1:8–19 and 1:20–33 establish a comparable viewpoint. One now reads the following chapters through the lens of the opening lessons, 1:8–19 and 1:20–33.[13]

An awareness of the role played by the opening two psalms may also help to account for the presence and order of 1:8–19 and 1:20–33. Not only is 1:20–33 the only example of prophetic speech in the book of Proverbs, but as prophetic speech it follows the opening discourse which is derived from the Torah. Even though one is reading the book of Proverbs, one gains access to Proverbs by starting with lessons drawn

---

establishing a context, i.e., Torah and Prophets, as the domain in which the Psalter is read, and by drawing a clear line between insiders and outsiders by means of examples drawn from the Torah and Prophets, the opening two psalms act as guides for the reading of the Psalter as a whole. Cf: G. Sheppard, *Wisdom as a Hermeneutical Construct*, 136–144, where he offers an analysis of the role Psalms 1 and 2 in the context of the Psalter. Sheppard likewise addresses the unique role that these two psalms play not only in the context of the Psalter as a whole but in the context of the canon. See Sheppard's extensive footnotes on pp 136–144 for references to other scholars who have discussed Psalms 1 and 2. More recently, G. H. Wilson (*The Editing of the Hebrew Psalter* [SBLDS 76, Chico, California: Scholars Press, 1985] 206) says: "The effect of the editorial fixation of the first ps as an introduction to the whole Psalter is subtly to alter how the reader views and appropriates the pss collected there;" and N. Gottwald (*The Hebrew Bible,* 526): "One entire category of psalms, called wisdom or didactic psalms, focuses proper prayer and worship on wholehearted adherence to the divine law (in many, if not all, instances this law is probably already the canonical Law). Psalms 1 and 2, which form a complementary introduction to the whole collection, epitomize this manner of praying and pondering the texts, for the Psalms have become testimonies to the proven power of fidelity to God's law in shaping righteous and happy lives in a just community. And even though the Davidic monarch heralded in Psalm 2, and elsewhere throughout the Psalms, was no longer reigning when Psalms was finally shaped, he was remembered and anticipated as the executor of justice in Jewish society so that the divine law might be embodied on earth."

[13] R. Van Leeuwen, "Liminality and Worldview," 128, says this about the theme established by Prov 1:10–19: "The end of sinners is death, and thus the parent sounds a theme that rings throughout 1–9 and the entire book . . . ."

first from the Torah then the Prophets. The ordering of the opening lessons in the book of Proverbs also suggests that as early as the book of Proverbs there is evidence of an evolving sense of a fixed body of authoritative scripture. By alluding first to traditions from Israel's past as recorded in scripture in the same order of Torah and Prophets, the final editing of the book of Proverbs identifies it as a companion piece to what later becomes canonical scripture.

We can also see a high degree of continuity between Proverbs 1 and 2. For example, the manner in which the parent opens and closes the discourse unit in 1:8–19, and the fact that the parent introduces wisdom's speech in 1:21–22, indicates that the concluding words in 1:32–33 are probably those of the parent. The probability that such is the case becomes clearer in Prov 2:1ff. No mention is made of wisdom as a separate figure. Instead, the figure of those people who take the wrong path, alluded to in Prov 1:8–19 and 1:20–33, clearly re-emerges in the parent's warnings to the son in Proverbs 2.

Primary concern is given to words/discourse (2:1) affiliated with ḥokmâ and těbûnâ, "wisdom" and "understanding." The parent's words are the conduit through which the son acquires "the fear of the Lord," and "knowledge" (cf. 2:5–6, 10). The emphasis upon "the fear of the Lord," and "knowledge," likewise singles out the same themes found in 1:7, the introductory motto of the book of Proverbs and in 1:29, wisdom's judgment upon the earlier inhabitants of Judah/Jerusalem. In addition, YHWH's wisdom and understanding are characterized as linṣôr ʾorḥôt mišpāṭ wěderek ḥăsîdāw yišnōr ʾaz tābîn ṣedeq ûmišpāṭ ûmêšārîm kol maʿgāl ṭôb, "guarding the *paths* of justice, and preserves the *way* of the saints. Then you will understand righteousness and justice and equity, every good *path*" (2:8–9).

The importance of the parent's words in Proverbs 2 relates directly to the theme that receives more attention in the following chapters of Proverbs—that of choosing the right "way"/"path" in order to avoid two kinds of people: "men" who perpetuate "evil" and the "strange/foreign woman."

In 2:12–19 the parent concentrates solely upon characterizing the men and the woman in very specific terminology. The immediate importance of the parent's words is how his/her discourse continues issues which have been raised in the opening two lessons in Proverbs 1. Only now the parent directs attention to the positive side of his/her teaching by calling attention to the source of wisdom and understanding; i.e., YHWH. The reference to "evil men" and the "strange"/"foreign woman" provides a foil for the parent's argument to follow his/her version of what constitutes wisdom and the fear of YHWH.

Prov 2:12–19 divides neatly into two sections: one dealing with the ways of the "wicked man" in vv 12–15 and the other with the "strange"/"foreign" woman in vv 16–19. Although the parent does not quote the words of the "wicked men" as in 1:11–14, we can detect a number of expressions which help to forge a common viewpoint in the parent's discourse between Proverbs 1 and 2:12–15. Most notably, the expressions *derek*, "way," *ʾōrḥôt*, "paths," and *nātîb*, "path," receive special attention in 2:12–15. If the son follows the parent's advice, then the son will be saved 2:12 *midderek rāʿ*, "from the *way* of evil," from men 2:13 *haʿōzēbîm ʾorḥôt yōšer lāleket bĕdarkê ḥōšek*, "who forsake the *paths* of uprightness to walk in the *ways* of darkness," 2:15 *ʾăšer ʾorḥôtêhem ʿiqqĕšîm ûnelôzîm bĕmaʿgĕlôtām*, "whose *paths* are crooked, and are devious in their *ways*."

The parent earlier warns the son "not to go in the *way* with them (i.e., "sinners"), hold back your foot from their *paths*," *ʾal tēlēk bederek ʾittām mĕnaʿ. raglĕkā minnĕtîbātām*, in 1:15, for their ways lead to the "paths," *ʾorḥôt*, of self-destruction, according to 1:19. In the initial lesson the "way"/"paths" are associated with Judah and the selling of Joseph.

As for the "strange"/"foreign" woman, mentioned for the first time in 2:16–19, her ways are described in terminology similar to the ways of the "evil men:"

> 2:18 *kî šāḥâ ʾel māwet bêtāh wĕʾel rĕpāʾîm maʿgelôteyhā*, "for her house sinks down to death, and her *paths* to the shades,
> 2:19 *kol baʾeyhā lōʾ yĕšûbûn wĕlōʾ yaśśîgû ʾorḥôt ḥayyîm*, none who go to her come back nor do they regain the *paths* of life."

In addition, where the "evil men" have *mĕdabbēr tahpukôt*, "perverted speech," in 2:12, the "strange"/"foreign" woman speaks *ʾămāreyhā heḥĕlîqâ*, "smooth words" (2:16)—an expression that has derogatory overtones within Proverbs 1–9.

In contrast to the ways of the "evil men" and "strange/foreign" woman, the parent alludes to the "way of the good," and the "paths of the righteous" in 2:20, implying that these "men" know the source of wisdom and the fear of YHWH. The parent augments his/her discourse by specifying that those who choose the "way of the good" will be the ones who "will dwell in the land" unlike the "wicked," and "treacherous," who will be "cut off," and "rooted out" of the land.

In 1:33 reference is made to "dwelling secure" and "being at ease:" *wĕšōmēay lî yiškān betaḥ wĕšaʾanan mippaḥad rāʿâ* "and he who listens to me will dwell secure and will be at ease, without dread of evil." We know from our traditio-historical analysis of 1:20–33 that the parent's discourse is playing on traditions from Jeremiah which reflect the question of dwelling secure in the land of Judah. Even though an added dimension of the land in 2:21 is made, the endings of 1:32–33 and 2:21–22 strike a similar chord. Where those who do not listen to words of wisdom are destroyed in 1:32–33, those who choose the way/paths of evil instead of wisdom and understanding will not have a stake in the land in 2:21–22. In other words, those who listen to words of wisdom "will dwell secure," *yiškān betaḥ* (1:33), and those who choose the path of righteousness "will dwell in the land," *yiškĕnû ʾāreṣ* (2:21). Furthermore, if the "son" heeds words of wisdom he will be "delivered" *nṣl*, 2:12, 16, from both the way of the "evil men" and the "strange"/"foreign" woman.

Because the parent frames his/her opening discourse in terms of traditions from the Torah and the Prophets, the opening chapter assumes a significant role in how the following chapter is read. Not only the allsuions to "paths" and "ways" in 1:8–19 and 1:20–33, but also the allusions to those in the past who took the wrong "paths"/"ways," affect our reading of the occurrences of the similar motifs of "paths" and "ways" in Prov 2:12–22. Read in conjunction with Prov 1:8–19 and 1:20–33, the parent's admonition to "receive my words, and treasure up my commandments," 2:1, is enhanced by the reutilization of select vocabulary and motifs found in 1:8–19 and 1:20–33. And key terms such as those relating to "ways" and "paths" help to focus the parent's discourse.

Other references to "ways"/"paths" can be found scattered throughout Proverbs 3 such as in 3:6, 17, 23, 31. In 3:31–33 the parent punctuates his/her discourse by enlisting YHWH's reaction to the "ways" of *ʾîš ḥāmās*, "a man of violence," *nalôz*, "a perverse man." Such a man is *tôʿăbat YHWH*, "an abomination to the Lord." We saw earlier that similar terminology is used to describe the man who sends "discord" among brothers in Prov 6:16–19.

Once again in Proverbs 4, the parent concentrates on the "way" of the "evil men" in comparison with the "way" that derives from wisdom and uprightness: *bĕderek ḥokmâ hōrētîkā hidraktîkā bemaʿgelê yōšer*, "I have taught you the *way* of wisdom; I have led you in the *paths of uprightness*" (4:11). In Prov 2:12–13, those "men" who engage in the "way of evil" are those *haʿōzĕbîm ʾorḥôt yōšer*, "who forsake the *paths of uprightness*." The "way of wisdom" stands in contrast to "path"/"way" of the wicked: *bĕʾoraḥ rĕšāʿîm ʾal tābōʾ wĕʾal tĕʾaššēr bĕderek rāʿîm*, "Do not enter the *path* of the wicked, and do not walk in the *way* of evil men" (4:14); and *wĕʾōraḥ ṣaddîqîm kĕʾôr nōgah hôlēk wāʾôr ʿad nĕkôn hayyôm derek rĕšāʿîm kāʾăpēlâ lōʾ yādĕʿû bammeh yikkāšēlû*, "But the *path* of the righteous is like the light of dawn, which shines brighter and brighter until full day. The *way* of the wicked is like deep darkness; they do not know over what they stumble."

As for the "strange"/"foreign" women mentioned for the first time along with the "evil men" in Proverbs 2, she is not mentioned again until Proverbs 5. However, where the ways of "evil men" are mentioned throughout Proverbs 1–4 (with the exception of the brief reference to the "strange"/"foreign woman" in 2:16–19), references to the "strange"/"foreign woman" are now discussed along with the ways of the "evil"/"wicked" man as they are first introduced in Proverbs 2:12–22.

In Prov 5:3 she is called the *zārâ* and in v 20 she is called the *zārâ/nokriyyâ* as in 2:16. Moreover, not only is her speech referred to as being "smooth," *ḥlq* (5:3), as in 2:16, but her *ʾōraḥ*, "path," and *maʿgĕlōteyhā*, "her ways," lead to *māwet*, "death," and *šĕʾôl*, "Sheol"(5:5–6)—expressions similar to the parent's earlier description of the *zārâ/nokriyyâ* found in 2:16–19 and the *ʾēšet kĕsîlût*, "foolish woman," 9:18–19, the concluding verses in Proverbs 9. Interestingly, YHWH sees *darkê ʾîš*, "the *ways* of a man," and *kol magĕlōtāw*, "all his *paths*," when he associates with the "strange"/"foreign woman" in 5:20–21 illustrating again the continuity within the parent's discourse.

In the parent's lengthy description of the seduction of the "young man without sense," in Proverbs 7, the woman, *zārâ/nokriyyâ*, 7:5, is again described as having *ʾămāreyhā heḥĕlîqâ*, "smoothed her words" (cf. 7:21). And as in the other references to her, *darkê šĕʾôl bĕtāh yōrĕdôt ʾel ḥadrê māwet*, "her house is the *way* to Sheol, going down to the chambers of death" (7:27), an expression very similar to 2:18–19 and 9:14, 18.

Lastly, references to "way"/"paths" appears to be a central aspect of Proverb 8. As in the other occasion when wisdom speaks in Prov 1:20–33, emphasis is placed upon the necessity of hearing in Proverbs 8. "Wisdom calls," *ḥokmâ tiqrāʾ*, vv 1, 4, and "understanding raises her voice," *ûtĕbûnâ tittēn qôlāh*, a combination similar to Prov 2:1. Wisdom/understanding implores "men" to "hear," *šāmaʿ*, vv 6, 32, 33, 34. Other references to speech such as *śĕpātay*, "my lips," v 6, 7, *ḥikkî*, "my mouth," v 7, *kol ʾimrê pî*, "all the words of my mouth," v 8, are further linked with *bĕʾoraḥ ṣĕdāqâ* "the way of justice," *nĕtîbôt mišpāt*, "paths of justice," v 20, *dĕrākay*, "my ways," v 32. By heeding wisdom/understanding in Proverbs 8, one receives not just *ʿōšer wĕkābôd hôn ʿātēq*, "riches and honor, enduring wealth," v 18 (the things promised by the "sinners" in 1:10–14), one also receives *ḥayyîm*, "life," and *rāṣôn meYHWH*, "favor from the Lord," v 35.

Prov 6:1–19 and Its Interrelationship
with Proverbs 5.

Given the parent's overriding interest in warning the son about the
evil ways of some men and women, we saw how the reutilization of
traditions from Genesis and Jeremiah in Prov 1:8–19; 1:20–33 help to
establish their words. As for Prov 6:1–19, these verses likewise have the
potential of recounting events from the past in order to illuminate issues
addressed by the parent. Contrary to P. Skehan's attempt to reestablish
what appears to be a natural order to the parent's discourse by
eliminating all of Prov 6:1–19,[14] there are clear indications within the text
which suggest a continuous reading between Proverbs 5:1–23 and 6:1–19.

Recently O. Plöger makes a case for the editorial combination of Prov
5:1–23 and 6:1–19. Like other commentators[15] who have pointed out how

---

[14] "Proverbs 5:15–17 and 6:20–24," 1: "According to any understanding of the text
which permits us to consider the entire section, chs. 5–7 *with the exception of 6:1–19*, as
the development of a single idea prepared for in 2:16–19, we should be concerned to
find, for such textual irregularities as exist, the explanation which least impedes the
harmonious development of thought"(emphasis added). R. B. Y. Scott, *Proverbs*, 55,
places Prov 6:22 after 5:15–19 and says that "apparently [6:22] belongs after vs. 19 [of
chap. 5]" (p. 58). R. Murphy, *Wisdom Literature*, 59, adopts Skehan's interpretation
and says: "6:22 is best read after 5:19."

[15] P. Skehan, "Proverbs 5:15–19 and 6:20–24," ignores 5:20–23 in his analysis. W.
McKane, *Proverbs*, 313: "The concept of *mûsār* which prevails in this chapter is that of
the international Instruction and, apart from vv. 21–23, there are no traces of
Yahwistic theological and moral categories. The reasoning which throws doubt on
3.32–35; 4.18ff. and the additions to 4.27 in LXX . . . also applies to these verses [5:21–
23]. They are located at the end of a chapter and so in a place where reinterpretative
expansion by means of motive clauses can be most conveniently made, and they
introduce a Yahwistic note which is absent from the remainder of the chapter. . . .
Verses 21–23 present a concept of *mûsār* (v. 23) into which there enters a theology and
moralism conspicuously absent from the remainder of the chapter. The man who dies
through his indiscipline is wrapped (*yiśgeh*) . . . in the shroud of his massive folly is
he who does not reckon with Yahweh's constant scrutiny of his ways, who becomes
the prisoner of his iniquities and is entangled in the cords of his sin. . . . Certainly the
idea of the all-seeing God occurs in *Amenemope* (xvii.9–12) and in the *Samas
Hymn* . . . , but I am confident that this passage redefines *mûsār* and *'iwwelet* in
Yahwistic terms." For 5:21–23 C. H. Toy, *Proverbs*, 116, says: "General concluding
reflection, similar to what is found at the end of chs. 1. 2. 3, without special bearing
on the body of the chapter, perhaps the addition of the final editor." Interestingly,
Toy comments that there may have been at one time an expressed antecedent for
"*him*" that has been lost. As Toy says: "The insertion of the words *the wicked*, in v 22,
appears to show that the reference in the *him* was thought to need explanation; and it
is natural to suppose that, when the verse was written, the reference was clear, that
is, that the antecedent of *him* had been expressed. The same thing is true of the *his* in

5:21–23 appear to be a later addition to Prov 5:1–20, he states: "Die verse [5:21–23] zeigen keinen unmittelbaren Zusammenhang mit dem Gedankengang des Kapitels, denn sie beigegeben sind."[16] Plöger, however, pursues the question of what role 5:21–23 plays in the larger context of Proverbs 5 and 6.

Plöger detects an unusual reference to the "all-seeing eye" of YHWH, ⁶ênê YHWH, in combination with the lesson concerning the "fremden Frau," "strange woman." Prov 5:21–23 is the only time in Proverbs 1–9 where such a combination occurs.[17]

In contrast to scholars who tend to pass over vv 21–23 in their interpretation of Proverbs 5 and 6, Plöger argues that vv 21–23 with their unusual reference to the all-seeing eye of God which watches over the "man" functions as a transition (Überleitung) which links Prov 6:1–19 with 5:1–20 and 6:20–35.[18] The reference to the "man" in 5:21–23 and a similar reference to the "man" found in Prov 6:1–19 forms the basis of his

---

the first line of v. 22—it has now no expressed antecedent"(*Proverbs*, 116). R. B. Y Scott, *Proverbs*, 51, places 5:21–23 at the end of Proverbs 4.

[16] *Sprüche Salomos*, 58.

[17] As Plöger says: "Denn in allen Passagen, die sich mit der fremden Frau befassen, bleibt eine Beziehung zu Jahwe durchweg unberücksichtigt, nicht aber in den Versen 21–23. Zwar könnenten die 'alles sehenden Augen' Jahwes daren erinnern, dass der Umgang mit der fremden Frau, der sich begreiflicherweise in Verborgenen abzuspielen pflegt, gleichwohl nicht verborgen bleibt (V. 21)" (*Sprüche Salomos*, 58).

[18] *Sprüche Salomos*, 58, 62. Plöger raises the question of what role 6:1–19 play in conjunction with Proverbs 5. Plöger's comments on the curious combination of Prov 5:1–23 and 6:1–19 bear repeating for they provide us with a fresh perspective on the text. Unlike other scholars who pass over Prov 6:1–19, Plöger asks why 6:1–19 appears here of all places and then offers a possible answer: "Warum dann aber an dieser Stelle? Auf diese Fragen soll besser nach der Auslegung des ersten Teiles von Kap. 6 eingegangen werden; hier sei nur ein Rückverweis auf Kap. 5 noch gestattet. Bei der Auslegung von Kap. 5 war die Vermutung geäussert worden, ob die abschliessenden Verse 21–23, die die wirkungsvolle Schlussfrage in 5,20 abschwächen, als eine Überleitung zu Kap. 6 in seiner jetzigen Form angesehen werden können. Die Feststellung, dass ein Mann aus Mangel an Zucht umkommt und in einem Übermass an Torheit in die Irre geht (5,23), könnte der Anlass gewesen sein, darüber Genaueres mitzuteilen, was nicht nur mit dem Thema 'Fremde Frau' zu tun hat, mit dem sich Kap. 5 beschäftigt. Und dies geschieht im ersten zuchtlose Mann 'Frevler' genannt wird (5,22), wird ein deutlicher Hinweis gegeben auf das Thema 'Fremde Frau' genannt worden war. Es könnte föderlich sein, unter diesem Aspekt die vier Spruycheinheiten in 6,1–19 zu betrachten. Eine unmittelbare Verknüpfung mag in dem Stichwort לְבַב zusätzlich au vermuten sein: Wie sich der Zuchtlose in seinen Verfehlungen verfängt, so verfängt sich der Bürgschaft Leistende, von dem in der ersten Einheit 6,1–5 geredet wird, in den Worten seines Mundes. Das könnte der Anlass gewesen wird, die Warnung vor Bürgschaftleisten an den Anfang des Kapitels zu stellen"(p. 62).

analysis. The mistakes made by the "man" with foreigners in 5:1–23 seem, for Plöger, to establish a common focal point with the reference to the "man" found in 6:1–5. And *lkd*, "to snare," in 5:22 and 6:2 acts as a *Stichwort* which binds 5:21–23 and 6:1–19.[19] Even though 6:1–19 do not address the issue of the "foreign"/"strange" woman, 6:1–19 continue the same focus upon the "man" which receives special attention in 5:21–23.

We can add to Plöger's analysis concerning the thematic relationship between Proverbs 5 and 6 on the basis of our interpretation for Prov 6:1–19. There we detected an underlying play in the text which links the parent's discourse with events regarding Judah's role in the Joseph story. We also saw how the shift to the third person in Prov 6:12–19 helps us to perceive the inner-biblical links between Proverbs and Genesis.[20] A similar shift to the third person occurs with Prov 5:21–23 where the *darkê ʾîš*, "ways of a man," are alluded to.

We also described the unique combination of going surety "for your companion," *lěrēʿekā*, and striking a bargain "with a stranger," *lazzār*, in Prov 6:1. Prov 6:1–5 concentrates solely upon the *rēʿa*, "companion," without further mention of the *zār*, "stranger." The initial lesson on surety functions as one of the textual indices for linking Prov 6:1–19 with Judah's role in the Joseph story.

The opening words of the parent in 6:1 also serves to connect Prov 5:1–23 and 6:1ff. Although the parent in Prov 5:1–23 does not mention the issue of "surety," *ʿrb*, the reference to the *zr* in 6:1 functions as another *Stichwort* between Prov 5:1–23 and 6:1–19. The parent's message in Proverbs 5 warns the son about involvement not only with the *nokriyyâ*, "foreign woman," (v 20) but also the *zārâ*, "strange woman," (v 3, 20) and the *zārîm*, "strange men," (vv 10, 17). The further warning about entering into a bargain arrangement with a *zār* in 6:1 thus suggests a relationship between the parent's lesson in Prov 5:1–23 and 6:1–19.

The juxtaposition of Prov 6:1–19 after Proverbs 5 lends itself to a broader inner biblical reading whereby the ambiguous references to the man in 5:21–23 are given a degree of specificity in Prov 6:1–19 by means of a creative interplay upon events within the Joseph story. And as Plöger has shown, there is evidence in the final redaction of Proverbs 5 which indicates an attempt to link Proverbs 5 and 6 together by means of a common focus on the "man," and the *Stichwort lkd*, "to ensnare."

We are adding to Plöger's analysis by referring to the shared expression *zār* in Prov 6:1, the attention given to the "man" in Prov 5:21–

---

[19] A. Meinhold, *Die Sprüche*, 108, also notices the literary device of *Stichwörter* which link Proverbs 5 and 6.

[20] O. Plöger, *Sprüche Salomos*, 66, also notes the shift to the third person that starts at 6:12.

23 and 6:12–19, and the comparable appeal to YHWH in passing judgment on the "man" in 5:21–23 and 6:16–19. The parent's lesson to the son to avoid associations with "foreign/strange" men and women (Proverbs 5) is supported by the allusive play on Judah's surety arrangement and the general background of events in the Jospeh story (Proverbs 6). When read in context with Prov 6:1–19 the identity of the "man" obliquely referred to in 5:21–23 is given a degree of specificity. Again, our interpretation of Prov 5:1–23 is based upon our earlier analysis of Prov 6:1–19 which offers a rationale for final canonical ordering of the text.

In sum, the consistent use of similar terms and phrases to describe certain kinds of men and women in Proverbs 1–9 serves as an index of the overall message of the parent to the son. According to the parent, more is at stake than general well-being in avoiding any sort of association with certain kinds of men and women outlined in the parent's discourse; one is dealing quite literally with a life and death situation which is likewise connected with dwelling securely in the land (1:33; 2:21–22) and fecundity (3:9–10). Even though the parent's discourse reaches the point of being repetitious because of how the text is saturated with similar expressions, one can likewise interpret such repetitiveness as an indication of the gravity of the situation which the son faces. And the stylistic use of the inclusio, traditions from the Torah and the Prophets, and the combined warnings of the parent indicates how the final form of the text is designed to alert the son as well as the reader to the overriding parental message.

6

Conclusion.

Our analysis of Prov 1:8–19; 1:20–33; and 6:1–19 illustrates the existence of inner-biblical interpretation within Proverbs 1–9. The textual linking of portions of Genesis and Jeremiah with Proverbs is evidence of an editorial practice found elsewhere in the Hebrew Bible whereby earlier traditions are refashioned in order to address issues in a new biblical context. The most immediate significance of our analysis pertains to the close interrelationship between the content of the book of Proverbs and biblical traditions related to events from Israel's history. Like other cases of inner-biblical interpretation documented by M. Fishbane in his book *Biblical Interpretation in Ancient Israel,* our examples from Proverbs add to the growing awareness of how earlier texts form and inform later traditions. The parent's discourse is framed in such a way that one hears both elements of the Torah and the Prophets in the context of Proverbs.

The later combination of wisdom with Torah and Prophets that we find in Sirach has a precursor within the opening chapters of Proverbs. Sirach then is not the first "wisdom" book to combine traditions found elsewhere in scripture. In place of overt references to persons and events from Israel's past as found in Sirach, Proverbs 1–9 reutilizes earlier biblical traditions. Within other non-canonical traditions besides Sirach such as the Wisdom of Solomon, we find that incidents from the Joseph story figure as important sources for didactic purposes. Moreover, rabbinic commentary from Genesis Rabbah and Midrash Mishle are helpful indicators of how early Jewish commentators perceived the interconnectedness of seemingly unrelated biblical traditions.

A clear play upon events affiliated with Judah either as a character within the Joseph story, or as the eponymous figure of Judah as a nation, emerges in our analysis. In each case the parent alludes to Judah in an unfavorable manner. In addition to the parent's direct address to the son, we also detect a play upon the discourse of someone else from within scripture—i.e, double-voiced discourse. But each example of discourse has been recast in such a way that potentially complimentary aspects of Judah have been overshadowed by the evil that is associated with him as a person or as a nation.

In Prov 1:8–19 the parent draws upon the words of the brothers from Genesis 37 when they sell Joseph to the passing Ishmaelites/Midianites. Through a combination of select terms and allusive imagery the parent brings to mind the earlier event in which Judah and his brothers conspire to rid themselves of Joseph. Even though the concluding words of the parent in vv 18–19 refer to "them," the summary-appraisal form in v 19 plays directly upon Judah's suggestion that there is no "profit," *bāṣāʿ*, (i.e., "ill-gotten gain") in merely killing Joseph. Judah's own involvement in the selling of Joseph has self-serving undertones. By a series of earlier events in which Simeon, Levi, and Reuben fall into disfavor in Jacob's eyes, Judah stands next in line once Joseph is removed. The selling of Joseph results in clearing the way for Judah to assume the primary place among the brothers in the family. But as we know from the context of the Joseph story, the plans of Judah and his brothers backfire. Instead of ridding themselves of Joseph and appearing innocent of any evil deed before their father, the true nature of their characters is revealed in the events which unfold within the Joseph story.

The parent's discourse in Prov 1:8–19 alludes to the same reversal of fortunes. The "sinners'" plans to "lie in wait for blood" and "let us wantonly ambush the innocent" for personal gain in 1:11–13, actually set in motion a series of unforeseen events which entrap them. The parent's words in 1:18, "but these men lie in wait for their own blood, they set an ambush for their own lives," are more than a rephrasing of the words of the "sinners" in 1:11.

The structure of the parent's speech draws a lesson from what happened to Judah and his brothers based upon tradition. In this regard, the overall import of the parent's discourse moves from alluding to earlier tradition to formulating a conclusion concerning others who engage in similar activity as expressed in 1:19. Precisely the concerns of the parent as contained in Proverbs 1:8–19 overshadow a wooden reutilization of the earlier traditions from Genesis. It is not enough to refer obliquely to events related to the selling of Joseph; the parent takes that same event and builds upon it in the context of his/her own discourse. In effect, events from the Joseph story figure as paradigmatic factors in the parent's discourse to the son, thus establishing a degree of continuity between events from Israel's past and the immediate concerns of the parent. By carefully crafting the discourse so as to draw upon earlier traditions, the parent signals to the reader the authority behind their words. Portions of Genesis are interpreted in a Proverbial context that results in an inner-biblical point of view.

In Prov 1:20–33, we find a similar combination of speech within speech that we encounter in Prov 1:8–19. Even though we uncover a play upon discourse from portions of Jeremiah, we are again presented a picture which alludes to Judah—in this case, the eponymous figure of Judah. After wisdom is introduced in vv 20–21, wisdom assumes a prophetic voice by recalling Jeremiah's words to the people of Judah in vv 24–31. Where the parent stands back, as it were, and allows the son and the reader to hear the words of the "sinners" in 1:11–14 (albeit refracted through the voice of the parent), wisdom introduces another level of discourse starting with 1:24 which plays upon Jeremiah's words to the people of Judah before the destruction of Judah and Jerusalem in 587 BCE.

The effect of a layering of discourse in 1:8–19 and 1:20–33 is to bridge the distance between the reader and persons from Israel's past. Such bridging is especially effective when wisdom shifts her voice from "you" plural in vv 24–27 to "they" plural in vv 28–31. The initial "you" in v 24, along with the significant combination of vocabulary pertaining to "calling" and the people's refusal to hear, pinpoints the object of wisdom's speech. By shifting the focus to an earlier generation in Judah's recent past and then referring to the same generation in the third person plural, "they," all within the same discourse, wisdom exercises a level of control over the reader's viewpoint. We stand with wisdom both in her direct address to the generation just before the destruction of Jerusalem (vv 24–27) as well as in a period afterwards when wisdom assesses her own refusal to hear and respond (vv 28–31). Instead of lamenting over the earlier generation's ruin, wisdom's speech trades upon their continuing recalcitrance. A combination of "you" and "they" speech, which refers to the same people but from different perspectives, is a common rhetorical device within prophetic discourse. Our awareness of the function of layers of speech further confirms wisdom's dependence upon earlier prophetic traditions as well as indicating the angle at which wisdom wants the son and subsequent readers to hear her voice.

An emerging common point of view between Prov 1:8–19 and 1:20–33 is discernible in the shared address to the *pth* "simple." In 1:10 the parent's words imply that the son is potentially "enticeable," i.e., "simple." In 1:22 *ḥokmâ* addresses her words directly to the *pĕtāyim,* "simple ones." As we indicated earlier, the book of Proverbs maintains a separation between *pĕtāyim,* "simpletons," and those who are called *lēṣîm,* "scoffers," and *kĕsîlîm,* "fools." The *pĕtāyim* are potentially reprovable unlike the *lēṣîm* and *kĕsîlîm.* The similarity between the opening address of the parent and wisdom suggests a redactional association between 1:8–19 and 1:20–33 whereby the reader is directed to hear a degree of similarity between the parent's and wisdom's speech.

Furthermore, both 1:8–19 and 1:20–33 end with a summation based upon the content of the immediately preceding verses. The summary-appraisal form in 1:19, introduced by the particle *kēn,* not only condenses the content in the previous verses into a brief but memorable statement, it also establishes a guide for behavior based upon recast traditions from Genesis. In the case of Prov 1:20–33, vv 32–33 similarly alert the son and the reader to the possibility of being like those addressed in the preceding verses by offering a summary statement introduced by the particle *kî.* Like Prov 1:8–19, the summary recorded in 1:32–33 alerts the reader to the seriousness of wisdom's speech by playing off an earlier discourse event—in this case discourse from the book of Jeremiah.

Our last example which we analyze in detail is Prov 6:1–19. Even though other commentators point out the unusual combination of content and forms in the seemingly unrelated four units of traditions (i.e., vv 1–5; 6–11; 12–15; and 16–19), our analysis uncovers a sophisticated level of editing for these verses. The text exhibits a high degree of unity by virtue of imagery associated with sleep, animate objects, body parts, references to speech, particular kinds of action, a familial context, and similar diction. Even though such topics as warnings against surety arrangements, the sluggard, and the industrious ant, are found only in the book of Proverbs, they contribute to the allusive nature of Prov 6:1–19. Specifically, the combination of traditions projects an organized discourse unit formed so as to allude to Judah and to events within the Joseph story. The parent's discourse is designed to warn the son about certain kinds of actions which will trap the son in undesirable circumstances. Again, events from the Joseph story provide the narrative matrix for arranging the traditions from Proverbs. Events from the past are useful only to the degree that they form and inform the parent's words to the son.

. Unlike our earlier examples from Prov 1:8–19 and 1:20–33, where the role of direct discourse plays a crucial part in our investigation, Prov 6:1–19 recalls events associated with Judah by means of the order of its combined themes, select phrases, and word plays. As 1:8–19 and 1:20–33 end on a note which specifies the outcome of similar kinds of behavior by pointing to someone else *via* third person speech, 6:19 also ends by identifying "the man" as someone who appears like Judah in the Joseph story. In view of our earlier examples with their retrospective commentary on Judah, Prov 6:1–19 in places reflects similar vocabulary and set expressions found in Prov 1:8–19 and 1:20–33, thus contributing to an emerging common point of view.

The importance of our analysis for Prov 6:1–19 is also reflected in our attempt to interpret it as a contributing component within the parent's discourse in Proverbs 5–7 which involves warnings about certain kinds of men and women whom the son is to avoid. In contrast to other scholars who treat Prov 6:1–19 as an interpolation with no connection to its surrounding context, we argue that the warnings about mixing with foreigners and strange/foreign women in Prov 5:1–23 is further broadened by Prov 6:1–19. The text now takes on a broader inner-biblical context by virtue of Prov 6:1–19 and its juxtaposition after Prov 5:1–23. Furthermore, our description of the editorial marks within the last verses of Proverbs 5 indicate an intended interlocking relationship between Prov 5:1–23 and 6:1–19. The warnings addressed to the son about a "man" whose ways are evil as in Prov 5:21–23 gain in importance by virtue of the inner-biblical context of 6:1–19 and its concerns with a "man" who resembles Judah in the Joseph story.

The above review is not meant to be exhaustive of the ways that our examples interconnect with other portions of the Hebrew Bible. As a brief summary, it is sufficient to call attention to some of the similar content shared by Prov 1:8–19; 1:20–33; 6:1–19 and how these verses play upon earlier traditions. Our concentration on these three discourse units plays an important role in establishing a point of view for the parent's discourse in Proverbs 1–9. Prov 1:8–19 stands in the important place as the opening didactic lesson in Proverbs 1–9. We know from other examples from the Hebrew Bible that the initial discourse in a text has the important role of introducing themes and content which are addressed elsewhere in the text.[1] The opening discourse introduces us to the "sinners" and not to the figure of wisdom. Moreover, 1:11–14 is the only place where we hear the "sinners" speak. Even though we do not hear the words of the "sinners" anywhere else in Proverbs 1–9, they do

---

[1] One has only to take note of such examples as the call of Jeremiah in Jeremiah 1, which introduces not only Jeremiah as a prophet like Moses, but also the themes of "to pluck up and break down, to destroy and to over throw, to build and to plant," 1:10, which appear in other strategic places in Jeremiah; or the introduction to Qoheleth and the motif of "vanity of vanities" which likewise is reiterated throughout the book of Qoheleth.

not disappear altogether. They figure as important characters elsewhere within the parent's discourse.

As for Prov 1:20–33, it is the only example in the book of Proverbs which employs prophetic content and forms of speech. The significance of these verses lies not merely in the combination of forms of prophetic speech but also in the content and historical significance of that speech. And as we have noted, Prov 6:1–19 has been treated by virtually every modern commentator (except O. Plöger) as an interpolation which does not add to the parent's discourse in Proverbs 5–7. We have argued instead that 6:1–19 does not stand as an erratic block within Proverbs 5–7. Even though Prov 5:1–23; 6:20–35; and 7:1–27 contain similar content concerning the ways of certain kinds of men and women, we note the significant role that 6:1–19 plays in these chapters. That role relates not only to the allusions to the Joseph story but also how 6:1–19 manifests themes found elsewhere in Proverbs.

In short, our studies of Prov 1:8–19; 1:20–33; and 6:1–19 demonstrate that the final form of Proverbs 1–9 reflects an editing processes found elsewhere within the Hebrew whereby earlier biblical traditions are reutilized and transformed in later scriptural contexts.

BIBLIOGRAPHY

Ackerman, J. S. "Joseph, Judah, and Jacob." *Literary Interpretations of Biblical Narratives*. Vol. 2. Edited by K. R. R. Gros Louis. Nashville: Abingdon, 1982.

Ackroyd, P. *Exile and Restoration, A Study of Hebrew Thought of the Sixth Century B.C.* Philadelphia: Westminster Press, 1968.

Aletti, J. N. "Seduction et Parole en Proverbes I-IX." *Vetus Testamentum* 27 (1977):129–144.

Alt A. "Zur literischen Analyse der Weisheit des Amenemope." *Vetus Testamentum Supplements* 3 (1960):16–25.

Alter, R. *The Art of Biblical Narrative*. New York: Basic Books, 1981.

Bakhtin, M. *Problems of Dostoevsky's Poetics*. Edited and translated by C. Emerson. Theory and History of Literature, vol. 8. Minneapolis: University of Minnesota Press, 1984.

———, *The Dialogic Imagination*. Edited and translated by C. Emerson and M. Holquist. Austin: University of Austin Press, 1981.

Barth, H. *Die Jesaja-Worte in der Josiazeit: Israel und Assur als Thema einer produktiven Neuinterpretation des Jesajauberlieferung*. Wissenschaftliche Monographien zum Alten und Neuen Testament, 48. Neukirchen-Vluyn: Neukirchener, 1977.

Barton, G. A. *The Book of Ecclesiastes*. International Critical Commentary. New York: Scribners, 1908.

Barucq, A. *Le Livres des Proverbes*. Sources Bibliques. Paris: J. Gabalda et Cie, 1964.

Bauckmann, E. "Die Proverbien und die Sprüche der Jesus Sirach." *Zeitschrift für die alttestamentliche Wissenschaft* 72 (1960):33–63.

180   PROVERBS 1-9: A STUDY OF INNER-BIBLICAL INTERPRETATION

Baumgartner, A. J. *Étude critique sur l'état du texte des Proverbes d'après les principales traductions anciennes.* Leipzig: Imprimerie Orientale W. W. Drugulin, 1890.

Baumgartner, W. *Israelitsche und altorientalische Weisheit.* Tübingen: Mohr, 1933.

———, "Die israelitische Weisheitsliteratur." *Theologische Rundschau* 5 (1933):259–288.

Beuken, W. A. M., S. J. *Haggai-Sacharja 1–8 Studien zur uberlieferungsgeschichte der Frünachexilischen Prophetie.* Assen: Van Gorcum and Comp. N. V., 1967.

Bickell, G. "Kritische Bearbitung der Proverbien." *Wiener Zeitschrift für die Kunde des Morgenlandes* 5 (1891):79–102.

Boström, G. *Proverbiastudien, Die Weisheit und Das Fremde Weib in Spr. 1–9.* Lund: C. W. K. Gleerup, 1935.

Boström, L. *The God of the Sages: The Portrayal of God in the Book of Proverbs.* Coniectanea Biblica, Old Testament Series 29. Stockholm: Almqvist and Wiksell International, 1990.

Buber, S. *Midrasch Mischle: Samlung agadischen Auslegung der Sprüche Salomonis.* Wilna: Druck v. Wittwe & Gebr. Romm., 1883.

Buchanan, G. "Midrashim Pretannaites, a propos de Prov I-IX." *Revue biblique* 72 (1965):225–239.

Budge, E. A. W. "The Precepts of Life by Amen-em-Apt, the Son of Ka-nekt." In *Recueil d'études égyptologiques dédièes á la mémoire de Jean-Francois Champollion.* Paris: E. Champion, 1922.

Bultmann, R. "Der religionsgeschichte hintergrund des Prologs zum Johannes-Evangelium ." In *Eucharisterion Festschrift* Hermann Gunkel N. F. 19 (1923) 1–26.

Camp, C. *Wisdom and the Feminine in the Book of Proverbs.* Sheffield, England/Decatur, Georgia: Almond Press, 1985.

Carroll, R. *Jeremiah: A Commentary.* London: SCM Press Ltd., 1986.

Causse, A. "Sagesse égyptienne et sagesse juive." *Revue d'Histoire et de Philosophie religieuses* 12 (1929):149–169.

Childs, B. "Psalm Titles and Midrashic Exegesis." *Journal of Semitic Studies* 1 6 (1971):137–150.

———, *Isaiah and the Assyrian Crisis.* Studies in Biblical Theology. Second series, n. 3. Naperville, Illinois: Alec R. Allenson, 1967.

———, "Midrash and the Old Testament." In *Understanding the Sacred Text. Essays in Honor of Morton J. Enslin.* Edited by J. Reumann. Valley Forge, Pennsylvania: Judson Press, 1972.

———, *Introduction to the Old Testament as Scripture.* Philadelphia: Fortress Press, 1979.

Clines, D. J. A., Gunn, D. M. "'You Tried to Persuade Me' and 'Violence! Outrage!' in Jeremiah XX 7–8." *Vetus Testamentum* 28 (1978):20–27.

Crenshaw, J. "Method in Determining Wisdom Influence upon 'Historical' Literature." *Journal of Biblical Literature* 88 (1969):129–142.

————, "Wisdom." In *Old Testament Form Criticism*. Edited by J. Hayes. San Antonio: Trinity University Press, 1974.

————, "Prolegomenon." In *Studies in Ancient Israelite Wisdom*. Edited by J. Crenshaw. New York: KTAV, 1976.

————, *Old Testament Wisdom: An Introduction*. Atlanta: John Knox Press, 1981.

Dahood, M. *Proverbs and Northwest Semitic Philology*. Roma: Ponticium Institutum Biblicum, 1963.

Daube, D. "A Quartet of Beasties in the Book of Proverbs." *Journal of Theological Studies* 36 (1985):380–386.

Delitzsch, F. *Das Salomonische Sprüchbuch*. In *Biblische Commentar über das AT*. Edited by W. Keil and F. Delitzsch. Leipzig:Verlag von S. Hirzel, 1873.

————, *Proverbs, Ecclesiastes, Song of Songs*. Translated by J. Martin. Grand Rapids: Eerdmans, 1986.

Diettrich, G. "Die Theoretische Weisheit der Einleitung zum Buch der Sprüche, ihr Spezifischer Inhalt und ihre Entstehung." In *Theologische Studien und Kritiken* 12. Gotha: Friedrich Andreas Berthe, (1908):475–512.

Drioton, E. "Sur la Saggesse d'Aménémópe." In *Mélanges bibliques rédiqués en l'honneur de André Robert*, edited by H. Cazelles. Paris: Bloud and Gay, 1957.

————, "Le Livre des Proverbes et la Sagesse d'Aménémópe." In *Sacra Pagina. Miscellanea biblica congressus internationalis Catholici de re biblica*. Edited by J.Coppens, A. Descamps, É. Massaux. Paris/Gembloux: Éditions J. Duculot, 1959.

Driver, S. R. *Introduction to the Literature of the Old Testament*. New York: Meridian Book, 1960.

Driver, G. R. "Problems in the Hebrew Text of Proverbs." *Biblica* 32 (1951):173–197.

————, "Abbreviations in the Massoretic Text." *Textus* 1 (1960):112–131.

Duesberg, D. H. *Les Scribes Inspires*. Paris: Desclée De Brouwer, 1938.

Eissfeldt, O. *The Old Testament: An Introduction*. Translated by P. R. Ackroyd. New York: Harper and Row, 1965.

Emerton, J. "A Note of the Hebrew Text of Proverbs i. 22–3." *Journal of Theological Studies* 19 (1968):609–614.

Erman, A. "Eine ägyptische Quelle der 'Sprüche Salomos'." *Sitzungsberichte der preussischen Akademie der Wissenschaften* 15 (1924):86–93.

Fichtner J. *Die altorientalische Weisheit in ihrer israelitisch-judischen Auspragung, Eine Studie zur Nationalisierung Der Weisheit in Israel*. Beihefte für *Zeitschrift für die alttestamentliche Wissenschaft*, 62. Geissen: Verlag von Alfred Topelmann, 1933.

————, "Zum Problem Glaube und Geschichte in der israelitisch-judischen Weisheitsliteratur." *Theologische Literaturzeitung* 76 (1951):145–150.

Fishbane, M. "Torah and Tradition." In *Theology and Tradition in the Old Testament*. Edited by D. Knight. Philadelphia: Fortress Press, 1977.

————, "Revelation and Tradition: Aspects of Inner-Biblical Exegesis ." *Journal of Biblical Literature* 99 (1980):343–361.

————, *Biblical Interpretation in Ancient Israel.* Oxford: Clarendon Press, 1985.

————, "'A Wretched Thing of Shame, A Mere Belly': An Interpretation of Jeremiah 20:7–12." In *The Biblical Mosaic, Changing Perspectives.* Edited by R. Polzin and E. Rothman. Philadelphia/Chico, California: Fortress Press/Scholars Press, 1982.

Fohrer, G. "Jeremias tempelwort 7,1–15." *Theologische Zeitschrift* 5 (1949):401–417.

Fowler, R. "Who is 'The Reader' in Reader Response Criticism?" *Semeia* 31 (1985):5–23.

Fox, M. "The Indentification of Quotations in Biblical Literature." *Zeitschrift für die alttestamentliche Wissenschaft* 92 (1980):416–430.

————, "Two Decades of Research in Egyptian Wisdom Literature." *Zeitschrift für ägyptische Sprache und Alterumskunde* 107 (1980):120–135.

Frankenberg, W. *Die Sprüche ubersetz und erklart.* Handkommentar zum Alten Testament. Göttingen: Vandenhoeck and Ruprecht, 1898.

Freedman, H., trans. *Midrash Rabbah, Genesis.* 3d ed. London/New York: Soncino Press, 1983.

Galling, K. "Koheleth-Studien." *Zeitschrift für die alttestamentliche Wissenschaft* 50 (1932):276–293.

————, *Die Fünf Megilloth.* Handbuch zum Alten Testament, 18. 2d ed. Tübingen: J. C. B. Mohr, 1969.

Gasser, J. K. *Die Bedeutung der Sprüche Jesu Ben Sira für die Datierung des althebräischen Spruchbuches.* Gütersloh: Druk und Verlag C. Bertelsmann, 1903.

Geiger, A. *Urschrift und Ubersetzungen der Bibel in Ihrer Abhangigkeit von der innern Entwicklung des Judenthums.* First edition, 1857. Frankfort-on-Main: Verlag Madda, 1928.

Gemser, B. *Sprüche Salomos.* Handbuch zum alten Testament, 16. Tübingen: J. C. B. Mohr, 1937.

Gerleman, G. "The Septuagint Proverbs as a Hellenistic Document." *Old Testament Studies* 8 (1950):15–27.

————, "Studies in the Septuagint: III Proverbs." *Lunds Universitets Arsskrift,* NF, Aud 1 Bd. 52, No. 3 (1956).

Gese, H. *Lehre und Wirklichkeit in der alten Weisheit.* Tubingen: Mohr, 1958.

Gilbert, M. "Le Discours menaçant de Sagesse en Proverbes 1,20–33." In *Storia e tradizioni di Israele,* pp. 90–119. Brescia: Paideia Editrice, 1991.

Goldin, J. "The Youngest Son or Where Does Genesis 38 Belong." *Journal of Biblical Literature* 96 (1977):27–44.

Good, E. "The 'Blessing' on Judah, Gen 49:8–12." *Journal of Biblical Literature* 8 2 (1963):427–432.

Gordis, R. "Quotations in Wisdom Literature." *Jewish Quarterly Review* 30 (1939):123–147.

———, "Quotations as a Literary Usage in Biblical, Oriental and Rabbinic Literature." *Hebrew Union College Annual* 22 (1949):157–219.

———, *The Book of Job: Commentary, New Translation, and Special Studies.* New York: The Jewish Theological Seminary of America, 1978.

Gottwald, N. *The Hebrew Bible—A Socio-Literary Introduction.* Philadelphia: Fortress, 1985.

Greenstein, E. "An Equivocal Reading of the Sale of Joseph." In *Literary Interpretations of Biblical Literature.* Vol. 2. Edited by K. R. R. Gros Louis. Nashville: Abingdon, 1982.

Gressmann, H. *Israels Spruchweisheit in zusammenhang der Weltliteratur.* Berlin: Verlag Karl Curtius, 1925.

———, "Die neugefundene Lehre des Amen-em-ope und die vorexilische Spruchdichtung Israels." *Zeitschrtift für die alttestamentliche Wissenschaft* 42 (1924):272–296.

Grumach, I. *Untersuchungen zur Lebenslehre des Amenemope.* MÄS 23. Münich: Münchener Universitätsschriften, 1972.

Hayes, J., ed. *Old Testament Form Criticism.* Austin: Trinity University Press, 1975.

———, and Miller, J. M., editors. *Israelite and Judaean History.* Philadelphia: The Westminster Press, 1977.

Hengel, M. *Judaism and Hellenism: Studies in their Encounter in Palestine during the Early Hellenistic Period.* Two volumes. Translated by J. Bowden. Philadelphia: Fortress Press, 1974.

Hermission, H.-J. *Studien zur Israelitischen Spruchweisheit.* In *Wissenschaft Monographien zum alten und nuen Testament* 28. Neukirchen Vluyn: Neukirchener Verlag, 1968.

Hertzberg, H. W. "Die Nachgeschicht altestamentlicher Texte innerhalb des Alten Testaments." In *Werden und Wesen des Alten Testaments.* Edited by P. Volz, F. Stummer, and J. Hempel. Beihefte für *Zeitschrift für die alttestamentliche Wissenschaft,* 66. Berlin: Topelman, 1936:110–121.

Hitzig, F. *Der Prediger Salomo's.* Leipzig: Wedimann'sche Buchhandlung, 1847.

Holladay, W. *Jeremiah 1: A Commentary on the Book of Jeremiah Chapters 1–25.* Philadelphia: Fortress Press, 1986.

———, "Prototype and Copies: A New Approach to the Poetry-Prose Problem in the Book of Jeremiah." *Journal of Biblical Literature* 79 (1960):351–367.

———, *The Architecture of Jeremiah 1–20.* Lewisburg, Pennsylvania: Bucknell University Press, 1976.

Humbert, P. "Les Adjectifs 'Zâr' et 'Nokri' et la 'femme étrangère' des Proverbes Bibliques." In *Mélanges Syriens* 1. Offerts à Monsieur René Dussaud. Paris: Librairie Orientalisk Paul Geuthner, 1939.

Isbell, C. D., Jackson, M. "Rhetorical Criticism and Jeremiah VII-VIII." *Vetus Testamentum* 30 (1980):20–26.

Iser, W. *The Act of Reading, A Theory of Aesthetic Response.* Baltimore/London: The John Hopkins University Press, 1980.

Janzen, J. G. *Studies in the Text of Jeremiah.* Cambridge: Harvard University Press, 1973.

Kayatz C. *Studien zu Proverbien 1–9: eine form- und motivgeschichtliche Untersuchung unter Einbeziehung ägyptischen Vergleichsmaterial.* WMANT 22. Neukirchen-Vluyn: Neukirchener Verlag, 1966.

Kevin, R. O. "The Wisdom of Amen-em-Apt and its Possible Dependence upon the Hebrew Book of Proverbs." *Journal for the Study of Oriental Research* 14 (1930):115–150.

Kristeva, J. *Desire in Language: A Semiotic Approach to Literature and Art.* Translated by T. Gora, A. Jardine, and L. S. Roudiez. Edited by L. S. Roudiez. New York: Columbia University Press, 1980.

Kugel, J. "The Bible's Earliest Interpreters." *Prooftexts* 7 (1987):269–283.

———, "A Feeling of Déjà Lu," *Journal of Religion* 67 (1987):66–79.

———, *The Idea of Biblical Poetry: Parallelism and Its History.* (New Haven/London: Yale University Press, 1981.

Kuhn, G. *Beiträge zur Erklärung des Salomonishen Spruchbuches. Beiträge zur Wissenschaft vom alten und neuen Testament* 16. Stuttgart: W. Kohlhammer, 1931.

Lagarde, P. A. de. *Anmerkungen zur griechischen Übersetzung der Proverbien.* Leipzig: A. A. Brockhaus, 1863.

Landes, G. "Creation Tradition in Proverbs 8:22–31 and Genesis 1." In *A Light Unto My Path: Old Testament Studies in Honor of Jacob M. Myers.* Edited by H. Bream, R. Heim, and C. Moore. Philadelphia: Temple University Press, 1974:279–293.

Lang, B. *Frau Weisheit, Deutung einer biblischen Gestalt.* Dusseldorf: Patmos-Verlag, 1975.

———, *Anweisungen gegen die Torheit Sprichworter—Jesus Sirach.* Stuttgart: Verlag Katholisches Bibelwerk GmbH, 1973.

———, *Wisdom and the Book of Proverbs: An Israelite Goddess Redefined.* New York: The Pilgrim Press, 1986.

Levenson, J. D. *Sinai and Zion: An Entry into the Jewish Bible.* San Francisco: Harper and Row, 1985.

Lewin, E. D. "Arguing for Authority, A Rhetorical Study of Jeremiah 1.4–19 and 20.7–18." *Journal for the Study of the Old Testment* 32 (1985):105–119.

Lieberman, S. *Hellenism in Jewish Palestine.* New York: The Jewish Theological Seminary, 1962.

Marbock, J. *Weisheit im Wandel: Untersuchengen zur Weisheittheologie bei Ben Sira.* Bobb: Peter Hanstein, 1971.

Mason, R. "The Relation of Zech. 9–14 to Proto-Zechariah." *Zeitschrift für die alttestamentliche Wissenschaft* 88 (1976):227–239.

Mays, J. L. "The Place of the Torah-Psalms in the Psalter." *Journal of Biblical Literature* 106 (1987):3–12.

McKane W. *Prophets and Wise Men.* Studies in Biblical Theology 44. Naperville, Illinois: A. Allenson Inc, 1965.

——, *Proverbs, A New Approach.* London: SCM Press, 1970.

——, "Functions of Language and Objective of Discourse According to Proverbs, 10–30." In *La Sagesse de l'Ancien Testament.* Edited by M. Gilbert. Paris-Gembloux: Leuven University Press, 1979:166–185.

Meinhold, A. *Die Sprüche. Teil 1: Sprüche Kapitel 1– 15.* Zürcher Bibelkommentare Altes Testament 16.1. Zürich: Theologischer Verlag, 1991.

Melamed, E. Z. "Break-up of Stereotype Phrases as an Artistic Device in Biblical Poetry." *Scripta Hierosolymitana* 8 (1961):115–144.

Michel, D. *Grundlegung einer hebräischen Syntax: Teil 1—Sprachwissenschaftliche Methodik, Genus und Numerus des Nomens.* Neukirchen-Vluyn: Neukirchener-V., 1977.

Middendorp, T. *Die Stellung Jesu Ben Siras zwischen Judentum und Hellenismus.* Leiden: E. J. Brill, 1973.

Mielzinger, M. *Introduction to the Talmud.* New York: Bloch Publishing Company, 1968.

Mitchell, H. G. *Zechariah.* International Critical Commentary. Edinburgh: T and T Clark, 1912.

Montefiore, C. G. "Notes on the Date and Religious Value of the Proverbs." *Jewish Quarterly Review* 2 (1890):430–453.

Müller, A., and Kautzsch, E. *The Book of Proverbs: Critical Edition of the Hebrew Text with Notes.* Leipzig: J. C. Hinrichs' Svhe Buchhandlung, 1901.

Murphy, R. "Wisdom's Song: Proverbs 1:20–33." *The Catholic Biblical Quarterly* 48 (1986):456–460.

——, "Assumptions and Problems in Old Testament Wisdom Literature." *The Catholic Biblical Quarterly* 29 (1967):101–112.

——, "Form Criticism and Wisdom Literature." *The Catholic Biblical Quarterly* 31 (1969):475–483.

——, *Wisdom Literature: Job, Proverbs, Ruth, Canticles, Ecclesiastes, and Esther.* Vol 13. The Forms of the Old Testament Wisdom Literature. Grand Rapids: Eerdmans, 1981.

Myers, J. *Ezra, Nehemiah.* Anchor Bible. Garden City, New York: Doubleday and Company, 1965.

Nachmias, J. ibn. *Kommentar zu den Sprüchen Salomos.* Berlin: Schriften des Vereins Mekize Nirdamim, 1911.

Nel, P. J. *The Structure and Ethos of Wisdom Admonitions in Proverbs.* Beihefte zur *Zeitschrift für die alttestamentliche Wissenschaft* 158. Berlin/New York: de Gruyter, 1982.

Neusner, J., trans. *Genesis Rabbah, The Judaic Commentary to the Book of Genesis, A New American Translation* Vol. 3. Atlanta: Scholars Press, 1985.

Newsom, C. A. "Woman and the Discourse of Patriarchal Wisdom: A Study of Proverbs 1–9." In *Gender and Difference in Ancient Israel*, edited by Peggy L. Day, pp. 142–160. Minneapolis: Fortress, 1989.

Nickelsburg, G. W. E. *Jewish Literature Between the Bible and the Mishnah.* Philadephia: Fortress Press, 1981.

———, *Resurrection, Immortality, and Eternal Life in Intertestamental Judaism.* Cambridge/London: Harvard University Press, 1972.

Nicholson, E. W. *Preaching to the Exiles: A Study of the Prose Tradition in the Book of Jeremiah.* Oxford: Basil Blackwell, 1970.

Nowack, W. *Die Sprüche Salomo's.* In *Kurzgefasstes exegetisches Handbuch zum Alten Testament.* Leipzig: Verlag von S. Hirzel, 1893.

O'Callaghan, R. T. "Echoes of Canaanite Literature in the Psalms." *Vetus Testamentum* 4 (1954):164–176.

Oesterley. W. O. E. *The Wisdom of Egypt and the Old Testament in the Light of the Newly Discovered 'Teaching of Amen-em-ope'.* London: Methuen and Co. Ltd., 1927.

———, *The Book of Proverbs with Introduction and Notes.* London: Methuen and Co. Ltd., 1929.

Patte, D. *Early Jewish Hermeneutic in Palestine.* Missoula: Scholars Press, 1975.

Pfeiffer, R. H. *Introduction to the Old Testament.* New York/London: Harper and Row, 1941.

Perdue, L. *Wisdom and Cult: A Critical Analalysis of the Views of Cult in the Wisdom Literatures of Israel and the Ancient Near East.* Society of Biblical Literature Dissertation Series, 30. Missoula, Montanna: Scholars Press, 1977.

Petersen, D. L. *Late Israelite Prophecy: Studies in Deutero-Prophetic Literature and in Chronicles.* Society of Biblical Literature Monograph Series, 23. Missoula, Montana: Scholars Press, 1973.

———, *Haggai and Zechariah 1–8, A Commentary.* Philadelphia: Westminster Press, 1985.

Petitjean, A. *Les Oracles du Proto-Zacharie, Un programme de restauration pour la communauté juive après l'exil.* Paris: Librairie Lecoffre J. Gabalda, 1969.

Plöger, O. "Zur Auslegung der Sentenzensammlungen des Proverbiabuches." In *Probleme Biblischer Theologie. Gerhard von Rad 70. Geburtstag.* Edited by H. W. Wolff. Munich: Chr. Kaiser Verlag, (1971):402–416.

———, *Sprüche Salomos (Proverbia) Biblischer Kommentar Altes Testament* XVII/I. Neukirchen Vluyn: Neukirchener Verlag, 1984.

Pohlmann, K. F. *Studien zum Jeremiahbuch.* Göttingen: Vandenhoecj & Ruprecht, 1978.

Polzin, R. *Moses and the Deuteronomist, A Literary Study of the Deuteronomic History*. New York: The Seabury Press, 1980.

——, "The Speaking Person and His Voice in 1 Samuel," *Vetus Testamentum* 36 (1985):218–229.

Pratt, M. L. *Toward a Speech Act Theory of Literary Discourse*. Bloomington/London: Indiana University Press, 1977.

Rabin, C. "מעט חבק ידים לשכב‎ (Prov vi, 10; xxiv 33)." *Journal of Jewish Studies* 1 (1949):197–198.

Redford, D. B. *A Study of the Biblical Story of Joseph*. Vetus Testamentum Supplements 20. Leiden: E. J. Brill, 1970.

Richardson, H. N. "Some Notes of ליץ‎ and its Derivatives." *Vetus Testamentum* 5 (1955):163–179.

Richter, W. *Recht und Ethos, Versuch einer Ortung des weisheitslichen Mahnspruches*. München: Kösel-Verlag, 1966.

Ringgren, H. *Word and Wisdom in the Old Testament*. Lund: H. Ohlsson, 1947.

——, *Sprüche/Prediger. Das Alte Testament Deutsch*, 16/1, 1962.

——, and Zimmerli, W. *Sprüche/Prediger*. Göttingen: Vandenhoeck and Ruprecht, 1980.

Robert, A. "Les attaches littéraires bibliques de Prov. I-IX." *Revue biblique* 43 (1934):42–68, 172–204, 374–384; *Revue biblique* 44 (1935):334–365, 502–525.

——, "Les Genres littéraires." In *Dictionnaire de la Bible, Supplement* 5 (1957):405–421.

Roth, W. M. V. *Numerical Sayings in the Old Testament. Vetus Testamentum Supplements*, 13. Leiden: E. J. Brill. 1965.

Rylaarsdam, C. *Revelation in Jewish Wisdom Literature*. Chicago/London: University of Chicago Press, 1946.

Sarna, N. "Psalm 89: A Study in Inner Biblical Exegesis." In *Biblical and Other Studies*. Edited by A. Altmann. Brandeis Texts and Studies. Cambridge: Harvard University Press, 1963.

Savran, G. "The Character as Narrator in Biblical Narrative." *Prooftexts: A Journal of Jewish Literary History* 5 (1985):1–17.

Schechter, S. and Taylor, C., eds. *The Wisdom of Ben Sira, Portions of the Book of Ecclesiasticus*. Reprint of the Cambridge Editions of the 1896 and 1899. Amsterdam: APA-PHILO Press, 1979.

Schmid, H. H. *Wesen und Geschichte der Weisheit, Eine Untersuchung zur altorientalischen und israelitischen Weisheitsliteratur*. Berlin: Alfred Töpekmann, 1966.

Schmidt, J. *Studien zur Stilistik der alttestamentlichen Spruch-literatur*. Münster: Verlag der Aschendorfschen Verlagsbuchhandlung, 1913.

Schürer, E. *The Literature of the Jewish People in the Time of Jesus*. Translated by P. Christi and S. Taylor. Edited by N. Glatzner. New York: Schocken Books, 1972.

Scott, R. B. Y. "Solomon and the Beginnings of Wisdom in Israel." *Vetus Testamentum Supplements* 3 (1955):262–279.

———, "Folk Proverbs of the Ancient Near East." *Transactions of the Royal Society of Canada* 15 (1961):47–56.

———, *Proverbs. Ecclesiates. A New Translation with Introduction and Commentary.* Anchor Bible 18. Garden City, New York: Doubleday, 1965.

———, "The Study of Wisdom Literature." *Interpretation* 24 (1970):20–44.

———, "Wise and Foolish, Righteous and Wicked." *Vetus Testamentum* 23 (1972):146–165.

Seeligmann, I. L. "Voraussetzungen Der Midraschexegese." *Vetus Testamentum Supplements* 1 (1953):150–181.

Seligman, C. *Das Buch der Weisheit des Jesus Sirach.* Breslau: Druck von Th. Schatzky, 1883.

Sheppard, G. *Wisdom as a Hermeneutical Construct: A Study in the Sapientializing of the Old Testament.* Beihefte für *Zeitschrift für die alttestamentliche Wissenschaft* 151. Berlin/New York: Walter de Gruyter, 1980.

Simpson, D. C. "The Hebrew Book of Proverbs and the Teaching of Amenophis." *Journal of Egyptian Archaeology* 12 (1926):224–240.

Skehan, P. "A Single Editor for the Whole Book of Proverbs." *Catholic Biblical Quarterly* 10 (1948):115–130.

———, "Proverbs 5:15–19 and 6:20–24." *Catholic Biblical Quarterly* 8 (1946):290–297. A revised form appears in *Studies in Israelite Poetry and Wisdom.* Catholic Biblical Quarterly Manuscript Series, 1, pp. 1–8. Worcester, Massachusetts: The Heffernan Press, 1971.

Skladny, U. *Die ältesten Spruchsammlung in Israel.* Göttingen: Vandenhoeck and Ruprecht, 1962.

Slomovic, E. "Toward an Understanding of the Exegesis in the Dead Sea Scrolls." *Revue Qumran* 7 (1969–1971):3–15.

———, "Toward an Understanding of the Formation of the Historical Titles in the Book of Psalms." *Zeitschrift für die alttestamentliche Wissenschaft* 91 (1979):350–380.

Snijders, L. A. "The Meaning of *zar* in the Old Testament, An Exegetical Study." *Oudtestamentische Studien* 10 (1954):1–154.

"זוּר/זָר." In *The Theological Dictionary of the Old Testament*, vol. 4. Edited by G. Botterweck and H. Ringgren. Translated by D. E. Green. Grand Rapids: Eerdmans, 1980.

Speiser, E. A. *Genesis: A New Translation with Introduction and Commentary.* Anchor Bible. New York: Doubleday & Company, Inc., 1964.

Steiert, F.-J. *Die Weisheit Israels - ein Fremdkörper im Alten Testament? Eine Untersuchung zum Buch der Sprüche auf dem Hintergrund der ägyptischen Weisheitslehren.* Freiburger theologische Studien 143. Freiburg: Herder 1990.

Sternberg, M. "Ordering the Unordered: Time, Space, and Descriptive Coherence." *Yale French Studies* 61 (1981):60–88.

———, "Point of View and the Indirections of Direct Speech." *Language and Style* 15 (1982):67–117.

———, "Proteus in Quotation Land: Mimesis and the Forms of Reported Discourse." *Poetics Today* 3 (1982):107–156.

Steurnagel, D. "Die Sprüche." In *Die heilige Schrift des alten Testaments*. Edited by E. Kautzsch. Tübingen: Verlag von J. C. B. Mohr, 1910.

Strack, H. L. *Introduction to the Talmud and Midrash*. New York: Atheneum, 1978.

Stulman, L. *The Prose Sermons of the Book of Jeremiah, A Redescription of the Correspondences with Deuteronomistic Literature in the Light of Recent Textcritical Research*. Atlanta: Scholars Press, 1986.

Thiel, W. *Die deuteronomistische Redaktion von Jeremia 1–25*. Neukirchen-Vluyn: Neukirchener Verlag, 1973.

———, *Die deuteronomistische Redaktion von Jeremia 26–45*. Neukirchen-Vluyn: Neukirchener Verlag, 1981.

Thomas, D. W. "Textual and Philological Notes on Some Passages in the Book of Proverbs." *Vetus Testamentum Supplements III, Wisdom in Israel and in the Ancient Near East*. Leiden: E. J. Brill. (1960):280–292.

Thompson, J. M. *The Form and Function of Proverbs in Ancient Israel*. The Hague: Mouton, 1974.

Toy, C. H. *A Critical and Exegetical Commentary on the Book of Proverbs*. International Critical Commentary. Edinburgh: T & T Clark, 1899.

Trible, P. "Wisdom Builds a Poem, The Architecture of Proverbs 1:20–33." *Journal of Biblical Literature* 94 (1975):509–518.

Van Leeuwen, R. C. "Liminality and Worldview in Proverbs 1–9." *Semeia* 50 (1990):111–144.

Visotzky, B. L. *Midrash Mishle: A Critical Edition Based on Manuscripts and Early Editions with an Introduction and Annotated English Translation of Chapters One through Ten*. Two volumes. Ph.D. dissertation, The Jewish Theological Seminary, 1982.

Volosinov, V. N. "Reported Speech." In *Readings in Russian Poetics: Formalist and Structural Views*. Edited by L. Matejka and K. Pomorska. Michigan Slavic Studies. Ann Arbor, Michigan: University of Michigan Press, 1978.

Volz, P. "Weisheit." In *Die Schriften des Alten Testaments*, III/2. Göttingen: Vandenhoeck & Ruprecht, 1911.

von Rad, G. "The Joseph Narrative and Ancient Wisdom." In *The Problem of the Hexateuch and other Essays*. London: SCM, 1984.

———, *Wisdom in Israel*. London: SCM Press, 1972.

Weingreen, J. "Rabbinic-Type Glosses in the Old Testament." *Journal of Semitic Studies* 2 (1957):149–162.

————, "Rabbinic-Type Commentary in the LXX version of Proverbs." In *Proceedings of the Sixth World Congress of Jewish Studies, Vol. 1.* Jerusalem: Jewish Academic Press, 1977.

Westermann, C. *Basic Forms of Prophetic Speech.* Translated by H. C. White. Philadelphia: The Westminster Press, 1967.

————, *Isaiah 40–66, A Commentary.* Philadelphia: Westminster, 1969.

White, H. C. "The Joseph Story: A Narrative which 'Consumes' its Content." *Semeia* 31 (1985):49–69.

Whybray, R. N. *Wisdom in Proverbs.* Studies in Biblical Theology No. 5. London: SCM Press, 1965.

———— "Some Literary Problems in Proverbs I-IX." *Vetus Testamentum Supplement* 16 (1966):482–496.

————, *The Intellectual Tradition in the Old Testament.* Beiheft zur *Zeitschrift für die alttestamentliche Wissenschaft* 135. Berlin/New York: de Gruyter, 1974.

————, "Yahweh-sayings and their Contexts in Proverbs, 10,1–22,16." In *La Sagesse de l'Ancien Testament.* Edited by M. Gilbert. Leuven: University Press, 1979.

Wiesmann, H. "Das Buch der Sprüche, Kap. 1." *Biblische Zeitschrift* 8 (1910):138–145.

————, "Das Buch der Sprüche, Kap. 6, 1–19." *Biblische Zeitschrift* 10 (1912): 242–247

Wildeboer, D. G. *Die Sprüche.* Leipzig/Tübingen: Verlag Von J. C. B. Mohr, 1897.

————, *Die Fünf Megillot.* Tübingen: J. C. B. Mohr, 1898.

Williams, R. J. "The Alleged Semitic Original of the *Wisdom of Amenemope.*" *Journal of Egyptian Archaeology* 47 (1961):100–106.

————, *Hebrew Syntax: An Outline.* 2nd ed. Toronto/Buffalo: University of Toronto Press, 1976.

Wilson, G. H. ""The Words of the Wise": The Intent and Significance of Qohelet 12:9–14." *Journal of Biblical Literature* 103 (1984):175–192.

————, *The Editing of the Hebrew Psalter.* Society of Biblical Literature Dissertation Series 76. Chico, California: Scholars Press, 1985.

Zimmerli W. "Zur Struktur der alttestamentlichen Weisheit." *Zeitschrift für die alttestamentliche Wissenschaft* 5 1 (1933):177–204. English translation, "Concerning the Structure of Old Teatment Wisdom," in *Studies in Ancient Israelite Wisdom.* Edited by J. Crenshaw. New York: KTAV, 1976.

————, "The Place and Limit of the Wisdom in the Framework of the Old Testament Theology." *Scottish Journal of Theology* 17 (1964):146–158. Reprinted in *Studies in Ancient Israelite Wisdom.* Edited by J. Crenshaw. New York: KTAV, 1976.

Appendix

Since the completion of my dissertation in 1988, further work has led me to the realization that Prov 1:1–6, the prologue, provides interpretive clues to help understand some of the peculiar features of Proverbs 1–9. As I have argued in chapters II, III, and IV the combination of direct discourse, vocabulary, imagery, phrases, word order, the sequencing of speech and description in Prov 1:8–19; 1:20–33; and 6:1–19 are crafted in such a way so as to create inner-biblical allusions to people and events from the Joseph story in Genesis and sections from the book of Jeremiah. The inner-biblical allusions are not overt but covert, not obvious but hidden, given not directly but indirectly, not identified but still identifiable. The following analysis of Prov 1:1–6 supplements my earlier work alerting the reader of Proverbs to different levels of reading found in sections of Proverbs 1–9.

The first hint that one is presented with a complex level of reading occurs in the opening verses of the prologue. The prologue addresses two separate groups of people. The first group is identified by the paired terms the *pĕtāʾyim*, "simple ones," and the *naʿar*, the "young man." Presented as beginners in the ways of wisdom, their goal is to be initiated into the ways of instruction, wisdom, wise dealing, justice, righteousness, and equity (Prov 1:2–4). As argued in my analysis of Prov 1:8–19 and 1:20–33 (chaps. II and III), special attention is given to those identified as the *pĕtāyim* (Prov 1:10, 22) as well as to the *bēn*, "son" (Prov 1:10). A distinct level of continuity is achieved between the prologue, its targeted audience, and the first two discourse sections of the book of Proverbs.

The second group addressed in the prologue are ḥākām, the "wise," and nābôn the "discerning," Prov 1:5. They are allotted a special role as those set apart in two distinct ways from the "simple" and the "young" in vv. 2–4. The first finite verb, yišmaʿ, 1:5, usually translated as a cohortative, begins the first complete sentence in the prologue. The verb yišmaʿ sets v. 5 apart from the string of infinitives in Prov 1:2–4. The NRSV, like numerous other translations, adds "also" to highlight further the distinctive place given to the "wise" and "discerning" as a specially targeted group: "Let the wise also hear and gain in learning, and the discerning acquire skill." Having already acquired a degree of wisdom, they are encouraged to deepen their wisdom.

The grammar of the text is not the only factor highlighting the unique place given to the "wise" and "discerning." According to the prologue they are to add not only to their learning and understanding, but they also are invited "to understand a proverb and a figure, the words of the wise and their riddles"(Prov 1:6). But as clear as the Hebrew is for Prov 1:6, numerous problems arise as how to understand and interpret mĕlîṣâ and ḥîdâ, translated as "figure" and "riddle" respectively. Where one can find numerous examples of "proverbs" and "words of the wise," in the book of Proverbs, commentators puzzle over the reference to "figures" and "riddles," especially since Proverbs 1–9 does not seem to have any. Proverbs 30 is a more likely source of examples for "figures" and "riddles." But it is difficult to decide in what way the content of Proverbs 30 qualifies as "figures" or "riddles."

The difficulty in interpreting these two words is compounded by the fact that the combination mĕlîṣâ and ḥîdâ is found only here and in one other place in the Hebrew Bible, Hab 2:16, which does not add any clarity to the meaning of these two words. Of the two mĕlîṣâ is the more difficult to interpret. If derived from mlṣ, then mĕlîṣâ means "smooth, slippery" (see, Ps 119:113). But in the larger context of the book of Proverbs it is difficult to understand just what is meant by describing words of wisdom that are "smooth" or "slippery," especially since mĕlîṣâ is not used elsewhere in the book.

A more likely interpretation is that mĕlîṣâ is a noun derived from lîṣ, "scorn." BDB defines mĕlîṣâ as a "satire, mocking poem,"(p. 539) a definition which has direct bearing upon my analysis of Prov 1:8–19, 1:20–33, and 6:1–19. In these three discourse units Judah as a person or as an eponymous figure is mocked and satirized. BDB's further definition of lîṣ as "speak indirectly or obliquely"(p. 539) indicates its part in communication that is not straightforward but esoteric. Through the speech of the parent and wisdom, and the verbal strategy of quotation which often mimics the object of scorn, messages are conveyed "indirectly" and "obliquely." As Bakhtin and Sternberg have argued (see above chaps. II, III, IV), one of the primary characteristics of reported discourse is its mimetic ability of bringing to mind the speech and behavior of another person in an indirect and oblique manner. As I have argued, the discourse in Prov 1:8–19; 1:20–33; and 6:1–19 conveys messages of ridicule indirectly. Moreover, the likelihood that mĕlîṣâ is derived from lîṣ is increased when we see that in Prov 1:22 wisdom cautions the son/hearer against acting like lāṣôn, "scorners." A thematic and verbal link is thus created between the prologue and wisdom's opening discourse. But this is not the only incident of a word derived from lîṣ. Words derived from lîṣ occur throughout the book of Proverbs.

As for ḥîdâ, BDB defines it as a "riddle, enigmatic, perplexing saying or question . . . of something put indirectly and needing interpretation . . ."(p. 295). Like mĕlîṣâ, ḥîdâ is concerned with a particular form of esoteric communication. Both mĕlîṣâ and ḥîdâ imply a high degree of skill not only on the part of the one who gives intentionally enigmatic instruction, but also skill on the part of the one invited to decipher a discourse's deeper meaning. According to Prov 1:2–6, not everyone is suited for esoteric instruction. It is reserved only for the "wise" and "discerning"(Prov 1:5–6).[1] As paired terms, mĕlîṣâ and ḥîdâ thus function as hermeneutic clues to the following discourse in Proverbs 1–9. Instances of enigmatic discourse require deeper interpretation than that given to other forms of instruction.

The question as to why the editor chose to teach in such an enigmatic, esoteric, indirect, and coded manner is in itself a riddle needing interpretation. But as a riddle, my analysis invites other scholars to take a closer look at the literary features and the inner-biblical connections of the book of Proverbs. Within the carefully crafted discourse of Proverbs 1–9 there may lie further clues to the meaning of wisdom and the book of Proverbs.

---

[1] James Crenshaw ("Wisdom," in *Old Testament Form Criticism,* ed. John H. Hayes [San Antonio: Trinity University Press, 1974] 240–241) says this about ḥîdâ that by extension applies to mĕlîṣâ: "Basic to the riddle is the ambiguity of language; it can only operate where words bear meanings that are common knowledge and at the same time conceal special connotations for an exclusive group." In a later work (*Old Testament Wisdom: An Introduction* [Atlanta: John Knox Press, 1981] 32) Crenshaw avers that mĕlîṣâ "seems to point in the direction of sayings which carry a sting hidden in their clever formulations, and may by extension refer to admonitions and warnings."